the HOMEBUYER'S KIT

Fifth Edition

Edith Lank with Dena Amoruso

DEARBORN™
TRADE

A **Kaplan Professional** Company

This publication is designed to provide accurate and authoritative information in regard to the subject matter covered. It is sold with the understanding that the publisher is not engaged in rendering legal, accounting, or other professional service. If legal advice or other expert assistance is required, the services of a competent professional person should be sought.

Vice President and Publisher: Cynthia A. Zigmund
Acquisitions Editor: Mary B. Good
Project Editor: Trey Thoelcke
Cover Design: KTK Design Associates
Typesetting: Elizabeth Pitts

Printed in the United States of America

01 02 03 10 9 8 7 6 5 4 3 2 1

Library of Congress Cataloging-in-Publication Data

Lank, Edith.
    The homebuyer's kit / Edith Lank with Dena Amoruso.—5th ed.
        p. cm.
    Includes index.
    ISBN 0-7931-4438-8 (pbk)
    1. House buying. I. Amoruso. Dena. II. Title.
HD1379 .L326 2001
643'.12–dc21   00-012910
                                                                      CIP

Dearborn Trade books are available at special quantity discounts to use as premiums and sales promotions, or for use in corporate training programs. For more information, please call the Special Sales Manager at 800-621-9621, ext. 4514, or write to Dearborn Financial Publishing, Inc., 155 N. Wacker Drive, Chicago, IL 60606-1719.

Praise for the Previous Editions:

"Edith Lank is real estate's Dear Abby."
   —*USA Today*

"Edith Lank is real estate's Q & A guru."
   —*The Boston Globe*

"Edith Lank is considered the Dr. Ruth of real estate. . . . It's Lank's soothing words which calm the remorseful buyer reeling from panic attacks after signing a real estate contract. It's her sage advice which catapults the prudent penny-saver into a real estate mogul. And it's her wit, charm, and clarity which distinguishes her columns."
   —*The Miami Herald*

"For most of us, the single largest purchase we will make in our lifetime is our home. Doing it right the first time is made considerably easier with this trilogy of homebuying/selling books [*The Mortgage Kit, The Homebuyer's Kit, The Homeseller's Kit*]. Lank, a syndicated columnist and real estate consultant, has painstakingly gathered the essentials and made them readable/practical. . . . Each of Lank's books is replete with payment/mortgage tables, glossary, charts, check-off lists, sample forms, and innumerable helpful hints and strategies for doing it right the first time."
   —*Library Journal*

"Now prospective homesellers can get experienced, practical advice on how to fix up, market and sell their home, from a leading real estate expert. *The Homeseller's Kit,* written by national real estate columnist and author Edith Lank, tells how to sell a home for the most money and with the fewest headaches."
   —*Bloomingdale (IN) Herald*

Contents

Preface

When our son and daughter-in-law called long-distance to say they were starting to look for their first home, I sat down at the typewriter (in those days we still used typewriters) and sent them ten closely typed pages of advice—everything I'd learned that could help first-time buyers—drawn from my experience in selling houses, teaching real estate at the college level, and answering thousands of queries that pour in every year to my syndicated newspaper column, and radio and TV shows:

- How do we start to buy a house?
- How much house can we afford?
- Should we wait to save up more down payment?
- Which mortgage plan is best?
- Where do you find a good agent?
- Do we need a lawyer?

When I got up the courage to ask my daughter-in-law over the phone a few weeks later if the letter was helpful, she answered, "Terrific! I've already lent it to three people at my office. Edith, make it into a book."

And here it is, five editions later, with Dena Amoruso coming on board now to add her expertise, especially about new homes and the Internet.

Buying a home, particularly your first one, is an adventure, like a trip to a foreign country. First off, there's the language problem—the natives use words like *easement, margin,* and *amortization* so fast you can't follow them. And they have strange customs as well. Is it polite to ask questions? Should you tip the driver?

It always helps to have a guidebook for the trip—here it is. Bon voyage, and have fun on your journey!

If you'd like to send me a postcard about your adventures, do write me at 240 Hemingway Drive, Rochester, NY 14620, or send e-mail to edithlank@aol.com.

1

Starting Your Homebuying

As we begin a new millennium, more American families than ever own their own homes—nearing 70 percent in recent surveys. But the makeup of those households is changing.

The nuclear family consisting of a stay-at-home-mom, working dad, two children, and the family pet has experienced some changes over the past two decades. Today, just 34 percent of U.S. households have kids under the roof. Single parenthood is commonplace, and mothers working outside the home make up the majority of family lifestyle scenarios. More and more unmarried people are buying homes, not worrying about waiting to tie the knot with a life partner before they invest. These unmarried couples, with or without dependents, now form a measurable segment of the home buying population.

In the 21st century, older homebuyers make up an increasing share of the market as well, affecting the design of new housing and creating trickle-down opportunities for younger homebuyers by way of the larger homes they leave behind. As the millennium began, one Baby Boomer began turning 50 every nine seconds. During the birth explosion of the Baby Boomer years (1946–1964) 76 million Americans were born. Today, they represent 28 percent of the population. In response to these statistics, hundreds of active adult and retirement communities have sprung up all over the United States, with an end to that trend nowhere in sight.

Real estate finance has also changed. Where Grandpa was offered a simple mortgage at a standard, fixed interest rate, today's buyer can choose from among hundreds of innovative loan programs, each designed to meet some borrower's particular financial need.

The desire to retreat from the pressures of an increasingly crowded society, inflation, upwardly spiraling taxes, the booming economy of the decade just closed, the need for self-expression, and the ever-increasing desire to "have it now"—all enter into the decision to buy a home. When you own your own home you can play the stereo at midnight, have a menagerie of pets, plant a garden, drive nails into the wall wherever you want, and use your own washer and dryer. And the portion of your monthly mortgage payment that goes to reduce the principal acts as automatic forced savings.

What Must You Have in Order to Buy?

It takes just three things to buy a house: some cash, dependable income, and good credit. And if you're lacking any of these three, no need to despair. Home ownership is still possible, because there are techniques for overcoming each problem.

Just be sure to level with the real estate agent you work with about your financial problems. A competent agent can recommend an appropriate financing strategy for your particular situation.

Shelter Two Ways: Income Tax

Deductions

These days, home ownership offers one of the few remaining tax shelters. Property taxes on one's home and even on vacation property are completely deductible. Interest paid on up to $1 million in loans to acquire or improve a home (or two homes) is deductible—and that more than covers most of us. If the value of one's property rises over the years, additional borrowing of up to $100,000 in equity loans, refinancing, or second mortgages also qualifies for federal tax deduction.

For homeowners in a 28 percent tax bracket, this means that Uncle Sam is making almost 28 percent of their monthly payment, with deductible property taxes and interest forming almost the whole of the payment in the first few years of the loan. Uncle's contribution shows up in the form of lower income tax owed or unexpected income tax refunds. Using the formula in Figure 1.1 will give you a rough idea of how much you could afford to spend on monthly mortgage payments. The calculation does not include further possible savings on state income taxes.

Exclusion

When you sell your home, you can take advantage of a delightful law that allows up to $500,000 profit for joint filers ($250,000 for a single homeowner) free of any federal income tax ever. The exclusion from capital gains tax, which went into effect for sales after May 7, 1997, can even cover previous, postponed tax on earlier home sales under the more complex laws in effect before that date.

This free lunch on the IRS is available to homesellers of any age, and you can do this more than once in your lifetime—theoretically as often as every two years. (There is even an exception to the two-year limit, if a quick move is needed because of a job change or illness.)

You must have owned and occupied the property as your main home for at least two of the five years before the sale. If only one spouse is the owner, the couple is still entitled to as much as $500,000 tax-free profit on the sale, but both must have occupied the property for the required two years.

How Equity Builds

Besides tax savings, in most areas you can expect some increase (appreciation) in the value of your home: an additional return on your investment, known as *equity* buildup. Price trends

FIGURE 1.1
Rent versus Mortgage Payment

This calculation arbitrarily assumes that 10 percent of your mythical mortgage payment would cover homeowners insurance and principal repayment, with the rest going for deductible interest and property taxes. It also assumes your top tax bracket (known to accountants as your *marginal tax rate*) is 28 percent. If your tax bracket is higher, your tax savings will be correspondingly higher.

A. Your present rent $_____
B. Multiply by 1.32   × 1.32
C. Equivalent monthly
   mortgage payment $_____

The result (line C) is a rough estimate of the amount you could spend for monthly mortgage payment (principal, interest, property taxes, and homeowners insurance) without being out any more money at the end of the income tax year than you are with your present rental.

in real estate vary with locale; brokers can estimate what might happen in your area over the next few years based on their local experience and observations.

Equity represents the amount you'd have if you sold your home and paid off any *liens* (financial claims) against it—usually the mortgage and any past due taxes. Put in the simplest of terms, if you buy a $180,000 house with $25,000 down and a $155,000 mortgage, your equity the day after you move in is $25,000. Equity is the money you have invested in the house—it's like money in the bank. Home appreciation has become so tangible in our society that tapping that equity for revolving loan consolidation debt, paying for college tuition, or buying more real estate has become commonplace in recent years, just like tapping one's savings account for further investment or other debts.

If the house goes up in value by 10 percent the next year, your interest rate is 8 percent and your debt is paid down (*amortized*) by $1,240 that first year, your equity has grown to $44,240 (market value, $198,000, less remaining debt of $153,760).

BUYER'S TIP

Financial advantages of buying your own home include:

- Income tax deductions for property taxes and mortgage interest

- Prospect of increase in value over the years

Real estate prices have varied considerably from one area to another, with the economic boom of the late 1990s figuring prominently in the equation. Low unemployment, more discretionary income, rising land values and construction costs, and low inflation have all been contributing factors. The real estate market is cyclical: A drop in prices eventually attracts new industries and turns into recovery. At one point the farm states may be badly hit, but prices may be skyrocketing on the East and West coasts; then the Midwest sees steady growth and increase in values while the coasts experience what stock analysts would dub a "stabilization" or "correction."

With the stock market boom and the advent of e-commerce, the late 1990s and the emergence of the 21st century created many new millionaires in the United States, a designation not nearly as uncommon as it was years ago. Property values in high-tech areas and major cities, such as California's Silicon Valley and parts of New York City, have exploded. What would cost a modest $150,000 in a small Midwestern town may be worth well over a million dollars in those areas. In general, however, it's almost always a good time to buy, because even minimum appreciation and tax savings will be a bonus.

If You Wait

Some buyers' first attempts at house hunting often trigger bewildering—and sometimes misguided—advice from parents, grandparents and well-meaning friends who have all had different experiences of their own. The Depression-era generation has painful memories of doing without, making it more difficult for them to relate to the "have it all" generations of today. They may advise you to put more money down, imparting thrifty, old-fashioned virtues that served them well, but unaware of the advantage of tax benefits and remaining as liquid as possible.

Even Baby Boomers, on the cusp of empty-nesting or early retirement, can give younger generations warnings about buying over their heads, anticipating ever-increasing expenses related to child care, consumerism, and educational costs for young families. Many financial gurus will admit, however, that even if you can't find or afford your dream home today, it may be best to buy whatever you can, as soon as you can, however you can. Then start building your savings. When you finally locate the perfect house, you'll have something to trade in on the deal.

BUYER'S TIP

To prepare for your purchase:

- Start reading classified ads in the real estate section of your newspaper, visit open houses, tour new home communities on weekends, and search the Internet for homes—all this even though you're not yet ready to buy.

- If you're a veteran, send for your VA certificate of entitlement so that the option is open to consider a VA loan when you're ready to purchase a home.

- Contact a credit bureau or check the Internet for a credit report on yourself, just to make sure that no mistakes turn up. If you don't like what you see, it's time to try to clean up any problem items. Several credit-counseling services, such as Consumer Credit Counselors, can help you with that process.

- Make an appointment with a lender and explain what your goals are. Then let the lender set up a plan for you to meet those goals after a review of your current income and debt situation. Also mention any anticipated increases in income, such as bonuses or incremental raises.

- Sock away extra cash; you'll be motivated to skip a vacation, a movie, or dinner out when you have a short-term goal like accumulating money for a down payment and closing costs.

(continued)

BUYER'S TIP

- Try not to buy anything on credit, and if you do, pay it off quickly. This is not the time to take on another car payment, buy a boat, or even apply for an additional credit card. If you find that you cannot avoid having to buy something on credit and can anticipate that need, make sure the lender you work with figures that debt into your qualifications to buy.

- Don't change lines of work. Lenders like to see a stable income picture, showing a demonstrated ability to earn an income in a particular field. Becoming a hairdresser, when your education and employment experience has been accounting for the past five years, is best done *after* you buy a house and not before. Changing jobs should be done only if the income for the subsequent position is equal to or greater than the previous one, and ideally in the same field.

- If someone is making you a large cash gift toward your purchase, try to get it into your savings account as soon as possible (hopefully several months) before you apply for a mortgage loan. Lenders like to see seasoned funds earmarked for a home purchase as early as possible.

2

You and the Broker

As you begin your house hunting, it helps to keep straight the various terms for real estate licensees.

Agent is a general term for anyone empowered to act for another. Many agents you meet have been hired by the seller and have special fiduciary duties to the seller (more on that important point later.)

Broker is a legal term for someone licensed by the state to negotiate real estate transactions and to charge for services.

Salesperson is the term for the holder of an entry-level license; a salesperson is allowed to assist a broker who is legally responsible for a salesperson's activities. In some areas the word *agent* may be used for a salesperson, as opposed to a broker. A salesperson may not operate without supervision and may collect fees only from the sponsoring broker as a share of commissions earned by the salesperson's efforts. In a new home purchase, the salesperson or *builder sales consultant* is generally employed by the builder to sell new home neighborhoods, with a license usually overseen by a "broker of record" within the building organization.

REALTOR® is a trademark designation (properly capitalized, like Xerox, Kleenex or Coke) for a broker (in some areas a salesperson) who belongs to a private organization called the local Association, or Board, of REALTORS®, a state board of REALTORS®, and the National Association of REALTORS®. REALTORS® subscribe to a code of ethics that goes beyond state license law, and usually sponsor a local Multiple Listing System, which offers access to houses listed for sale by many different firms.

REALTOR-ASSOCIATE® is the term used by some boards of REALTORS® for salespersons associated with member brokers.

So as you start your search for the best agent, should you prefer a salesperson or a broker? There's something to be said for each. In general, you can expect a broker to have more education and experience. On the other hand, some long-time salespersons remain at that status simply because they prefer not to go into business for themselves. And you could run into a well-trained, highly motivated newcomer with the time and enthusiasm to do a first-class job for you.

Law of Agency

The law of agency clearly sets out the broker's duties to the *principal* (also known as the *client*), the one who retains and (usually) pays the agent. These *fiduciary* duties are complex, but they boil down to one thing: The agent must put the principal's interest first, above anyone else's, including the agent's own interest. Among the specific duties involved are the following.

- *Obedience to the principal's instructions* unless they are illegal. (Examples of instructions an agent would not obey: "Don't show the house to any Lithuanians." "Keep quiet about the broken furnace.")
- *Loyalty to the principal,* which strictly interpreted (it sometimes isn't) includes obtaining the highest possible price for the property and never suggesting any offer under the listed price.
- *Confidentiality,* which prohibits the seller's agent from sharing with you details of the seller's financial or family situation, unless of course the seller has authorized such action to encourage offers. Whether the seller has received previous offers, and for how much, is also confidential information.

- *Notice,* a duty that obliges the seller's agent to forward to the principal (seller) any fact that it would be in the seller's interest to know, whether or not the seller knows enough to inquire. *This one is of vital importance for you to understand.*

BUYER'S TIP

When house hunting, keep in mind that a seller's agent is *obligated* to tell the seller anything known about you that could benefit the seller.

So Where Do You Stand?

Unless you specifically hire your own buyer's broker to represent you (more on that later), none of these duties is owed to you.

"Yes," you say, "I know those are the duties of the listing agent. But I'm dealing with a different firm that cooperates through the Multiple Listing System. My broker is the selling agent, and that's different."

No, it isn't. Both firms may be agents for the seller. The second one, the one you're working with (let's not say "your agent") is cooperating with the first firm and the seller. You are merely a third party in that relationship, a customer rather than a client.

It can be scary to realize this, but things aren't as bad as they seem.

First, the law does require the broker to be honest, straightforward, and trustworthy with third parties. Your questions will receive honest answers, although sometimes an honest answer might be, "I am not allowed to tell you whether the seller is facing foreclosure; I must keep financial information confidential."

Besides answering your questions honestly, agents and sellers have an obligation to volunteer information about any serious (material) hidden defects you aren't able to see for yourself. State laws differ, though, on whether they must also tell you about past problems that don't technically affect the real estate, such as suicide or murder on the premises, illness of the seller, and the like.

Second, you will receive a great deal of service (see list in the next chapter) paid for by the seller, because without this service to buyers, the property might never be sold.

And finally, you can take heart from the fact that, as a practical matter, many seller's brokers end up violating their duty to the seller. A good agent empathizes with you, wants you to find what you want at a price you can afford, and may emotionally adopt you. If brokers didn't to some extent identify with the buyer, not much real estate would get sold!

How to Protect Yourself

If the agent is duty-bound to put the seller's interest first (and there's only one first place), how should this affect your relationship with the broker?

First, realize that no confidentiality is owed to you. It's practical to reveal your financial situation if you expect to get effective service, but you may want to keep some information to yourself. The broker who knows that you would pay more "if we have to" is, strictly speaking, obliged to convey that information to the seller. Saying "but don't tell the seller that" won't help because the agent does not have any special obligation of obedience to you. *Never reveal the highest price you are willing to pay to a seller's agent.* Assume that whatever you say will be (or at least should be) transmitted to the seller.

Take advantage of the fact that you must receive honest answers to your questions. In a few states you are entitled to a seller's written disclosure of defects, but elsewhere, "Are you aware of any defects in this house?" is a good all-purpose query to ask of both seller and broker, preferably in front of witnesses.

Buyers' Brokers

What's to stop you from retaining your own broker, someone obligated to put your interests first and legally bound to help you obtain the property at the lowest possible price?

Nothing.

Almost unheard-of in years past, brokers who represent buyers are now found in every real estate market, and you should have no trouble locating one.

BUYER'S TIP

In dealing with a seller's agent:

- Do not reveal the highest price you are willing to pay on a particular property.

- Do ask whether the seller or agent knows of any defects in the property.

- If you have retained an agent, but are looking at homes without your agent along, always disclose to the selling broker that you are represented by your own agent.

- If you are looking at new homes and have an agent, make sure he or she is with you on your first visit to the community. (See Buying a New Home)

When you have specifically engaged a buyer's broker, those fiduciary duties are now owed to you, and sellers become merely customers. Your agent must keep *your* information confidential and obey *your* orders, such as "If they don't accept our offer, give them one for $5,000 more."

The buyer's broker is duty-bound to tell you anything that would be useful to you ("I'm not sure, but I've heard the seller needs a fast deal") and to help you obtain the property for the lowest price.

How are such brokers compensated?

The buyer's broker may ask for a signed contract and nominal retainer to compensate for time invested; sometimes the retainer applies against eventual commission or even the purchase price of the property. If no property is purchased within the contracted time, the retainer may be forfeited. (See Figure 2.1)

Sometimes, however, the buyer's broker maintains a verbal agreement with buyers, with a commitment to inform them of available properties and show them everything in the areas and price ranges they seek. The broker does this with the understanding that the buyers will not engage the services of any another agent for that purpose and that they will use the buyer's agent to represent them no matter what property they buy. It's pretty much a matter of trust and loyalty, based on faith in the agent's professionalism and expertise, and the buyer's willingness to use him or her exclusively.

In theory, the buyer who specifically hires a broker should pay for the service. In real life, however, it usually works out that the seller pays the originally agreed-upon commission, a designated amount of which goes to the buyer's broker, so that the house gets sold.

Proponents of the system like it because it sets up an adversarial situation similar to that in which the parties retain two different attorneys, each working on his or her own client's behalf.

Buying a New Home

In the usual production (tract) home purchase, the sales consultant represents the seller, who, in this case, is the builder of the home. Many builders offer a co-op fee, or commission, to any brokers who introduce them to a buyer on the first visit to the builder's community, should that introduction lead to a closed sale.

If you tour new homes without an agent and opt to buy one on your own, there is an implied (but not official) responsibility on the part of the builder's sales consultant, even though he or she

FIGURE 2.1   Sample Buyer's Broker Contract

SAMPLE   Only Buyer Representation Contract   SAMPLE

REAL ESTATE BUYER REPRESENTATION CONTRACT
(Short Contract Form. For purpose of Buyer hiring licensed real estate agent to represent,
negotiate, and advocate Buyer's interests in acquiring real estate property.)
*This is a legal instrument. If not understood, legal, tax, or other professional counsel should be
consulted before signing by Buyer.*

_____, ____City, State/Province. This _____day of _____, 19____.

"Buyer" _____ appoints
_____
(Broker's Company Name and Address)
**"Broker" as Buyer's only agent to acquire interests in real estate property as described in section 2
("Property") and under terms specified in this Contract.**
1. Effect of this Only Buyer Representation Contract. Buyer agrees to conduct all activities in this
property purchase through Broker. Broker represents only this Buyer's interests. Broker earns
compensation upon Buyer's acquisition of Property.

2. Property Description. Property shall substantially be as follows or as otherwise acceptable to Buyer:

3. Contract Duration. This Contract shall begin_____, 19___ and shall continue until the
earlier of _____, 19___, or completion of the property purchase.

4. Broker's Services. Broker will be 100% loyal to Buyer 100 % of the time in this transaction; will be
trustworthy; and will protect and promote Buyer's interests.

5. Broker's Compensation. Buyer agrees to pay Broker a maximum fee which will not exceed the
greater of $_____ or _____% of the purchase price of Property. This maximum fee
includes a nonrefundable earnest money deposit of $_____ due and payable upon signing
this contract.

6. Disclosure of Buyer's Identity. Broker ( ) does or ( ) does not   have Buyer's permission to
disclose Buyer's identity to third parties without prior written consent of Buyer.

7. Other Buyers. Broker may show properties in which Buyer may have interest to other prospective
buyers represented by this Broker without breaching any duty or obligation to this Buyer.

8. Buyer's Right to Terminate this Contract. Buyer has the right to unilaterally terminate this
contract, in writing, for any unsatisfactory condition of Broker service. Buyer may not, however, assign
rights or obligations under this contract to defeat any of Broker's rights.

9. Entire Contract. This written contract is the entire contract. Any modifications must be in writing
signed by both parties and attached to this contract.

Accepted _____   _____
                (Broker)   (Buyer)
By _____   _____
                                                                            (Buyer)
Address: _____   **Address:** _____

Phone/ Fax/ e mail _____   **Phone/ Fax/ e mail** _____

SAMPLE ONLY from bmiller@onlybuyers-re.com SAMPLE ONLY

represents the builder. This means that the sales consultant works diligently to assist both you and the builder, addressing both sides' concerns. The builder's agent is not ultimately obligated to take your instructions, however, because the agent does not, in fact, represent you.

Builders often post signs on their sales office doors warning buyers who are working with agents to have their agents along on their first visit. The builder believes that its elaborately decorated model homes, signage, advertising, builder Web site or on-site agent can also be the *procuring cause* of an eventual sale, saving them an agent commission. Some builders will refuse to compensate any agent introduced after their buyer's first visit for this reason. If you wish to remain loyal to your agent, make sure that he or she is available to escort you personally to any new home communities.

Discount and FSBO Brokers

Some sellers who are willing to perform part of the brokerage work themselves list their property with *discount brokers,* or *fee-for-service brokers.* These agencies offer a seller a limited list of services for a reduced commission or per job fee. You'll need to understand this relationship because if you run into one, you, as a buyer, will be expected to do part of the work yourself. The discount broker may assist by making viewing appointments for you, but will probably send you to tour these *FSBO* (For Sale by Owner) houses on your own. You may also be offered less help with mortgage financing, and end up viewing homes while the owners are present, sometimes an uncomfortable experience.

Other types of discount brokers include those on the World Wide Web who offer both buyers and sellers "cash back at closing" such as e-Realty.com or ZipRealty.com. These sites will list states in which they are permitted to operate. (One never knows how long selected dot-coms will survive in the ever-changing and fiercely competitive cyber-world, so check on the viability of any mentioned in this book.)

Fee-for-service brokers are those who sell individual services, such as a market analysis, represent the buyer or seller at closing, or recommend pricing all at a set fee, with no other obligations involved.

When sellers engage the services of a discount FSBO (pronounced fizz-bo) brokerage, the primary responsibility of selling the home is left in the owner's hands. Some owners who engage discount brokers may also offer a buyer's broker a commission (broker co-op) or flat fee for bringing them a real buyer. In this case, as the buyer you can have the services of your own agent to help you through a possible purchase of this type, if you are so inclined. FSBO agencies usually offer owners the option of listing their homes in the Multiple Listing Service for a set fee. And, even though the discount brokers offer a list of other services, owners generally do their own marketing, such as placing classified advertising, creating flyers and holding open houses.

Pure For Sale by Owner Properties

Owners who handle the sale of their own property, without aid of fee-for-service brokers or any licensed help involved, have gained steam over the past few decades, now using the Internet to gain exposure for their marketed property. Whereas predictions heralded the Internet as the perfect medium for sale-by-owner *anythings* (because it was generally a free way of marketing things), the road for FSBO sites has not been a smooth one, due to inconsistencies and a lack of real estate marketing expertise on the part of the owners themselves, who try for a while to sell on their own and then give up and list with a licensed agent.

Blanche Evans, author of *HomeSurfing.net: The Insider's Guide to Buying and Selling Your Home Using the Internet*, says that FSBO sellers usually don't take into consideration the hundreds of dollars professional agents spend up-front to gain exposure for their listings. She points out that the biggest professional real estate Web sites are Realtor.com, HomeAdvisor.com, and HomeStore.com, all of which display thousands of homes for consumers to view, compare, and learn about from their personal computers. FSBO listings, which are sparse and usually poorly displayed on discount broker and commercial Internet sites (some without photos) just don't seem to gain enough buyer attention or offer the volume of listings for the average consumer to sustain serious, consistent interest in them. According to Evans, as of the printing of this book, two of the largest Web sites (to remain unnamed here) to promote FSBOs were in severe financial trouble.

Some homeowners sell by owner for the satisfaction of tackling a new challenge, some are sophisticated in the ways of buying and selling real estate, but most are not doing this just to pass the saved commission on to you. They usually plan to sell their homes for fair market value, pocketing whatever they may have otherwise paid out in commissions as extra profit in return for their efforts. Selling by owner is not as easy a task as it sounds on the surface, and many FSBO owners customarily give themselves a certain time limit in which to sell their own homes, with a back-up plan to list their home with an agent if their efforts prove unsuccessful. FSBO owners are customarily approached by many local agents for that reason, some of whom may even give them advice in the hopes of garnering the listing when the time comes to leave it in the hands of a professional.

It's important to know that, should you buy a home directly from an owner, unless you hire a buyer's broker, you will probably have to negotiate face-to-face. You may also feel the need to seek the services of an attorney or agent to help you with the written contract. You will be on your own for advice on financing options and for help with your mortgage application. Be sure to have a building inspector look over the property and generate a report before making a final commitment to buy, or have this *contingency* (condition of purchase) written into the purchase agreement.

Some of the situations that are conducive to FSBO purchases are:

- The property is unique and you feel strongly attracted to it.
- The home seems underpriced for the area (the owner may not have had an appraisal or advice on pricing it properly). In that scenario, be prepared to act promptly; some investors lie in wait for unwary FSBOs and jump as soon as underpriced property hits the market.

It may be difficult to begin house hunting searching primarily for FSBOs, particularly if you are a first-time buyer. And until you have a good grasp of the values in your area and the entire home buying process, dealing with principals instead of professionals can be frustrating. If, however, you have bought and sold several homes in your time and think you've found your dream home in FSBO clothes, try to gather as much information and advice on the property as you can, and see how comfortable you feel with this type of arrangement.

Yet Other Arrangements

We're not quite finished with the roles real estate agents can play. Known in different states by different names, the *transaction broker* (TB) works to fill in the blanks where other types of agents don't. When someone is needed to represent neither the buyer nor the seller, but remain in a neutral stance, the transaction broker may be elected. This broker usually has no fiduciary duties, but can offer expertise and negotiate between parties. The law, in states that provide for this status, usually requires simple, honest, straightforward dealing, but may set up varying other duties as well. Find out, if considering the use of a TB, whether confidences are kept and just what the agent's duties would be.

The *dual agent* is allowed to represent both parties, as might take place if you visited an open house without any agent representing you and bought the house through the seller's agent, who, by the way, would be more than happy to help. In essence, you may surmise that a dual agent can represent both buyers' and sellers' interests, but as mentioned earlier, true representation of a buyer is almost impossible when the seller directly or indirectly pays the commission for both. The role of the dual agent and whose interests are represented has been hotly debated and is still a point of controversy in many real estate markets. However, there are many competent agents who fill these shoes regularly, representing the interests of both buyer and seller with professionalism and appropriate confidentiality.

Choosing an Agent

You will meet agents by answering advertisements, calling the phone numbers on lawn signs, and visiting open houses. You will see advertising for them on bus stop benches, in real estate Web sites and by direct mail campaigns. Best of all, perhaps, is a name suggested by a relative or a friend who has had a good experience—but only if the agent in question specializes in the area and type of house you want.

In a strange town, you can write or e-mail queries to the local chamber of commerce asking for maps and information; you will probably then hear from several local real estate brokers interested in working with out-of-towners. If you study the local newspapers, you will discover which agents are active in the areas you like. If you are relocating with your company, chances are they will put you in touch with agents who are part of their relocation network and probably already have a proven track record with their relocation department in your target area.

If you don't hire a buyer's broker and you deal with sellers' agents, you might be tempted to play the field, thinking that you'll get many people out there looking for your dream house. In reality, though, the buyer who works with many brokers is working with no one. The first time an agent calls to tell you about a house that just came on the market and hears, "As a matter of fact, we saw that with someone else this morning," your name is crossed off the to-do list. If you plan to use sellers' brokers and find a good one, stick with him or her.

Tests to Apply

Here are a few tests to apply when judging a broker:

- *Does the broker explain your state's law of agency at your first meeting and make it clear for whom he or she is working?*
- *Does the agent return phone calls promptly?* This simple question is a good screening device, whether you're look-ing for a broker, lawyer, or plumber. In these days of cell phones, pagers, voicemail, and e-mail, there is no excuse to be out of touch.
- *Does the agent explain things so you can understand them?* This attribute is especially important for first-time buyers. If you can find an agent who is a born teacher, you are in luck. (The fact is, many brokers *are* former teachers.)
- *Does the agent seem ready to invest time in you?* Where the broker is holding an open house that's on the market, does he or she just wave you through, asking as you leave whether you're interested in that house and letting it go at that? You want someone who, if not busy with other pros-pects, shows you the house in a professional manner, asks questions about your needs and wants, and offers to sit down and discuss other places on the market if you're not interested in the house you're touring.
- *Does the agent seem to have knowledge of the Internet?* Some agents carry a laptop computer with them wherever they go and are able to pull up pertinent information and new listings on the spot. A computer has become a valuable hi-tech sales tool and a convenient and ready resource for savvy brokers these days. If Internet communication is important to you, ask agents if they e-mail their clients with information on new listings as they appear.

- *Does the broker suggest an initial session in the office, rather than simply meeting you at the house you called about?* To get good service, you need a sit-down financial analysis and discussion of your whole situation in a confidential and professional setting.
- *Does the agent ask questions about your finances soon after meeting you?* This may not be proper etiquette in ordinary society, but it's the mark of an efficient broker who aims to give you good service. Suggesting a prequalification or a full loan preapproval is better yet, so that you have placed yourself in a position of strength and credibility as a buyer. If you haven't already spoken to a loan agent, the agent may suggest someone with whom he or she has a track record of success.
- *Does the broker explain up front if he or she is acting as a seller's agent?* In most states, this information must be given to you in writing upon first contact.
- *When suggesting potential houses for the first time, did the agent show you listings that convince you that he or she has been listening and understands what you are looking for?* If you're shown houses with the wrong number of bedrooms or ones clearly out of your price range, this may not be the agent for you.
- *Does the agent seem familiar and up-to-date on local conditions?* Does he or she have maps of the area, handouts about schools, local activities, property tax rates, and other information that shows knowledge and interest in the area?

The worksheet in Figure 3.1 can help you evaluate brokers.

Once you find a broker with whom you feel comfortable, one who inspires confidence, stick with him or her. Tell your broker about other firms' ads that interest you, Web sites (URLs) with homes that caught your eye, even about FSBOs, so that the agent can investigate and report back to you. Ask for advice before visiting open houses on your own. And if you have the agent's phone numbers, don't hesitate to use them. Real estate agents are accustomed to evening and weekend calls. Service is what they sell, and they welcome any sign that you intend to utilize it.

FIGURE 3.1
Worksheet for Evaluating Brokers

YES or NO	Agent 1	Agent 2	Agent 3
Returns phone calls/is accessible			
Follows up on contacts			
Uses office interview			
Understands your needs			
Runs financial analysis			
Suggests a meeting with a lender			
Uses an interview sheet			
Seems computer/Internet savvy			
Uses Multiple Listing System			
Cooperates with other agents			
Knows the community			
Inspires confidence			
Knows both new and resale home markets			

Using a Lawyer

Customs in real estate vary tremendously from one area to another. In some states, you may be told that no one uses lawyers for real estate transactions except when something goes wrong or you just want to seek legal advice about your purchase. In the states located mostly in the West, Midwest, and South, *escrow companies* act as neutral third parties, assisting both buyers and sellers in residential real estate transactions. Title companies (sometimes combined with escrow firms) in these states make sure you have clear title to the property and and that the deed is recorded so that the property is legally in your name.

In other states, attorneys are used for handling the paperwork and the closing on your house. The law does not require that you have legal counsel in these states, but it is wise to proceed with professional legal help on your side. Even in states where they are not required for general real estate functions, lawyers are useful not so much for getting you out of trouble as for heading off trouble before it starts.

An attorney can make sure that the sales contract protects your interests, intervene if problems arise before closing, and review documents so that you get proper credit at closing (in some states called *settlement*) time.

You can find a real estate attorney by asking the broker to suggest two or three names, check out some large law firms and ask who specializes in real estate law, or search the Internet for sources.

In states where attorneys are used for real estate purchases, contact the attorney you have chosen early on and explain that you're starting to house hunt, and inquire about the fees for handling an eventual purchase. He or she will probably suggest at what point to touch base once again, unless you have some legal matters to clear up before going ahead with the purchase of a home.

Escrow and Title Companies

Where escrow companies handle buyer and seller paperwork, most *escrows* (the period following the initial contract and before the closing or settlement takes place) can be opened or started up by a simple phone call or by having an agent drop off the signed contract itself at their offices. Escrow and title firm selection, as with every other aspect of real estate, is negotiable, but most buyers try to use the same firms for both buyer and seller, just to make it simple. New homebuilders may use the same companies for all their new home subdivisions, taking advantage of reduced fees due to the volume of escrows they handle. These discounted fees are usually attractive to their buyers as well.

Ask your real estate agent how real estate purchases are handled in your state in this regard.

What the Agent Does for You

The average person assumes that a real estate agent's job is to help find a house, but that's only the tip of the iceberg. The typical broker will spend a considerable amount of time bringing you into agreement with the seller and, most important, helping you arrange to finance your purchase. In a new home purchase, your agent can research the builder and the new home warranty, offer advice on choosing a home site and floor plan, and help with your design center choices and loan application.

You can expect a fairly lengthy list of services, even if you are using the seller's broker.

- *Analysis of your financial situation.* Don't be offended by what appear to be personal questions. A good agent asks them at the beginning because a lending institution will ask them later on. Your agent is also interviewing *you* to assess if you are financially ready to purchase a home, and deciding whether to take you on as a client. During a first conversation, the broker is already forming a strategy for financing your purchase based on the various mortgage options outlined in Chapter 7. In a resale (used home) purchase, just don't reveal the top price you're prepared to pay, even though the agent may already have figured out just how much house you are qualified to buy based on your income, debts, and down payment information.
- *Education in basic real estate principals.* Brokers expect to spend extra time with first-time homebuyers. Some seasoned homebuyers have not been through the purchase of a home in quite a while, making the same explanations necessary. You have a right to insist that every step be made clear so that you feel comfortable with the process.

- *Recommendation of a specific price range.* Without those figures, all of you—sellers, agent, and yourself—may just be spinning your wheels.
- *Orientation to a new community.* If you are moving to another town, send for the local newspaper (the weekend papers are usually where most real estate ads appear) or find their community Web sites. You can also contact a few firms you find in the process and ask about what part of town may be best for your price range. You may receive long-distance phone calls, e-mails, maps, or new home brochures. Your agent can set up motel reservations for a visit. At that time, your agent can chauffeur you around, checking out neighborhoods, schools, and shopping, while also arranging a time-efficient tour of potential homes in your price range.
- *Information about different locations.* The agent is prohibited by law (the federal Fair Housing Act) from answering questions regarding race, religion, familial status, or handicap of residents in any given area. They may, however, offer school test scores and expenditures, or guide you to Web sites with demographic information or crime statistics.
- *Screening of listings.* The agent will show you any house on the market, being careful not to limit your choice by the use of subtle steering based on any of the prohibited criteria mentioned above. A good agent is a skilled matchmaker, however, who listens instead of talking and then helps you narrow down available listings, thus making efficient use of your time.
- *Showing property.* The agent will set up appointments for house inspections and (unless representing a discount broker) will accompany you. During the tours, don't be afraid to ask questions. The agent will have a wealth of data on each house you see, including knowledge of lot size, property taxes and assessment figures, age of the house, square footage, heating and air conditioning systems, and the like. If you are also looking at new homes, the agent will have researched the new home communities, be able to discuss their amenities, understand the options in each floor plan,

and know how to get information on the future of the area. The agent may also have knowledge of home construction and can give you a recommendation on some of the technical aspects of your purchase.

- *Estimation of ownership costs.* When you are seriously interested in a specific house, your agent will sit down to help you figure out how you could buy it and what it would cost you each month. If your proceeds for the down payment are coming from the sale of a previous home, he or she can discuss the timing of your move and the readiness of the next property.

- *Contract negotiation.* The agent will prepare either a binding purchase contract or (in some areas) a preliminary memorandum of agreed terms, including provisions for financing, contingencies, or special terms. The broker negotiates differences between what you want and what the seller wants until you and the seller reach a meeting of the minds. In a new home purchase, your agent can try to negotiate for *builder incentives* (seller-paid credits used for financing or upgrade options) or even haggle over the price of the home if the builder is enticed by a quick reduction of inventory. Depending on whether it is a seller's market or a buyer's market at the time, it may be difficult to get the builder to negotiate. Except in, perhaps, a custom home purchase, most new homebuilders have their own purchase agreements, which are computer-prepared and presented by their own consultants. Your agent will be present for this and help advise and guide you along the way.

- *Set up the various inspections and help clear contract contingencies.* Your agent will make sure you have all the necessary inspections arranged that are specified as part of your negotiated contract, such as the pest, roof, pool, and electrical or structural inspections. The agent will make sure that you have resolved all of your buyer-related contingencies within the time frame allowed in your purchase agreement.

- *Liaison with your escrow officer, loan consultant, or attorney.* The broker works closely with your lender, attorney, or escrow officer, keeping a watchful eye on the progress of the transaction from the moment you sign a purchase agreement.
- *Financing expertise.* Some agents don't even consider looking for homes for their clients these days without a lender's loan prequalification or preapproval of their buyers (see Chapter 7), giving them even more bargaining power when it comes time to make offers. After the purchase, the agent will help you with your loan application and keep in close touch with the lender, checking the status of your loan approval frequently to be able to point out any red flags along the way. Your agent can recommend several lenders and suggest a variety of loan programs that suit your needs, but you need not feel tied to the same lender who gave you your original prequalification letter or certificate if you find another more suitable later on. The choice of which loan consultant and which loan program to use is ultimately up to you.
- *Closing escrow/settlement.* Local customs vary, but in many areas the broker attends the closing session. In a few places, agents even effect the transfer of title (ownership).
- *Recommend local services.* Agents network with a variety of local businesses and can be a resource for their buyers. Your agent can locate moving companies, day care providers, housekeeping services, and gardeners, and help you set up utilities. Consider your agent your new neighborhood's "ambassador" and let him or her roll out the red carpet for you.

4

What Can You Spend for Your Home?

Buying a home is not as simple as it was in past generations. Where postwar couples could partake in the American Dream making the mortgage payment their primary goal every month, today's homebuyers tend to bring some additional debts and more complex financial portfolios to the table.

Most buyers finance homes with mortgages these days, and interest rates fluctuate considerably more than they did in our parents' generation. Economists wait for quarterly reports on what the Federal Reserve will do with interest rates when certain economic factors are considered regarding unemployment, housing starts, and returns on investments. What follows is anybody's ball game.

Current thinking about home affordability at any given time concentrates more on the monthly costs of home ownership as they compare with income and debts than any other factor.

Income is not the only criterion. Equally important in today's debt-driven society is the amount of your other obligations. Each lending institution and each loan program has its own guidelines. The same indebtedness considered excessive to one loan underwriter may be acceptable to another. Outstanding student loans, life insurance payments, or child support may affect your allowable mortgage payment—or they may not.

BUYER'S TIP

- If you are planning to finance a home purchase with a mortgage, don't finance major purchases, such as a new car, with loans that will reduce the amount of the mortgage for which you qualify. Don't apply for more credit.

- Don't change your line of work, and try not to change jobs unless it is for the same or higher income.

First List Your Income

When estimating your allowable mortgage payment, include all the income of anyone who will be on the title to the house (see Figure 4.1). Unmarried persons may pool their income to buy a house together, just as a married couple can. If you are self-employed, average your past two years' income from that source. Do not include one-time events like inheritances, insurance settlements, and capital gains.

Next, list your monthly debt payments. Most lenders don't care about debts that will be paid off within ten months, so omit those. List actual monthly payments in Figure 4.2. Don't forget outstanding student loans or child support payments, if any.

Qualifying Ratios

Lenders figure your allowable mortgage payment many different ways. Some calculations even take into account your particular income tax payment and number of dependents. In general, though, you will hear about lending institutions' *qualifying ratios.* A typical ratio might be 28/36 or (more generous in the amount you could borrow) 29/41.

FIGURE 4.1
Listing Your Income

	Owner 1	Owner 2
Salary (gross)		
Self-employment income		
Second job income (gross)		
Dividends		
Interest		
Pension/401k		
Social Security/Disability		
Rental income		
Court ordered child support, alimony		
Other		
Total	_____ A	_____ B
Total Income (A + B) = $ _____		

It's important to note that even if you fall within the qualifying ratios of any loan program guidelines, you are the only person to decide if the *discretionary income* (what is left after you have paid your mortgage payment, regular debt payments, utilities and other bills each month) remaining each month would be enough for you and your family to feel secure. Don't permit well-meaning real estate agents, eager loan officers, family, or friends to pressure you into making financial decisions, even when you're getting green lights in all directions.

FIGURE 4.2
Listing Your Monthly Payments

	Owner 1	Owner 2
Car payment		
Furniture/Appliance loans		
Boat/RV loan		
Major credit card payments		
Department stores/other credit cards		
Equity lines/personal loans		
Student loan		
Child support/Alimony		
Other		
Total	_____ A	_____ B

Total Debt Service (A + B) = $ _____

Let's examine Figure 4.3. The first part of the ratio is the percentage of your gross monthly income the lender will allow as a maximum monthly payment on housing only. With a 28/36 ratio, you would be allowed to spend 28 percent of your monthly gross income on a mortgage payment.

Using a 28/36 ratio, a buyer with monthly gross income of $4,000 would be allowed up to $1,120 for monthly mortgage payment. You can perform the calculation for yourself.

The calculation in Figure 4.3 uses a ratio of 28/36. Local brokers or your loan agent can tell you if other ratios are currently in use in your area.

FIGURE 4.3
Maximum Monthly Payment (A)

Using 28%:

Your monthly gross income	$ _____
Multiply by 28%	× 0.28
Maximum monthly payment	$ _____ (A)

Lenders figure the allowable payment two different ways, however, and the second calculation (shown in Figure 4.4) takes into account your other ongoing debts. The second part of the ratio (36 percent) allows a higher percentage of monthly income for a mortgage payment, but that's because it must also cover other monthly debt payments.

The same buyer, with a monthly gross income of $4,000, might have $400 in current debt payments. Applying the ratio (36 percent) yields $1,440 a month available for total debt service. Subtracting present monthly payments of $400 qualifies the borrower for up to $1,040 in mortgage costs.

Lenders calculate both ways and then take whichever result is the lower, more conservative one. That's why you don't want to go into debt for a new car while you're house hunting. If you find you cannot avoid taking on another debt (your car is falling apart) and can anticipate how much you may be paying monthly on it, be sure to tell your lender so it is included in your qualifying ratios. Also discuss whether putting less money down on the house and paying off debt with the same money is a better way to go.

Whichever is lower, calculation A or B, is a rough estimate of the figure lenders will use for your maximum permissible monthly payment, PITI (principal, interest, taxes, and insurance).

FIGURE 4.4
Maximum Monthly Payment (B)

Your monthly gross income	$ _____
Multiply by 36%	× 0.36
Maximum monthly debt service	$ _____
Subtract present payments	$ _____
Available for monthly payment	$ _____ (B)

How Much Will This Carry?

PITI refers to the four standard components of a monthly mortgage payment: *principal, interest, taxes,* and *insurance.* With some mortgage plans, lenders collect these last two amounts each month on a prorated basis (one-twelfth of your yearly property taxes and one-twelfth of your homeowners insurance premium), for an *impound* (*trust* or *escrow*) *account.* Those tax and insurance bills go directly to the lender, which will pay them with your money, set aside in a separate account. Lenders are concerned about those particular bills being met, to protect the security for their loan. If your lender is not requiring an escrow account, but you feel more comfortable with the idea of forcing yourself to pay these prorated expenses each month, you may request an impound account be set up (some lenders may charge a nominal fee for this).

In the previous example, where $1,040 was the maximum PITI payment because the borrower had substantial other debts, how much could this buy? For starters, for how much of a mortgage loan could the borrower qualify?

FIGURE 4.5
How Much for Monthly Debt Service?

Your maximum monthly payment (from last worksheets)	$ _____
Subtract monthly property tax (from agent's estimate)	− _____
Subtract typical insurance	− _____ 30 _____
Principal and Interest Payment	$ _____

Property taxes and insurance differ from one house to another. Interest rates differ from one loan program to another. And, of course, the amount of cash available for down payment will make a difference. It's relatively simple to make the calculation when you already have a particular house in mind. Nevertheless, you can get a rough estimate at this point.

You'll need information (available from any agent or by calling the county assessor's office) on average property tax bills in the price range and neighborhood you're eyeing. Homeowners insurance is a simpler matter, because the whole calculation is a rough estimate anyway; $30 a month might be used.

Assuming that property taxes average $2,400 a year in the neighborhood under consideration, the calculated mortgage payment would run: $1,040 maximum payment, less $200 a month for taxes, less $30 a month for insurance, leaving $810 a month for principal and interest. Run the calculation for yourself in Figure 4.5, using the lower of the two final figures from your earlier calculations.

The next question: How much will that borrow? Again, the answer depends on several factors: loan program chosen, interest rate, term (number of years the loan is to run). Assuming a 30-year

FIGURE 4.6
How Much Can You Borrow?

Principal and interest (from Figure 4.5)	$ _____
Divide by monthly cost per thousand at current rate, 30-year term (from Appendix A)	− _____
Multiply by $1,000	× 1,000
Maximum Mortgage Amount	$ _____

fixed-rate mortgage and interest rates around 7.5 percent, the calculation comes from Appendix A. Locate 7.5 percent interest, for 30 years; 6.99 indicates that each $1,000 borrowed will cost $6.99 a month. How many thousands will $810 carry? Divide $810 by $6.99. The rounded off result, 115.88, indicates that $115,880 is the maximum mortgage for which the buyers qualify (see Figure 4.6).

So in what price range should our hypothetical buyers look? If they have $30,000 available for a down payment and can borrow $115,880, they can buy houses in the $145,880 range. For practical purposes, they could look anywhere under $160,000, because one never knows what sellers will take, and the whole calculation is rough anyway, until exact property taxes and interest rates are known (see Figure 4.7).

One caution: Now that you've done all this work, don't be surprised if a skilled agent or loan consultant, with a knowledge of current interest rates, ratios for specific loan programs, and property taxes, comes up with something different.

FIGURE 4.7
How Much for a House?

Maximum mortgage amount (from Figure 4.6)	$ _____
Plus available down payment	+ _____
Estimated Purchase Price	$ _____

The figure is only a rough estimate. You can safely look at houses priced 10 percent lower or higher than that price.

For buyers putting less than 20 percent down, *private mortgage insurance* (PMI) indemnifying the lender against default may be required, adding to your monthly figures. Some home purchases also require homeowners association fees as well.

5

Costs of Home Ownership

The monthly mortgage payment is, of course, the largest cost of home ownership for most people. If you buy at a time when interest rates are relatively low, you will probably opt for a fixed-rate mortgage. In that case, you can calculate at the start exactly what you'll pay each month for principal and interest for perhaps 15, 20, or 30 years.

When interest rates climb, more borrowers choose adjustable-rate mortgages. If you know the lifetime cap or ceiling on your interest rate, you can calculate the worst case right at the beginning—the highest monthly charge you could ever have if interest rates shot through the roof during the term of your loan. These mortgage types are discussed in greater detail in Chapter 7.

The next two items in the standard PITI payment are taxes and insurance, which can be handled in one of two ways. You may meet those bills on your own, or the lending institution will handle them for you, either by design or by request, as mentioned earlier.

Escrowing Taxes and Insurance

If your home were ever seized and sold for unpaid back taxes, the lending institution would be left with no security for its mortgage. If the house burned to the ground, only the vacant lot would remain as security. So your lender has a direct interest in seeing that you pay your taxes and insurance premiums on time.

With some mortgages, including all VA and FHA loans, an *escrow account* (*reserve, impound, trust* account) is set up for you by the lender. Each month, along with your principal and interest payment, you send one-twelfth of your anticipated property tax and homeowners insurance cost. As the bills come due, they are sent to your lender, who pays them on your behalf.

Your lender is allowed to keep not only enough to pay the next bill due, but also a two-month surplus as a precaution. In about half the states, you are entitled to interest on your escrow account on certain types of mortgages.

You will receive regular reports, monthly or yearly, on the status of the escrow account, which is, after all, your own money. At regular intervals, usually yearly, the account will be analyzed and your payment adjusted up or down, depending on whether the account shows a surplus or deficit.

This adjustment can be a surprise to the homeowner with a fixed-interest mortgage, who expected monthly payments to remain at exactly the same amount for the full term of the loan. It is, of course, taxes and insurance costs that change, not—with a fixed-interest loan—the underlying principal and interest portion of the payment.

About Insurance

The *mortgagee* (lender) will require that you keep *hazard insurance* (fire and similar risks) on the property in an amount sufficient to cover the loan and in areas where it may be required, flood insurance as well. As a prudent homeowner, you will want wider coverage, and for a larger amount.

Rebuilding after a fire, even partially, can sometimes cost more than your original purchase price. And you need personal protection for risks that don't concern your lender—liability for a guest who is hurt on your property, for example.

Your best bet is a *homeowners policy,* which puts many kinds of insurance together in a package. The least expensive, called basic or HO (homeowners)-1, covers fire, windstorm, explosion, smoke, glass breakage, and other perils, including three very important ones: theft, vandalism, and liability.

More expensive is the broad form, HO-2, which adds several more items, largely connected with plumbing, heating, and electrical systems. *Comprehensive insurance* (all-risk) covers even more items and is considered a luxury item. HO-6 is used for condominiums and cooperatives. State regulations dictate the specific coverage in the various policies.

Besides asking what is covered by the policy you buy, it's important to find out what is *not* covered (earthquakes, floods, laptop computers, musical instruments, bottles dropped from airplanes). If you have lots of expensive computer equipment or a valuable collection of jewelry, you may want to pay an additional premium for riders covering those items.

B U Y E R ' S   T I P

When buying homeowners insurance, you should consider:

- Insuring for full replacement cost

- Increasing the deductible to reduce premium payments

Replacement versus Depreciated Value

Suppose your ten-year-old roof is damaged by fire so badly that it must be completely rebuilt. How much is fair for the insurance company to pay you?

You now will have a brand-new roof instead of the old one, which was halfway through its useful life. It could be argued that you are entitled to only half the cost of a roof. On the other hand, you couldn't buy a half-used roof; you had to spend the money for a completely new one. Through no fault of your own, you had an expense you hadn't counted on.

It's important to inquire whether the policy will pay full replacement cost, which should be your goal. Sometimes the answer depends on the dollar amount of your coverage; sometimes an inexpensive rider ensures replacement value.

One way to economize on insurance cost is to opt for a larger deductible. This is the portion of your loss you agree to pay yourself. You wouldn't want the bother of filing claims for $150 losses in any event, and you're not buying insurance as a money-making proposition. Agreeing to handle a larger amount of any loss on your own can cut premiums considerably.

About Taxes

In some areas, property taxes remain the same when ownership of a house is transferred, so you can be sure that the tax bill the seller received last year will be the one you receive next year, except for any communitywide increases. In other areas, the *assessment* (valuation of the house for tax purposes) changes to reflect your purchase price. Next year's taxes would be based on that figure. It's a simple matter to inquire which system is followed in the areas you are considering.

Make sure that you know the *true tax* figure on any house you are considering buying. The present owner may have some tax abatement; various possibilities differ from one state to another, but could include senior citizens' discount, veterans' tax exemption, and preferential treatment for religious organizations.

On the other hand, the seller's tax figure may be higher than the true tax figure. In some localities, for example, unpaid water bills are added to the tax bill. On rare occasions a seller who neglects property could have costs for grass-cutting and even repairs by the city added to the tax bill.

Find out whether taxes in your state are paid in advance, for the coming fiscal year, or in arrears, at the end of the tax year. If you are considering a brand-new house, remember that present taxes are probably based on the value of the vacant lot; the exact amount you will be paying may or may not be established at the time you buy. Investigate when you may be hit with a *supplemental property tax bill,* if this is the case.

Other Costs

Inquire whether trash collection is included in taxes and if there is any extra charge for services such as sidewalk snowplowing. How are you billed for sewer and water charges? Ask the sellers about their utility and fuel bills for the past year or, better yet, for two years. If this is not possible, call the utility company and ask for a rate survey for a recent month on the street you're considering.

Some areas have special school assessments tacked on to the property bill when the usual property taxes are not enough to fund the maintenance and building of the area's schools. This information must be disclosed by the seller or homebuilder at the time of purchase.

Some authorities recommend setting aside 2 or 3 percent of the purchase price for annual maintenance. It's impossible, of course, to set any rule, because the age and present condition of houses vary so widely.

Include in your calculation of monthly costs the prices of basic telephone service and cable TV, which also will vary. Compare costs on homes you may be considering (see Figure 5.1).

Repairs versus Improvements

Improvements (in real estate terminology) are considered permanent additions that increase the value of your home. Every homeowner should keep a permanent file detailing all expenses for improvements, including bills, checks, and receipts. The Internal Revenue Service considers your cost basis for the house to include not only the original purchase price but also money spent on improvements.

FIGURE 5.1
Monthly Cost of Home Ownership

	Present Rental	House 1	House 2	House 3
Address				
Principal and interest				
(Rent)				
Property taxes ($\frac{1}{12}$)				
Insurance ($\frac{1}{12}$)				
Trash collection				
Water, sewer				
Heating and cooling				
Electricity				
Basic telephone				
Cable TV				
Reserve for repairs				
Total				

Repairs and redecorating are not considered improvements. Patching the roof is a repair; installing a completely new roof counts as an improvement. Repainting your living room doesn't count; painting a new addition to the house does. Other improvements can include fences, driveway paving, a new furnace, new wiring, landscaping your backyard, adding a pool or spa, finishing a basement, and adding new rooms or bathrooms.

Risk of Overimproving

Few improvements increase the resale value of your property by the amount you spend on them; buyers may like the idea of a finished basement but seldom want to pay anything extra for it. Depending on the location of the property and neighborhood price levels and expectations, an in-ground swimming pool may add value or may actually be a detriment when time to sell comes. Make improvements for your own satisfaction, not necessarily as investments.

Remodeling kitchens and bathrooms when they are outdated are among the wisest investments, as long as you don't go hog wild and make them worthy of *Architectural Digest* when you live on a Beaver Cleaver street.

The Internet is chock-full of remodeling sites and links to others. Try HomeStore.com or NAHB.com (National Association of Home Builders) as a starting point.

Be cautious about converting bedrooms to other uses by removing closets from those rooms, or cutting a four bedroom house down to two bedrooms without the possibility of putting those bedrooms back, should you someday want to sell your home. Appraisers generally give less value to homes that are not universally appealing or will take too much work to resell. Because your home is an investment, try to consider its value to future buyers, since no one knows what the future holds. If you must use a bedroom as a den, hobby room, or home office, stash the closet doors in the garage for future reconversion, just to be safe.

It is financially unwise to overimprove a house beyond its neighbors. When you decide to sell such a house, it's almost impossible to recoup your investment. A given street will support only a given price range; after that, buyers with more to spend want to live on a more prestigious street. As you house-hunt, keep in mind that any planning for alterations and additions is risky if it will make yours the most expensive house on the street. On the other hand, you may pick up a bargain from owners who have put too much money into their home and can't get it out.

6

What Sort of Home?

You may be sure of the kind of home you want now, but think about the future as you begin your search. Unless you are willing to move every few years, try to anticipate some of the changes that may lie in your future.

Nature-loving newlyweds may come into the agent's office asking for "an old house—we don't care if it's rundown because we can do some work on it, but it has to be in the country on five acres." (There's something mystical about five acres; no one ever requests four acres or six and a half.)

The agent faces a problem immediately, because it can be difficult to find financing for a rundown house. And a few years later the couple may come back to the office, having found themselves isolated with two infants and nary a babysitter in sight.

"Please," they say, "this time show us something in the middle of a tract full of toddler playmates and baby-sitting teenagers."

On the flip side, Americans are a more transient bunch than ever before, with the average householder moving an average of seven times during his or her life. Seeing your home as an investment that may be sold someday will make you want to retain its desirability and broaden its appeal so that if the time comes to sell it, you can get top dollar in a shorter marketing time.

Ideas about housing design can change also. The couple with the toddlers will be delighted with a family room open to the kitchen so that the tots can be supervised while the cooking is going on. But ten years later, the same parents may be longing for a family room located down a flight of stairs, around a corner, and with a soundproof door.

Every house is a compromise. Before you start looking, accept that you will eventually give up something you now consider important: the mature trees, the open fireplace, the guest room. You'll fall in love with one special house and suddenly decide you can live without a sunny backyard after all.

Keeping a Marriage Together through It All

The emotional aspect of buying a home can be extremely intense. Women view their homes as nests, men as their castles and investments. If buying a home with a spouse or partner, it may be wise to talk about what kinds of compromises may be in order, creating less room for conflict when the time comes to choose.

Analyzing the ratings in Figure 6.1, establish your own priorities: factors that are essential, those on which you will compromise if necessary, and those that don't matter at all. Then use Figure 6.2 to fill out the profile of your needs and wants, and to consider housing factors common in your area.

Consider Traffic Patterns

Keep in mind a few basics about floor plans as you inspect houses. Stand in the entrance and try to imagine yourself going about the daily routine. Consider, for example, a hypothetical trip home with bags of groceries. Where will you park? Will you have to carry the load up stairs? Must you go through the living room? Is there a handy counter near the refrigerator for unloading?

If you have an infant and you sleep with your door open, you'll want to stay within earshot. Many buyers with small children reject floor plans with master bedrooms on a different level than other bedrooms for that reason. In a year or two, though, you may value a private, quiet bedroom. It may be desirable to have the

FIGURE 6.1
What Matters Most to You?

Before you start house hunting, consider which factors are most important to you. Rate on a scale of 1 (unimportant) to 10 (very important):

Proximity to work	_____	Storage space	_____
Quality and proximity of schools	_____	Room for hobby	_____
Condition/age of house	_____	Room for entertaining	_____
Type/age of roof	_____	Home office	_____
Fireplace(s)	_____	Ease of maintenance	_____
Landscaping, view	_____	Mature trees	_____
Garage requirements	_____	Light and sunshine	_____
Number of bedrooms	_____	Sidewalks	_____
Number of baths	_____	Lot size and usability	_____
Pool or spa	_____	Expandability	_____
Computer wiring	_____	Security system	_____
Large kitchen	_____	Breakfast nook	_____
Deck, patio	_____	Formal entry	_____
Separate dining room	_____	Workshop	_____
Family room/great room	_____	Formal living room	_____
Community pool	_____	Neighborhood park	_____
Gate guarded	_____	Ample guest parking	_____
Active adult (over 55)	_____	Tot lot	_____
Neighborhood rules (CC&Rs)	_____	Other	_____

master bedroom separated from the others by a zone of closets, hall, or baths. (The best floor plans incorporate such buffers for all bedrooms.)

If the front door opens directly into the living room, a house in colder climates may eventually need an enclosed foyer to shield the occupants and the thermostat from icy blasts. If you don't like the idea of visitors regularly checking out your living areas from the front door, there is even more of a reason to buy a home with a true entry foyer.

Then imagine yourselves in midsummer, eating out on the patio. Will it be easy to serve from the kitchen, without risking spills on the living room carpet en route?

Check the kitchen for sufficient counter and cupboard space. Double-check for a place to put things down, not only next to the refrigerator but also at the stove, sink, and dishwasher. Even if you are resigned to a small Pullman kitchen and plan to eat in the dining room, look for enough space in the kitchen for a high chair, a bottled water dispenser, or a stool for a chatty guest. If there is a kitchen island, check out its use as an eating area as well. Make sure there is enough clearance for refrigerator doors to open, room for "help with the dishes," and enough overhead lighting.

Give a house extra points if you don't have to go through a living room or family room to reach other areas. A dead-end living area makes for better relaxation and tends to stay neat. Check out potential furniture placement in each room. Is there an entire wall of windows and doors, making furniture placement difficult? Can you face your bulkier pieces towards an entertainment wall without blocking traffic?

Garages and their dimensions have become extremely important in these days of SUVs, sophisticated recreational toys, and two- or three-car families. They are particularly important for breathing room in home areas where basements are not prevalent, such as the southern and western United States. In many areas, three-car garages are the norm in all but the smallest of new homes, with third stall flexibility giving rise to boat storage, a workshop, a home gym, a bonus room, or, even a third car! Sometimes the storage space for kids' toys and future garage-sale items is enough of a reason to opt for extra garage space for many homebuyers. Increasingly, municipalities are holding new homebuild-

FIGURE 6.2
Your Personal Profile

Analyzing the ratings in Figure 6.1, establish your own priorities: factors that are essential, those on which you will compromise if necessary, and those that don't matter at all.

Absolute Musts	Nice to Have	Don't Matter

ers to stricter and stricter guidelines as to the "streetscape" (the look of the neighborhood) of garage-dominant new home communities, encouraging builders to incorporate side-loading, back-loading or recessed garages.

Orientation is also important. Especially in the Sun Belt areas, evaluating where the sun will hit during certain times of the day can mean the difference between faded carpeting, more costly energy use, a swimming pool that sits in the shade most of the day, or the need for solar screens.

Look for the convenience of an outside entrance if the home has a basement and see if there is a service door to the garage. An engineer's inspection can help you evaluate conditions, which is particularly valuable with an older home. But you are the only one who can judge whether a floor plan fits your lifestyle.

See Figure 6.3 for an illustration of common home architectural styles.

FIGURE 6.3   Architectural Styles

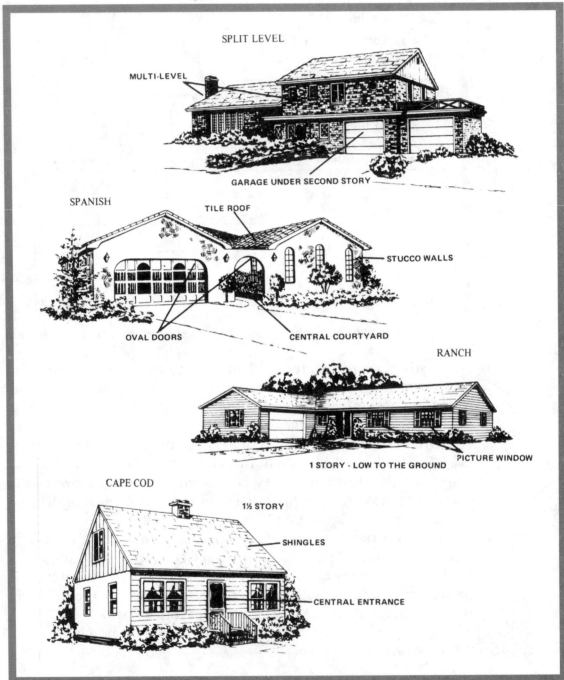

FIGURE 6.3 Architectural Styles (Continued)

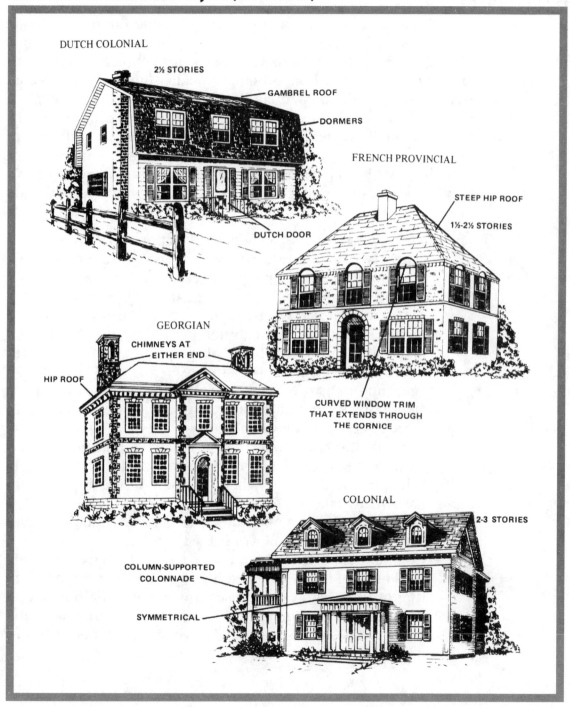

A Brand-New House

At one point every home was new. Production (tract) home-builders usually offer several floor plans, options to each floor plan, and several elevations (facades) for each one. Along with groups of speculative homes built by smaller builders, homes constructed on builder-owned land account for up to 80 percent of new single-family homes sold, according to the National Association of Home Builders. The remaining 20 percent or so are custom homes, made to order for individual landowners.

There are both positive and negative points to buying either a new home or one resale (previously lived-in). On the positive side of new home purchases:

- New homes are an original reflection of their owner's tastes. No one has ever smoked in, cooked in, or lived in a new home. Brand-new appliances, heating and air-conditioning systems, roofs, carpeting, and energy-efficient windows are but a few of the attractive features. Prepared home offices, custom cabinetry, the latest in decorating materials, and useful floor plan options, such as master bedroom sitting areas, walk-in closets with full built-in storage, and bonus play areas, can all be ordered by the buyer.
- New homes are built to stricter energy codes, resulting in more energy efficiency and cost-savings.
- Many in the real estate industry believe that new homes tend to appreciate faster than homes in older, more established neighborhoods, where the bulk of the appreciation has already taken place.
- New home areas sometimes offer newer schools, newer shopping areas, and newer infrastructure.
- Common experiences can create a rapport between neighbors moving into a new neighborhood. With everyone putting in their backyard landscaping, unpacking boxes, and decorating their homes at the same time, there tend to be fewer cliques within the neighborhood. Everyone seems to need each other at once.

- Areas where new homes are built can also offer more high-tech wiring for a growing number of telecommuters, home-based businesses, and home entertainment junkies.
- New homes can also be specially designed for handicapped homeowners with fully accessible elements.
- Some new home areas are master-planned with carefully designed amenities, such as tot lots for kids, soccer and softball fields, hiking and biking trails, perimeter walls or security gates, and community pools and clubhouses.

One of the more recent trends is for adults 55 and older to flock to the new active adult communities popping up all over the country, located not far from urban centers. Some of these active retirement and empty-nester neighborhoods feature golf courses and other recreational facilities. Even leading edge Baby Boomers who want the convenience and amenities these neighborhoods offer are happy to dispense with streets peppered with kids' toys and replace their second car with a golf cart.

On the negative side of new home purchases:

- Taxes may be higher. Special bonds and assessments for schools, road widening, and common lighting and landscaping are more prevalent in new home areas.
- Although not always the rule, new home areas don't offer the lush, established trees and landscaping you may find attractive in older areas.
- Spending your first few years putting in some landscaping, buying window coverings, installing patios, and making your home livable to your own tastes may result in "Hole in the Pocket" syndrome. Some of these things must be done with used homes also, but not usually with the urgency felt in a new home purchase, where all is bare to begin with.
- Depending on the builder's schedule, the weather, and the availability of labor and building materials, you may have to wait up to six to nine months for a new home to be built from the ground up. Delays in any one of these factors can throw off your plans to have the kids in school by a certain date or get the family settled before the holidays. You have to be willing to roll with the punches.

- If you change your mind on anything during the process of construction, you'll run into construction cut-off times, after which the builder may charge you an arm and a leg to make an alteration to the original plan.
- You'll pay full-cost for anything extra you do to a new home, unlike the purchase of a home that's even just a few years old, where a previous buyer put in the pool, enclosed the patio, did some decorating, added window coverings, or added built-in cabinetry.
- You may spend the first year or so working through the kinks of a new home purchase by dealing with the builder's warranty department. Chunks of concrete in the plumbing, previously unnoticed anomalies in the paint, walls, trim, or installations may have to be dealt with.

When shopping for a new home, it's important that you or your agent do your homework, not only evaluating the criteria already mentioned, but also checking out the reputation of the homebuilder, its new home warranty, and any applicable taxes that may apply. Make sure you can live with neighborhood restrictions, such as those prohibiting RV storage, basketball hoops hanging from garage doorframes, cars regularly parked on driveways, or satellite dishes. These rules are usually referred to as the CC&Rs (*Covenants, Conditions, & Restrictions*) and need a careful review before you make a commitment to buy. Never buy a new home in an area where you have mentally planned ahead to ignore any or all of these rules. After all, the reason some people decide *not* to buy in a given neighborhood (like too many rules) may be the same reasons others thought it was just the place for them.

The Internet is now an excellent source of information for new homebuyers. HomeStore.com and its subsidiary, Home-Builder.com, are sites endorsed by the NAHB (National Association of Home Builders), just as Realtor.com (with the same family of sites) is endorsed by the NAR (National Association of REALTORS®) Also popular is NewHomeNetwork.com, promoted by a consortium of newspaper conglomerates. For more technical sources, check out Builderonline.com, the Web site for the industry-popular *BUILDER* Magazine. Don't forget to spend an evening roaming around NAHB.com, where one can see what is going on in the home building industry nationwide. Individual homebuilders host their own Web sites as well. Some of these sites are linked to larger ones, but if you type the homebuilder's name in any search engine, you will probably hit pay dirt. There, you can check out the builder's homes being offered in areas that may interest you, as well as read about the builder's history and style, and the building components they deem important.

Having a custom home made to order is the dream of many a homebuyer. Most work themselves up to this purchase, which can be rewarding if done with eyes wide open. If this is an option for you, interview several area-known custom builders. You can call your local Homebuilders Association for referrals or a list of those in your area. It's important to see physically homes they have already built (and not just pictures of them). If possible, speak to some of the builder's clients for personal testimonials before proceeding. Communication, trust, and a good rapport with your contractor are probably the most important factors in this oftentimes time-consuming and tedious process. The result, however, may be worth the inherent frustrations involved in tackling such a project on your own.

Owning a Co-op, Condominium, or Town House

In areas where land is at a premium, cooperatives, town houses, and condominium apartments may be attractive alternatives to more expensive housing. Many empty nesters and busy young professionals also enjoy the absence of outside chores. Multifamily living offers the advantages of owning a home without the constraints of single-family homeownership. The Internal Revenue Service treats co-ops and condos exactly as it does single-family houses.

Cooperatives

The cooperative is the older form of ownership, found mainly in New York City, Chicago, and a few other areas. The owner of a co-op does not own any real estate. Rather, the buyer receives two things: (1) shares in a corporation that owns the entire building and (2) a proprietary lease for the particular living unit being bought.

These shares and the lease are classified not as real estate but as personal property. They may be borrowed against, however, to assist with the purchase, and the IRS will treat the loan as a mortgage. The owner of a co-op owes no property tax on the individual living unit. Instead, the monthly payment includes a share of taxes the cooperative pays on the entire building. It also includes a share of the cooperative's payment on the one large mortgage on the entire building, as well as the usual maintenance costs.

Tenant-owners in a cooperative building depend on each other for financial stability. For that reason, most co-ops require that prospective buyers be approved by the board of directors.

Because a large part of the monthly charge goes toward property taxes and interest on the underlying mortgage, the prospective buyer can expect a certain percentage of that expenditure to be income tax deductible at the end of the year. If you are interested in a cooperative, you will be told what percent of the monthly charge is deductible. Inquire also about the dollar amount of liability you will be taking on for your share of the existing mortgage on the whole building. This will be in addition to any loan you place to buy your shares.

Condominiums

The term *condominium* refers not to an apartment, but rather to a form of individual ownership. The buyer of a condominium receives a deed and owns real estate, just as a single house is owned. In the case of a condominium, the buyer receives complete title to the interior of the apartment ("from the plaster in") and also to a percentage of the common elements—the land itself, staircases, sidewalks, swimming pool, driveways, lawns, elevators, roofs, and heating systems.

The condo is classified as real estate. The buyer may place a mortgage on the property and will receive an individual tax bill for the one unit. In addition, monthly fees are levied to pay for outside maintenance, repairs, landscaping or snow removal, recreation facilities, and the like.

Town house ownership is a hybrid form of condominium and/or cooperative, and can take many forms. Typically, the unit owner has fee simple (complete) ownership of the living space and the land below it, with some form of group ownership of common areas. The individual may or may not own a small patio or front area and may or may not own the roof above the unit.

What to Check: Condos and Co-ops

Before investing in either type of living arrangement, you should be furnished with a daunting amount of material to read. Look it over carefully. Enlist the aid of an agent, an accountant, and/or an attorney to review the material. You are particularly interested in six things:

1. *The financial health of the organization you will be joining.* Does it have substantial reserves put aside to cover major renovations and replacements?
2. *The condition of the building(s).* Is it likely to need a new roof, elevators, boiler, or windows, for which you would bear a share of the responsibility?
3. *The covenants, conditions, and regulations you must promise to observe.* Could you rent out your apartment, paint your front door red, have a roommate under the age of 55, or eventually sell the unit on the open market?
4. *The percentage of owner-occupancy.* Traditionally, more homeowners and fewer tenants is preferred.
5. *Any liens or judgments against the property and their type.* These make it more difficult to sell the unit when you are so inclined.
6. *Any pending litigation against the builder.* This makes it almost impossible to get financing.

Use Figure 6.4 to rate the units you are considering.

Manufactured Housing

Manufactured housing has come a long way since its "trailer" days. In fact, many consumers do not fully appreciate what they are seeing when they are looking at manufactured housing. The

FIGURE 6.4
Checklist for Judging Condos, Co-ops, or Town Houses

	#1	#2	#3
Address			
Condo, co-op, or town house			
Square footage			
Number of bedrooms			
Garage			
Fireplace, extras			
Price			
Monthly charges			
Percent deductible			
Financial stability			
Reserves			
On a scale of 1–10:			
Floor plan, layout			
Condition			
Kitchen			
Bath			
View, windows			

umbrella term *modular* has also been used to describe these types of dwellings, but modular can refer to anything from build-it-yourself log cabins to luxury homes that are factory-built as modules on an assembly line.

Modular manufacturing techniques sometime have advantages over the sticks and mortar trades. They can be built year-round, installation times can be cut considerably, they are ideal for remote and rural areas, they can be easily customized, and they can cut waste and the environmental impact made by traditional types of home construction.

Manufactured housing leaves the factory in a variety of stages, to be assembled and completed on the home site. Some are precut and paneled. Other types arrive in modules that are joined together, complete with plumbing, floor coverings, cabinetry, and electrical and insulation systems installed at the plant. Immensely popular in some European countries, manufactured housing is gaining in popularity in both the United States and Canada.

You may be limited in finding lenders who offer loans on manufactured homes. Check with a mortgage company or manufactured-home dealer about which lender can help.

Not all neighborhoods permit manufactured homes to be placed on their home sites. Find out if the area you have in mind for a home of this type will permit this kind of construction.

Mobile Homes

Mobile homes are still popular in many parts of the United States. One attraction is the lower initial cost, as compared to a single-family home. Again, check zoning before considering the location of a mobile home, and investigate financing carefully. Mobile homes are regarded as personal property, and qualify for regular mortgage loans only if on a permanent foundation, and on land that is owned, not rented.

Choosing the community in which you buy may be more important than selecting the individual home itself. Talk with the occupants of the mobile home area that interests you, and find out how cooperative the management is. Give some consideration as to the pride with which the community is kept by both its occupants and its management.

7

Financing Your Home Purchase

Did you ever wish you could take the final exam in a course just for fun at the first session, to see how much you knew before you started? Right now, go ahead and try the following quiz (Figure 7.1), prepared by the Mortgage Bankers Association of America.

If you score ten or higher, the Mortgage Bankers Association says that you are "an informed consumer with a head start on shopping for the mortgage that is right for you."

If you score less than ten—fine. It proves that you will profit by reading on.

Broker Plans Strategy

Within the first few minutes of conversation, an agent probably begins, almost unconsciously, to plan a strategy for financing your purchase. Those seemingly impertinent questions about your salary, cash on hand, and present debts are important in helping you find the right way to buy your home.

Buying for All Cash

A purchase for all cash is, of course, the simplest and quickest method. It is also the most welcome to a seller and, in a normal open market sale, should be worth a concession on price.

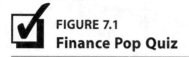

FIGURE 7.1
Finance Pop Quiz

1. According to most mortgage lenders, you could qualify for a mortgage amount of about four times your gross annual salary.
   True   False

2. What is the maximum amount that homeowners may borrow to purchase and/or improve a first and/or second home, and take full federal income tax deduction for the interest?
   A. $100,000
   B. $1 million
   C. $500,000
   D. There is no limit.

3. A 15-year fixed-rate mortgage saves you nearly 60 percent of the total interest costs over the life of the loan when compared to a 30-year fixed-rate mortgage.
   True   False

4. Mortgage lenders refer to a homeowner's monthly payment as "PITI" because:
   A. Homeowners should be pitied because of their monthly payments.
   B. It includes principal, interest, taxes, and insurance payments.
   C. *Piti* is French for *mortgage payment.*
   D. PITI is short for "Pay It on Time In full."

5. A jumbo loan is:
   A. A mortgage that is really too big for you to afford
   B. A loan that you pay monthly for a time and then pay one "jumbo" payment on the remaining principal
   C. A mortgage that is larger than the limits set by Fannie Mae (Federal National Mortgage Association) and the Federal Home Loan Mortgage Corporation (Freddie Mac)
   D. A loan to buy a house with more than four bedrooms

Source: Reprinted by permission of the Mortgage Bankers Association of America.

FIGURE 7.1   (Continued)

6. A *buydown* refers to:
   A. A discount on the home price so you can afford it
   B. A discount on the loan's interest rate during the first years of the loan to make financing easier to qualify for
   C. The purchase of a home in a southern resort area
   D. Buying a cheaper house than you live in now; also called a *trade-down*

7. Typical closing costs can range from:
   A. 1–3% of the loan amount
   B. 3–8% of the loan amount
   C. 8–10% of the loan amount
   D. 10–15% of the loan amount

8. A biweekly mortgage (a loan on which you pay half the monthly payment amount every two weeks) shortens the life of a 30-year loan by about:
   A. 10 years
   B. 5 years
   C. 15 years
   D. It doesn't shorten the life of the loan; it just decreases interest costs.

9. A convertible mortgage is one that
   A. allows you to buy a car with the house.
   B. allows the homeowner to decrease the loan's interest rate without refinancing the mortgage.
   C. can be used like a giant credit card.
   D. allows you to make an adjustable-rate mortgage into a fixed-rate mortgage.

10. Lenders normally recommend refinancing a mortgage if:
    A. The market rate is two or more percentage points below the rate on the loan.
    B. The homeowner has no equity in the property.
    C. The homeowner doesn't want to pay any taxes.
    D. The homeowner has a convertible mortgage.

FIGURE 7.1 (Continued)

11. Mortgages backed by the Federal Housing Administration (FHA) require what size down payment?
    A. 0% (nothing down)
    B. About 3–5% of the loan amount
    C. About 10–20% of the loan amount
    D. More than 20% of the loan amount

12. When discussing *points,* your lender means:
    A. The things you really like about your new house
    B. Prepaid interest; each point equals 1 percent of the loan amount
    C. A rating system used by lenders to qualify applicants
    D. The number of traffic violations that show up on your credit report

13. What is a deed of trust?
    A. Money you receive before you have actually qualified for the loan
    B. A special document waiving your right of rescission
    C. A document used in place of a mortgage in some states
    D. A special mortgage you can get if the lender knows you

14. A VA loan is:
    A. A long-term, low- or no-down payment loan guaranteed by the Department of Veterans Affairs
    B. A loan on a home sold at a discount because it has been "Vacant and Abandoned"
    C. A loan on which the homebuyer pays a 1 percent premium
    D. A loan for an animal hospital funded by the Veterinarians of America

15. A title search:
    A. Examines the homebuyer's background to see if he or she is descended from royalty
    B. Examines municipal records to determine the legal ownership of a property
    C. Looks for books in the public library that tell about housing finance
    D. Verifies a property's past owners

Answers: 1. False; 2. B; 3. True; 4. B; 5. C; 6. B; 7. B; 8. A; 9. D; 10. A; 11. B; 12. B; 13. C; 14. A; 15. B.

You may run into an unusual situation that calls for immediate action—a seller facing foreclosure, for example. Sometimes when a divorce or death in a family occurs, owners are ready to accept a bargain price in return for quick cash. If you can take advantage of such an opportunity, resist the temptation to act without professional or legal advice. You may need to sign an immediate purchase offer promising prompt settlement, but your own broker or lawyer should ensure that the offer protects you properly.

Without the protection of a mortgage lender's investigation, you need assurance that you are receiving clear, trouble-free title, that taxes are paid to date, that the seller has the right to transfer the property to you, and that you aren't taking over old financial claims along with the real estate.

In such emergency situations, the buyer often must accept the physical condition of the property "as is." You may want to bring in a building inspection engineer before your purchase contract becomes firm so that you know what you are getting into.

Buying with Nothing Down

You've seen those hot-shot speakers on cable TV, with operators standing by to take your money for the privilege of video-training you to buy property with no down payment. Can you really buy real estate with nothing down?

Yes, indeed.

There are several ways, and they're not secret. You don't need to send $299 for the books and tapes. Any good real estate broker knows the techniques and can tell you whether a particular plan fits your circumstances.

Veterans can place VA loans with nothing down and do it on houses valued to $203,000, if they qualify to carry the payments. If the seller agreed, a VA loan could even be placed with the seller paying all the buyer's closing costs.

For those with limited income who want to live in rural areas, the Farmers Home Administration (FmHA) makes no-down-payment loans on modest properties, discussed later in this chapter. Monthly payments with FmHA can be subsidized, depending on family income, with as low as 1 percent interest.

Then—particularly with income property, where the owner doesn't need to get the money out right away—you can always look for a seller who will turn the property over to you and carry the mortgage—and if you look really hard, perhaps do it with nothing down.

Picking a Mortgage

For the usual purchase, a smorgasbord of mortgage types is available for your consideration. At any time, perhaps 200 different loan programs will be offered in the typical community. Dozens of terms describe particular mortgages: FHA, VA, assumable, portfolio, conventional, convertible, and adjustable-rate mortgages (ARMs), just to name a few. Your agent contemplates this dazzling array, trying to fit your needs with current offerings. To ask, "Which is the best loan program?" is like walking into a pharmacy and asking, "Which is your best medicine?" Choosing the right loan involves taking into consideration the following:

- Proposed down payment
- Your income and future prospects
- Current interest rates
- Type and condition of the property
- Costs and fees
- Price range of homes you want to consider
- Your personal debt portfolio
- Your credit scores

When you're offered a loan at a particularly favorable rate, inquire about closing costs. Certain costs are standard: appraisal of the property, credit check, and other legitimate charges. Most leaders charge an origination fee, which covers their cost of doing business; paying it up front or seeing it absorbed into the interest rate is the trade-off you'll usually face. Any other fees should be questioned and compared with other lenders'.

Mortgagor and Mortgagee

To speak of "getting" a mortgage, by the way, is inaccurate. A mortgage is a financial claim against your real estate. You give that to a lending institution, along with a bond or note, which is a personal promise to repay. In return, the lender gives you money—cash. You do the mortgaging; you are the mortgagor. The lender takes your mortgage, holds your mortgage, and is the mortgagee.

Some who have trouble with the terms find it helpful to remember that *borrower* and *mortgagor* both have two *o*s. *Lender* and *mortgagee* have two *e*s each.

In some states, a *deed of trust* is used instead of a mortgage. If your state is one of these, for practical purposes you can consider *deed of trust* and *mortgage* to be interchangeable terms.

Portfolio Loans

In looking for the right mortgage plan, it helps to understand the difference between *portfolio loans* and those intended for sale on the secondary market.

Years ago, banks took part of their depositors' savings, lent it out on mortgages, collected monthly payments, and when enough money was returned, made more loans. This procedure is the exception these days. The bank that uses such a system is said to be making portfolio or nonconforming loans, keeping the mortgages as assets in its own portfolio.

If you have an unusual situation (complicated self-employment income, for example, or the desire to pay your own property taxes and insurance instead of through the lender's escrow account) find out which local lenders are currently making portfolio loans. On these loans underwriters can be more flexible, making exceptions to their usual rules, subject only to state laws and their own judgment. Portfolio loans are sometimes called nonconforming (because they are not tailored to the requirements of the secondary market), or jumbo loans if they are for larger amounts than the secondary market will buy.

The Secondary Market

These days, most other mortgages are bundled into large packages and sold to big investors in what is known as the *secondary market*. Among the buyers are large insurance companies, banks and pension funds, and most important, organizations specifically set up to warehouse mortgages, like the Federal National Mortgage Association (Fannie Mae).

Borrowers may not know that their mortgages have been sold if the original lender retains the servicing—collecting payments, handling paperwork, and forwarding the money. In other cases, particularly when the buyer of the packaged mortgages is another bank, borrowers may be instructed to send their payments directly to the new mortgagee. Many borrowers feel betrayed when they find they are dealing with out-of-state institutions instead of their friendly local bank, but the system allows lenders to recoup their investment immediately and to channel more mortgage money back into the community.

Lenders are required to notify you, before commitment, how likely your loan is to be sold on the secondary market.

When Fannie Mae, which owns perhaps one mortgage in 20 in this country, announces that it will buy packages of certain types of loans, lenders around the country quickly bring their loan programs into compliance. Other national standards are set by the Government National Mortgage Association (Ginnie Mae) and the Federal Home Loan Mortgage Corporation (Freddie Mac).

All of this can affect your search for the perfect mortgage. When you find that most lenders have identical upper limits on the amount they'll lend, or analyze your income in the same way, they are probably conforming to the requirements of the secondary market in order to sell your loan.

Other Lenders

Don't be surprised if your mortgage lender turns out to be something other than the traditional bank—savings bank, commercial bank, or savings and loan institution. While those entities are

---

BUYER'S TIP

When choosing a mortgage to suit your financial situation, find out about:

- How much down payment is required

- Both the interest rate and the annual percentage rate (APR)

- Standard closing costs (and any extra fees the lender may charge and why)

- The possibility that your mortgage will be resold on the secondary market

---

still very much in the mortgage business, there are many other players.

Mortgage bankers (mortgage companies) are in business solely to make (originate) mortgage loans and handle the ensuing monthly paperwork (servicing). Unlike traditional banks, they take no depositors' savings and offer no checking accounts. They are active in the secondary market, selling packages of mortgages and turning the proceeds over to make more loans. Mortgage banking firms have become a large part of the lending industry.

Mortgage brokers, on the other hand, make no loans at all. Their role is to bring borrowers and lenders together. If you have an unusual situation or special needs, they can be particularly useful because they keep current with the offerings of many different lenders, much like insurance brokers who search multiple lines of insurance for their clients.

Credit unions are often overlooked in the search for the right lender. If you belong to one, mention this fact to the broker with whom you are working, and investigate for yourself whether your credit union offers mortgage loans. In some instances, favorable terms are available.

So What Are Points?

As with everything else, there are good points and bad points. Bad points are the ones you pay; good points are the ones someone else pays.

Points can be described as the fees charged by lending institutions as extra up-front, one-time lump-sum interest when a new loan is placed.

Each point is 1 percent of a new loan. If you buy a house for $150,000 and borrow $120,000, one point would equal $1,200 (not $1,500). Two points would be $2,400. The term is sometimes used interchangeably with percent, as in "You'll have a two-point cap," which means that you'd have a 2 percent cap.

Points are usually paid at final settlement when the loan is actually made. *Zero point loans*, however, are not uncommon, with the points financed into the loan, giving you a slightly higher debt. Don't assume in this case that points magically disappear, unless they are paid by another party entirely. Arranging for a zero point loan is not a bad option if you are short on closing funds, and don't mind the higher monthly payment.

Sometimes you can pay extra points in return for special favors—a lock-in guarantees that you'll receive the rate in effect when you apply for the loan, no matter what has happened to rates in the meantime. Or you may be charged extra for an extension if you don't close within a given period after the bank commits to making the loan.

When rates are fluctuating rapidly, some borrowers have been known to apply at two different lenders: one with the rate locked in, and one without. For whichever loan isn't eventually chosen, the wheeler-dealer may owe some up-front money for appraisal or credit report fees. Lenders are less than pleased at the prospect, but it could give the applicant a chance to choose the more favorable loan at the last minute.

On new construction, builders will usually not permit their own in-house or preferred lenders to lock in an interest rate until they have received a firm completion date for the new house, so that their buyers are not left with expired rate locks if the home's construction schedule is delayed. This is usually within 30 days of completion. If you are using your own lender to buy a builder's home, be extremely careful that you don't lock your rate too soon, or you may be out of luck if there is a delay in the home's completion (unless, of course, interest rates fall while you're waiting).

Points may be paid by buyer or seller, depending on their agreement. Points paid by you as the buyer of your own residence are income tax deductible as interest, in the year they are paid. Points you pay to purchase income property must be amortized (deducted bit by bit over the years) along with other costs of placing an investor's loan.

Points paid by the seller are one of the expenses of selling, and reduce the seller's capital gain on the sale. The buyer, however, is allowed to take points paid (even those paid by the seller) as an income tax deduction for interest expense for that year.

Annual Percentage Rate

Which is better, an 8 percent, fixed-rate loan for 30 years with payment of one point plus a half-percent origination fee, or an adjustable-rate mortgage for 20 years, currently at 5 percent, with four points up front?

First, of course, you must decide whether you have a gambler's instinct and will enjoy following interest rates and taking a chance on next year's payment being higher or lower. If rates are currently at the lower end of their inevitable cycle, you might prefer a fixed-rate loan (see Figure 7.2).

But trying to compare rates on such different loan programs, with varying closing costs, is (as your algebra teacher used to say) like working with apples and oranges.

To aid the consumer, lenders are required to quote you an annual percentage rate (APR), which takes into account points and certain closing costs.

FIGURE 7.2
Checklist for Comparing Fixed-Rate Mortgages

	Loan 1	Loan 2	Loan 3	Loan 4
Lending institution				
Phone number				
Application cost				
Interest rate				
Points				
Term (years)				
Monthly payment (P&I)				
Loan-to-value ratio (required down payment)				
Private mortgage insurance?				
Monthly cost				
Qualifying ratio				
Prepayment penalty				
Buydown?				
Lock-in?				
Biweekly?				

Suppose you do pay 6 percent, but with four extra points in a lump sum at closing. Clearly, your rate is really more than 6 percent. It's not six plus four, because you pay those four points only once, not every year. But it's more than six. How much more? That's the APR. Not all lenders calculate it in the same fashion, but it is useful for comparison shopping.

Conventional Mortgages

Loans agreed on between you and the lender, without any government intervention except for state banking regulations, are known as conventional mortgages. Because banking theory holds that it is unsafe to lend more than 80 percent of the value of the property, the standard conventional loan requires 20 percent down. With a 20 percent down payment, you have an 80 percent loan-to-value ratio (LTV).

If you are putting less than that down on a conventional loan, you will be asked to carry private mortgage insurance (PMI). This insurance, for which you pay a small premium, protects the lending institution in case the loan goes sour and the property can't be sold for enough to cover the debt. Because this lowers the lender's risk, you can sometimes borrow with as little as 5 percent down (95 percent LTV).

Low documentation (Low-doc), no-documentation, or express loans are also available, and have become popular with many who wish to minimize the amount of personal financial information given to a lender in exchange for a sizable down payment. If you are making a large down payment (usually 25 percent or more), the lender may waive most of its usual paperwork for verifying income or employment, checking on reserves and credit standing only.

Understanding Adjustable-Rate Mortgages

Until the early 1980s, almost all mortgages had a fixed rate, with the borrower knowing in advance exactly what the monthly payment would run for principal and interest over the full 25 or 30 years of a loan.

As interest rates began to skyrocket and finally hit 18 percent, lenders found themselves locked into unprofitable long-term commitments to keep their money lent out at rates like 5, 6, and 7 percent. This led to serious problems for lending institutions, and many were reluctant to make any further fixed-interest loans.

What emerged was the *adjustable-rate mortgage* (ARM). The ARM shifts the risk of rising interest rates to the borrower, who also stands to benefit if rates drop during the period of the loan. It is often chosen when interest rates are high; when rates drop, many borrowers prefer to lock in long-term, fixed-rate loans. Those who plan to remain in a house for only a short time may opt for an ARM.

To choose wisely, the borrower must shop around, asking about the details of each ARM loan to find the one best suited to his or her own situation (see Figure 7.3).

Judging adjustable-rate mortgages requires understanding of a whole new vocabulary.

Index. The interest rate on your loan may go up or down, following the trend for interest rates across the country.

To keep things fair, your lender must key the changes to some national indicator of current rates. The index must be outside the control of your lender, and it should be a figure you can check for yourself, as published in the business sections of newspapers.

The most commonly chosen indexes are the rates at which investors will currently lend money to the government through purchase of U.S. Treasury notes and bills. The index used for your ARM loan might be the rate on sales of one-year, three-year, or five-year Treasury obligations ("one-year T-bills . . .").

Another index might be the average mortgage interest rate across the country for the preceding six months (Federal Home Loan Bank Board Cost of Funds). This index changes more slowly than, for example, the one-year T-bill. It could work for or against you, depending on the general direction of rates.

Margin. If Treasury bills are the chosen index, and they are selling at 6 percent interest, your lender will not make mortgage loans at that rate. Rather, you will pay a specific percentage above the index.

If you are offered a 2 percent margin, you would pay 8 percent. If at the time of interest adjustment, Treasury bills had gone to 7 percent, a 2 percent margin would set your mortgage rate at 9 percent. If they had dropped to 5.5 percent, your interest would drop to 7.5 percent.

FIGURE 7.3

Checklist for Comparing Adjustable-Rate Mortgages (ARMs)

	Loan 1	Loan 2	Loan 3	Loan 4	Loan 5
Lender					
Phone number					
Term (years)					
Adjustment period					
Index					
Margin					
Initial rate					
Today's true rate					
Points					
Adjustment cap					
Lifetime ceiling					
Application fee					
Loan-to-value ratio (LTV)					
Qualifying ratio					
Buydown (yes or no)					
Negative amortization (yes or no)					
Convertibility?					
When, at what cost?					
Assumability?					
At what cost?					

Cap. The word is used in two ways. First, your loan agreement may set, for example, a 2 percent cap (limit) on any upward adjustment. If interest rates (as reflected by your index) had gone up 3 percent by the time of adjustment, your rate could be raised only 2 percent.

When choosing an ARM, ask what happens in the above example. Is the extra 1 percent saved to be used for "catch-up" at the next adjustment, even though interest rates might have remained level? Or will you have negative amortization (see below)?

The second use of the word is synonymous with *ceiling*.

Ceiling. A ceiling (sometimes also called a lifetime cap) is an interest rate beyond which your loan can never go. Typically, you may be offered a five-point ceiling. This means that if your loan starts at 8 percent, it can never rise beyond 13 percent, no matter what happens to national interest rates. A ceiling allows you to calculate your worst case.

Worst case. If your 30-year adjustable loan for $85,000 now costs $510 a month for principal and interest at 6 percent, and if your ceiling is 5 percent, the worst that could ever happen is that your interest rate would rise to 11 percent. You can and should calculate in advance what that could cost you–$809 a month.

Negative amortization. Regular amortization involves gradually paying off the principal borrowed, through part of your monthly payments. If, however, your monthly payments aren't enough to cover even the interest due, negative amortization is a possibility.

Suppose that interest on your loan should total $700 a month. For some reason, however, your monthly payment is set at $650. The shortfall, $50 a month, may be added to the amount you have borrowed. At the end of the year you'd owe not less, but about $600 more than when you started.

Negative amortization could result from an artificially low initial interest rate, or it could follow a hike in rates larger than your cap allows the lender to impose.

Not all mortgage plans include the possibility of negative amortization. Sometimes the lender agrees to absorb any shortfalls. But ask if it is a possibility, and in what fashion, before choosing a specific ARM.

Floor. Different ARM plans may or may not set a cap on decreases in your rate, either at each adjustment period or over the whole life of the loan. With a floor, you could calculate the best case for your loan—your lowest possible payment if interest falls deeply during the life of the loan.

Convertibility. If your mortgage offers this attractive feature, you have the best of both worlds. You can choose to convert your adjustable-rate mortgage to a fixed-rate loan if you'd like.

With some plans, you can seize any favorable time (when fixed rates are generally low) during the life of the mortgage; more commonly, you can make the choice on certain anniversaries of the loan. Cash outlay for the conversion is low compared with the costs of placing a completely new mortgage: one point, or 1 percent of the loan, is typical. Be sure to inquire what it would be. You may, however, pay a slightly higher interest rate all along, in return for the option.

Initial interest rate. With most ARM loans, the rate during the first year, or the first adjustment period, is set artificially low to induce the borrower to enter into the agreement—a teaser or come-on rate. Buyers who plan to be in a house for only a few years may be delighted with such arrangements, especially if no interest adjustment is planned for several years. Other borrowers, however, may end up with negative amortization and payment shock.

The prudent borrower asks, "If you were not offering this initially lower rate, what would my true interest be today? If things remained exactly the same, what rate (and what dollar amount) would I be paying after the first adjustment period?"

Payment shock. The borrower who starts out with an artificially low rate may easily carry initial payments.

Suppose, however, that the rate eventually rises to the full ceiling allowed. Result: a bad attack of payment shock, leading in some cases to foreclosure and loss of the property. After many bad experiences, most lenders require borrowers to qualify to carry the payments at next year's rate, even if this year's is low.

Adjustment period. This is the length of time between interest rate adjustments. Typically made at the end of each year, adjustments might also be made as often as every six months or as infrequently as every three or five years.

With some loans, interest rates may be adjusted although monthly payments are not. This could result in negative amortization or, if rates had gone down while payments didn't, in faster reduction of the principal owed.

Principal. This is the amount you borrowed; the amount still remaining on the debt at any given time.

Buydown. An up-front, lump-sum payment of interest may bring down the interest rate charged on a loan. In some cases, the lower rate lasts for the whole life of the loan. In a 3-2-1 buydown, however, interest is reduced 3 percent for the first year of the loan, 2 percent the next year, 1 percent the third year. After that, interest reaches normal levels. Virtually any loan program can be bought down.

30 or 15 Years

Thirty-year mortgage loans are still the most popular, even though borrowers often choose 20-year and even 15-year mortgages. Monthly payments on a 15-year loan can run about 20 percent higher than on the same loan figured on a 30-year basis. You would need about 20 percent more income to qualify for the shorter loan. On the other hand, you'd make payments only half as long and cut your total interest cost considerably.

The 15-year mortgage operates like enforced savings, because it requires you to pay off the debt faster. It may be appropriate if, for example, your children will be starting college in 15 years, at a time when you'd like to have your house free and clear.

It does tie up your money, however. If you have the discipline, there's nothing to stop you from putting that extra money, each month, into your own investment plan, where you can tap it as needed and where it will earn extra interest. Talk to your loan consultant about how to make a 30-year fixed-rate loan give you the same (and even better) benefits than a 15-year loan by making extra principal payments, or by tacking a certain amount onto your monthly payment. By opting for the 30-year loan, you won't be forced into the larger monthly payment, and you'll have the flexibility of paying down your principal and interest on your own terms.

From an income-tax point of view, paying off a mortgage early is more or less a wash, because the money you use to pay it off could otherwise be earning taxable interest elsewhere. Make your decision on how large a mortgage, and how fast a payoff, is feasible in view of your particular financial situation. Income tax considerations should not enter into that particular decision.

Biweekly Mortgages

Some mortgage plans involve biweekly mortgage payments: half a monthly payment is automatically deducted from your checking or savings account every two weeks. This plan not only adds up to the equivalent of 13 payments each year instead of 12; it also reflects faster payoff of principal with a corresponding saving in interest, and could cut the length of a 30-year fixed-rate mortgage to less than 22 years.

With an adjustable-rate mortgage, where payments are recalculated at the start of every new period, the length of time on the mortgage will not change. Instead, each new monthly payment will be lower than otherwise scheduled, because extra principal has been paid off.

FHA Mortgages

The Federal Housing Administration (FHA), an agency of the Department of Housing and Urban Development (HUD), was established to help homeowners buy with low down payments. Lenders can safely make loans of up to 97 percent of the value of property, because the FHA insures them against loss in case of foreclosure.

If FHA loans are used in your area, they can be a fine way to go. The money comes not from the government but from local lenders, so if none in your locality is handling FHA mortgages, you're out of luck. The loans are not intended for expensive property, but upper limits in high-price areas are raised from time to time.

For inexpensive property, down payments can be lower than 3 percent; in any case, it runs less than 5 percent. FHA loans may be placed on single-family to four-family dwellings and are intended for owner-occupants.

Insurance premiums (to protect the lender in case of default) are due in a lump sum at closing and can run up to 1.5 percent of the loan. Because most FHA buyers don't have extra cash at closing, the mortgage insurance premium (MIP) can be added to the amount of the mortgage loan. If you pay off your FHA mortgage within the first few years, a portion of your MIP is returned. In addition to the one-time MIP, borrowers pay one-half percent of the outstanding balance each year. The number of years this extra premium is charged depends on the size of the down payment; minimum-down loans require the extra charge over the longest period. When a first-time buyer agrees to go through mortgage counseling, some special FHA programs discount the original MIP.

The FHA bases its loans on the value found by authorized FHA appraisers and sometimes requires certain repairs (items concerned with the preservation of the property and with health and safety) before the loan will be granted.

In addition to the standard FHA program, #203-b, others are available in certain areas. FHA 203-k, for example, lends money to cover both the cost of a home needing rehabilitation and the money needed for repairs.

Your real estate broker will know whether any or all of these programs are available in your community—or you can sit down with the Yellow Pages open to "Mortgages" and spend a couple of hours calling around yourself.

The outstanding feature that has made FHA loans particularly desirable in the past is their assumability by the person to whom you might sell your property. New regulations, however, limit this advantage; see the discussion on assumability that follows.

For a comparison of various loan programs, including conventional, FHA, and VA options, see Figure 7.4.

VA Is for Veterans

The most attractive benefit of VA loans is the possibility of no down payment. Beyond that, the loans are assumable (with the restrictions listed below in the discussion of assumptions).

As with FHA mortgages, the money comes from a local lender; the Department of Veterans Affairs (VA) contribution is to guarantee the loan at no cost to the veteran. While FHA loans require low down payments, VA loans may be made for the entire appraised value of the property (100 percent LTV)—nothing down. In 1997, the VA guaranteed loans as high as $203,000.

To qualify, the veteran must have a discharge "other than dishonorable" and one of the following:

- 180 days' active (not reserve) duty between September 16, 1940 and September 7, 1980
- 90 days' service during a war (the Korean, Vietnam and Persian Gulf conflicts are considered wars)
- Six years' service in the National Guard

For those enlisting for the first time after September 7, 1980, two years' service is required. In-service VA mortgages are also possible.

VA loans may be used for single-family to four-family houses, owner-occupied only. Eligibility for such mortgages does not expire. If one's first VA loan is paid off and the property sold, full eligibility is regained.

At closing, a funding fee is paid directly to the VA.

FIGURE 7.4

Cost Comparisons of Different Mortgage Loans

	Conventional					FHA 203-b	VA
	Fixed 30-Year	Fixed 15-Year	Buydown	Biweekly	Adjustable Rate		
Minimum Down	Some Plans 5% Down					3%–5%	0%
Mortgage Insurance	If Less than 20% Down					Upfront, Some Yearly	No
Maximum Loan	"Jumbo" Loans Sometimes Available					Moderate, Varies by Area	$203,000
Easier Qualifying	Somewhat		Yes		Yes	Yes	Yes
Faster Payoff		Yes		Yes			
Monthly Payment	Level	Level	Lower, Rises	Level	Lower, Can Rise or Fall	Level	Level
Assumability						Yes	Yes
Comments				Automatic Withdrawal from Checking		Repairs Sometimes Required	

Farmers Home Administration (FmHA)

In rural areas, direct mortgage loans can sometimes be obtained from the Farmers Home Administration (FmHA, Department of Agriculture). If your income falls within specific limits (fairly low, depending on family size), you can buy a modest home on no more than one acre, with interest payments tailored to your income.

The program is intended for those who cannot obtain financing elsewhere. The money is allotted to local offices quarterly. At any given time, some offices will have money available; others will have waiting lists. The FmHA processes mortgage applications before you've found a house, then notifies you as money becomes available.

Assumable Mortgages

An *assumable mortgage* is one that can remain with the property when it is sold. This results in considerable savings for the next buyer; no outlay for the costs associated with placing a new mortgage—items like appraisal of the property, mortgage tax, etc.

A high assumable mortgage, or one at a low interest rate, is therefore worth a premium, and contributes extra value to property on the market.

FHA loans made before December 1, 1986, and VA loans made before March 1, 1988 are completely—freely—assumable. This means that you, or anyone the seller chooses, can take the loan along with the real estate, just as it stands. Neither you nor the house need pass any evaluation by the lending institution, which has no say in the matter. Closing costs are negligible, interest rates will not change, and the transaction can be closed and settled as soon as the parties wish.

In areas where prices have risen, of course, these older loans represent only part of the value of the property. You must pay the seller the rest of the purchase price in cash, unless you can persuade the owner to take back financing. The seller who does that agrees to hold a second mortgage for part of the purchase price, or even—in rare instances—for the entire missing amount (nothing down!).

You'd have to look pretty good financially before a seller would enter into such an arrangement, because even though you take over the payments on the loan and ownership of the property, the seller retains liability for that FHA or VA debt if anything goes wrong. You can arrange to relieve the seller of future responsibility, however, if you are willing and able to prove to the lender's satisfaction that you are financially qualified to carry the mortgage payments on your own, as described below.

BUYER'S TIP

The advantages of an assumable mortgage may include:

- No points

- No change in interest rate

- Low closing costs

Newer FHA and VA loans are classified as "assumable with bank approval." To take over the newer FHA mortgages, the next borrower must be qualified (income and credit) to the lending institution's satisfaction. Once that's done, if payments are made promptly, the original borrower retains liability for only five years. With new VA mortgages, the person assuming the loan (who need not be a veteran) must always qualify with the lender before an assumption. A charge of no more than $500 may be made for the paperwork.

Besides FHA and VA loans, many adjustable-rate mortgages also have assumability features, which allow for considerable savings on closing costs. ARMs differ; most stipulate that the new borrower must qualify with the lender and that the interest rate may be adjusted upon assumption. Some charge is made for the privilege; one point might be typical.

Private Mortgages

Private mortgages typically come from one of two sources. A seller may agree to hold financing, lending you money on a first mortgage, or, if the property already has one, on a second (typically shorter-term) loan. Or a family member may agree to lend you part of the purchase price. It is prudent to keep things on a businesslike basis, offering the property as security for a regular mortgage.

Family members may offer low-interest or no-interest loans, but the Internal Revenue Service takes a dim view of them. It likes to see a private mortgage loan made at either the 9 percent or the *applicable federal rate,* an index published monthly by the government, which follows current trends in interest rates. If the mortgage rate does not meet that standard, the IRS will *impute* the interest and tax the lender as if it had been received anyway.

Land Contracts and Lease Options

A *land contract* is a type of layaway installment plan for buying a house. Typically it is sought by a buyer who does not have enough down payment to qualify for a bank loan or to persuade the seller to turn over title (ownership). You move in, make monthly payments to the seller and take care of taxes, insurance, and repairs exactly as if you owned the place. Title does not transfer to you until a specified time, perhaps when you make the final payment. With some land contracts, you receive title when you have made enough payments to constitute 20 percent equity.

Equity is defined as the amount the owner "has in" the property—roughly, market value minus mortgages owed.

A *lease-option* differs from a land contract in that you are not bound to buy the property. Instead, you move in as a tenant and typically pay a flat amount in return for an option—the right to purchase at a given price within a given time (one year, two years)—if you so choose. If you choose not to buy, you simply remain as a tenant for the duration of the lease. Who pays for what expenses, and whether any of your rent goes toward the purchase price, are negotiable items.

Any land contract or lease-option requires extra-careful consultation with your own attorney before you sign anything. Such contracts can vary considerably in their provisions, and you must have someone on your side making sure your interests are protected. Either type of contract should be recorded—entered in the public records to notify the world at large of your rights in the property.

Balloon Mortgages

Suppose an 80-year-old seller is ready to take back a $100,000 mortgage on the house you are buying from him. It might be because the house could not meet bank standards and he is unable to do the necessary repairs. It could be because he'd prefer a regular monthly income to realizing a lump sum, or it could be because you have unusual circumstances (just starting your own business) that don't let you qualify for a bank loan.

At that age, he doesn't like the idea of making a 30-year loan (not realizing that he could simply leave the remainder of the mortgage to his heirs). He will be comfortable only if he can count on seeing all his money within ten years.

But if you pay at the proper rate for a 10-year loan, your monthly payments will be more than you can handle. So you offer the seller a *balloon mortgage*. Your payments will be calculated, principal and interest, as if you were paying on a 30-year schedule. But at the end of ten years, whatever you still owe will be immediately all due and payable.

Because during the early years of a loan most of the monthly payment goes for interest, you will not reduce the principal much over those ten years. You will still owe about 90 percent of the original loan (see Appendix B). That final balloon payment will be a big one.

How will you meet it? The expectation is that your finances will have straightened out, you will have built up equity (the money you've paid off plus any increase in value), the house will have been repaired, and you can place a mortgage with a regular lending institution at that point. Or the old gentleman may still be in good health and so dependent on your prompt and regular checks that he agrees to renew the loan.

Building Your Own Home

Financing new construction is easiest if you are working with a large custom builder, who may finance the construction or may help you arrange a construction loan that later converts to a mortgage. If you are buying a home site, you will find banks reluctant to lend on vacant land. You'll have to buy for cash or persuade the seller to hold a mortgage.

Once the land is paid for, you can count it toward equity to help qualify for another loan. Construction loans are most readily obtained after you have taken all the necessary steps to have your plans and lot approved by local authorities, and if you are working through a recognized contractor. Do-it-yourselfers, particularly those on a shoestring, may find it very difficult to obtain financing.

In-House and Preferred Builder Mortgage Companies

Many large national production homebuilders, and even some smaller local builders, have their own lenders, often bearing the same name as the builders themselves. Those builders who own their own mortgage companies may offer incentive credit dollars (kind of like play money for upgrades, options or loan costs) for buyers to use if they keep their loan in-house instead of using an outside lender. It's important to know that you cannot be forced to use their lender; no seller or builder can make you use a particular mortgage company. They can, however, sweeten the pot by thousands of dollars—so much that it may be difficult to walk away from what they are offering.

Why do builders spend so much to keep their buyers in-house? One reason is that an in-house lender is a profit center, just as the builder's design center is meant to reap a higher profit margin for upgrades. Another reason is the amount of control the builder has knowing precisely where all 250 of its homebuyers stand with their loan approval statuses, instead of trying to get reports from 250 different companies. Loan agents, sales consultants, design personnel, and construction managers usually meet once a week around the same table to compare notes on sales, timing, construction status, and loan status on each home. The in-house lender's first and almost only priority is its builder's buyers, unlike other lenders who make loans for a variety of other types of buyers.

A *preferred lender* is usually one with which a particular builder has a partnership or business relationship and understanding, much the same as the in-house variety.

In either of these scenarios, compare how much the builder incentive money will help you to get into your new home, or whether their rates are slightly higher than others and you may be paying more over 30 years than you would ordinarily have chosen to do. If everything's equal, make your decision from there. If not, go outside, and pass up their offer of incentive money.

A Note on Mortgage Preapproval

If you want to impress a seller (and maybe negotiate a concession on the purchase price), consider obtaining a loan approval before you've even found the house.

Being preapproved for a loan differs from the prequalifying process you may go through with a real estate agent, or on your own following the steps in Chapter 4. As mentioned earlier, it's more and more common for buyers to contact a lending institution for a check on how much they might be qualified to borrow. Others explore various mortgage lender Web sites for guidance.

Obtaining preapproval, however, is a more formal process. The lender will investigate and verify your credit, assets, debts, and income. You'll end up with a written statement that the institution stands ready to make a mortgage loan, assuming that the house you choose meets its standards and that a last-minute check on your financial status when the loan is to be made does not hamper an approval. Of course, this appeals to a seller, who can be certain from the start that you're as good as gold. You'll be as welcome as an all-cash buyer.

The preapproval statement or certificate should not be offered to the seller's agent until after your offer is accepted, however, because it usually specifies the ceiling loan amount or highest purchase price for which the buyers are qualified, a figure you will not want to divulge unless you have to.

8

House Hunting

Inspecting houses is a tiring and confusing process. If you look at more than four in a morning or afternoon, you'll end up with your head in a whirl. And if you look at several new home communities, with three or four model homes each, you may lie in bed that night, trying vainly to remember whether it was the brick ranch, the two-story Mediterranean, or the Craftsman style tri-level that backed up to the busy street. You'll be totally unable to recall which house or model home had the kitchen with the center island. It can be helpful to take along a Polaroid, video, or digital camera (often an agent has one or can borrow one from the office).

Ask the agent for data on each property, and take it back with you. To concentrate fully on the house, take notes when you have finished, possibly when you are back in the car. Jot down your impressions right on the computer printouts, builder brochures, or copies of the listing sheets for the houses you inspect.

If you then note the things you disliked about the place or which features really appeal to you, sorting them out later becomes easier. Figure 8.1 is a sample worksheet with space for rating various features of a home from 1 to 10. A rating of 1 is the lowest.

You may want to mark up a street map of the area, locating the houses you view and also noting schools, religious institutions,

FIGURE 8.1
Comparing Houses

Address	Price	Lot Size	Construc-tion	Roof	Driveway	Land-scaping	Square Feet	No. Bedrooms	No. Baths
275 Isabell	110,000	School Near	2-story Wood	New shingle	Gravel	Big Trees	1,550	3 1-small	1½
		6	5	8	2	4		4	4
27W245 Patricia Ln. Winfield	125,900	Nice Open High	Ranch Brick	10 yrs. old shingle	B.T.	Good	1,900	3	3
		9	9	5	6	8		6	8
135 Marian Pl. Carol Stream	129,900	Sloping Lot	Ranch Wood	9 yrs. old shingle	B.T.	Fair	2,000	3	2
		5	4	6	6	5		6	6

FIGURE 8.1
Comparing Houses (Continued)

Dining Room	Kitchen	Deck, Patio	Garage	Heat, AC	Fireplace	Basement	Plumbing Electricity	Water	General Appeal	Total Rating
Dining/ Living	Old cabinets	breeze-way	1-car	Window AC Gas	None	Dry unfinished	OK	City	Older home in fair shape	71
4	5	6	3	5	1	4	6	6		
Yes	Small D.W.	Yes	2-car	Central AC Gas	In L.R. Wood Stove	Finished	OK	OK City	Nice house, good view	110
5	5	8	6	6	9	8	6	6		
Yes	Good D.W.	screened porch	2-car	Central AC Gas	None	Finished	OK	City	Very pleasant house	89
5	6	8	6	6	1	7	6	6		

shopping areas, approximate commute times, parks, and other important items.

For your own peace of mind, prepare ahead of time for your house-hunting adventure. If possible, leave the little ones with a friend, relative or sitter for the initial house-hunting trips—at least until you have narrowed down your choices. This will save your sanity, give you more quality time with your agent or for your search, and can eliminate pit-stops and the inevitable boredom that sets in with small children while touring homes.

Where Are the Bargains?

Yes, bargains are out there, and after you've been looking a while, you'll be able to spot them.

As you park across the street from the house on Robin Circle, your agent says apologetically, "Now, I want to warn you: there are a lot of kids in this house, school's out, and it doesn't show too well." Without moving from the car, you can see an old pickup truck in the driveway, a shaggy lawn, rusted toys on the front walk, old flyers beginning to get moldy under the shrubs and a torn screen door.

A disaster?

No, perhaps an opportunity.

When you locate such a house, if it has had decent maintenance (as opposed to housekeeping), then you may have stumbled upon a bargain. Houses that have been rented out sometimes fall into this category.

Most buyers cannot see past sloppiness. Perhaps without even knowing why, they'll feel that "the place doesn't have good vibes." As a result, the house on Robin Circle may stay on the market for months and may eventually sell for as much as 10 percent under true market value.

Conversely, as you walk into a spotless house, try to ignore the smell of baking cookies wafting through the place, your favorite music playing softly, and the flowers on the designer coffee table. Of course, such a house has probably had fine care and it could be a pleasure to move into. Still, when the sellers move out, you will be left with just three things: the location, the floor plan, and the condition.

Elaborately decorated model homes are notorious for distracting you with the fluff while little acrylic signs point out included, optional, and decorator features that you may or may not catch as you walk through. They tend to sell the sizzle and not the steak, so pay all the same attention to practicality, value, and suitability that you would with any previously lived-in home. With new homes, pick the sales consultant's brain and if you're serious about a particular floor plan, ask that he or she take you on a personally escorted tour to explain just what the base price of the home really includes. If at all possible, ask to see an empty production home.

If all factors—apart from surface appeal—seem right to you, don't hesitate: act quickly on it. If you hesitate, the next time you decide to get serious about it, the house may have sold. If a home has also been underpriced, quick action is indicated, as described in the next chapter. A properly priced house that shows well and has all the right stuff going for it also sells quickly.

In a new home scenario, the builder may have run out of that particular plan and won't have one until months from now, in the next phase of homes.

When it comes to decorating and housekeeping, concentrate on the substance. Pay attention to location, layout, and basic condition. Location can't be changed, floor plan can be altered only at some expense, but the last factor—condition—can be remedied. Just be sure, if there's a problem, that you know what you're getting into. An engineering report can tell you exactly what to expect.

More Bargain Situations

Often, bargains can also be found when a seller is under pressure. The seller's broker won't—or shouldn't—reveal that the house is near foreclosure or the seller is going bankrupt. But you can see this for yourself sometimes—for example, in a divorce situation, or if she's on the new job in Chicago and he's here alone with three

---

BUYER'S TIP

When house hunting, it is best to:

- Take notes, video, or photographs to record details

- Get detailed descriptions from the agent or builder

- Mark features such as schools, parks, or shopping centers on a map

- Keep in mind the difference between good (or poor) maintenance and housekeeping

- Focus on location, layout, and basic condition of the property

- Not let the hype of model homes affect you emotionally

---

kids. Such sellers may be ready to deal and ready to trade a price concession for a quick sale.

Where the owner has died, an executor is sometimes amenable to any reasonable offer in return for a prompt, trouble-free winding up of the estate. An older person, suspicious of workers and short on cash, may not want to bring a long-time home up to standards required by a lending institution; sometimes a broker can help you work out a mutually beneficial arrangement to solve that impasse.

With new homes, bargains can generally be found when the builder has inventory homes available or is at the tail end of a new home project. An *inventory home* is one that the builder has nearly or completely finished, forcing the builder into a sizable monthly mortgage payment on the unit. Sometimes these are homes the builder has built on speculation and will sell quickly. Other times it is a home some other buyer has ordered, only to cancel due to unforeseen circumstances, leaving the builder to cope with reselling it. The house could have a location or lot size that is not popular with other buyers, or could have had upgrades installed by its previous buyer that don't suit a large cross-section of homebuyers.

Above all, the way to buy a bargain is to buy promptly. The buying public is a sensitive judge of value. A house that is mistakenly underpriced will be snapped up quickly. For that reason, it's sensible to invest some time in learning the market and helpful to locate a broker in whose advice you have confidence.

Location, Location, Location

Before you get very far into your house hunting, someone will tell you the oldest real estate adage (almost the only real estate adage) that the three most important factors in the value of a house are location, location, and location.

It's true, too. A house costing $1.5 million in Beverly Hills might sell on a comparable lot in the suburbs of Peoria, Illinois, for $150,000. Never in the history of this country have geographical differences in home prices been so marked. Closer to home, you know that a modest home in the most expensive suburb is worth much more than the identical house in a poor inner-city neighborhood.

The classic advice is to buy the modest house on a more expensive street. Such a house is easy to resell, and its value will hold up well, for there are always buyers eager for the prestige of that particular neighborhood. And remodeling or adding to it is possible because alterations won't push it out of the price range for that area.

On the other hand, the most luxurious house on the street won't ever repay the original owner for the money invested. No matter how elegant it may be, buyers with money to spend will aim at another, fancier neighborhood.

In one way, then, an over-improved house represents an opportunity for the buyer who wants lots of space and luxury features and isn't worried about resale value. If you think that you will live in the house for a long time and if you like the area, you may be able to pick up a great deal for your money.

Where, then, are the bargains?

- Sloppy houses, but otherwise well maintained
- Family situations of stress: divorce, death, illness
- Property overimproved for its neighborhood
- The modest house on a prestigious street
- A builder's inventory home or one in the closeout of a new home community

Choosing a Neighborhood

If you are moving across town, you probably know what area suits your lifestyle best. Coming to a new community, however, requires research. Real estate brokers must, by the nature of their work, help you narrow your choices if you are ever to settle on one house. Rigorously regulated by the fair housing laws, however, brokers and new homebuilders hesitate to characterize neighborhoods or give you opinions on school systems. If any of their assumptions are based on the forbidden factors—race, color, religion, country of origin, sex, disability—they could face charges of illegal steering (using subtle means to ensure that you end up where they think you should).

Brokers and builders can, however, furnish solid data, and a good agent will have it available: per-pupil expenditure in various school systems, number of graduates going on to four-year colleges, and the like.

One good way to learn about a new community is to subscribe to its local newspaper or find its chamber of commerce Web site. With new homes, pull up new home Web sites and see which builders are active in that area. Review these resources carefully, and you'll begin to get a feeling for neighborhoods. In the end, you will have to decide yourself just what areas you'll want to consider.

Using the Internet

The Internet is full of Web pages describing various communities, placed there by different sources, including local real estate brokers, newspapers, builders, and municipalities themselves. Exploring the Net for any particular location can yield important information. You can also find current listings of homes for sale, information on master-planned areas, and descriptions of various real estate firms.

Though Web addresses come and go, one of the most comprehensive is the National Association of REALTORS® sponsored Realtor .com, part of HomeStore.com, which also includes HomeBuilder .com (for new home searches), and sites for remodeling and apartment rental as well. The Internet Real Estate Directory <ired.com> offers links to thousands of real estate sites. Inman News Service <inman.com> and Realty Times <realtytimes.com> both carry valuable and constantly updated material on the real estate market.

Looking Over an Older Home

In newer homes, regional and universal building codes have vastly improved things like plumbing, electric systems, and HVAC (heating, ventilation, and air conditioning) systems. Houses more than 20 years old, however, require extra-careful inspection. You won't (and can't) inspect in detail every house you see, but when you're seriously considering making an offer on one, go over it carefully.

Start with the outside of the house. Depending on the norms for the part of the country in which it is located, does it have easy-care features—built-in sprinklers, self-storing storm windows, full fascia gutters and downspouts? How soon might the place need a coat of paint, new siding, or fresh trim?

Examine the roof; binoculars can be of help here. Look for missing or curled shingles or loose roof tiles, patched spots, or bent or uneven flashing. Moss growing on the roof indicates a moisture problem. If in midwinter every other roof on the street bears a load of snow while this one is clean, you are looking at a house with inadequate insulation.

BUYER'S TIP

Before you make an offer, inspect carefully, looking for:

- Features that indicate ease of maintenance

- Adequate insulation and good condition of the roof

- Signs of termites

- Unobstructed gutters and attached downspouts

In termite areas (Southeast, Southwest), look for mud tubes where wooden parts of porch or foundation adjoin the ground. Poke exposed wood to see if it is solid.

Downspouts should be firmly attached. Gutters lose points if they have little trees growing out of them. If they need only repainting, that's a minor matter, but gutters with holes in them will need replacing. See Figure 8.2 for a diagram showing the location of all the various physical components of a house.

Electric Service

Remember that many homes built around the turn of the century didn't originally have any electric service. If the initial installation hasn't been updated, it can be inadequate for anything beyond the light bulbs, refrigerator, and flatiron it was originally designed for. The proliferation of appliances these days calls for plenty of outlets. You want 100-amp service at minimum; 220 amps for electric stoves, some clothes dryers, and air conditioners. Look for an outlet every 12 feet on a long wall so that any six-foot cord can be plugged in without using an extension cord. Small rooms should have at least one outlet on each wall.

Be alert for any tangle of extension cords, which can signal inadequate outlets. Examine the fuse box. If you find circuit break-

FIGURE 8.2   House Diagram

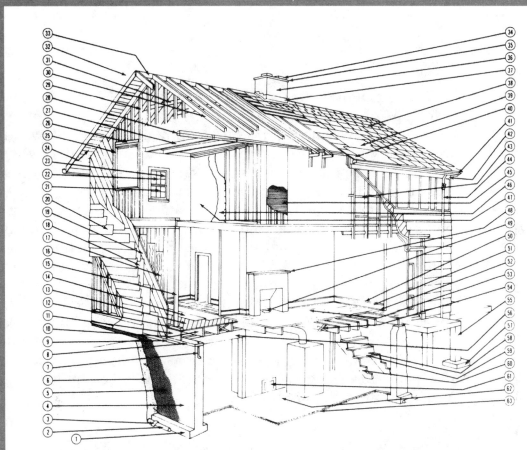

1. FOOTING	22. MUNTIN	43. FIRESTOP
2. FOUNDATION DRAIN TILE	23. WINDOW SASH	44. DOWNSPOUT
3. FELT JOINT COVER	24. EAVE (ROOF PROJECTION)	45. LATHS
4. FOUNDATION WALL	25. WINDOW JAMB TRIM	46. PLASTER BOARD
5. DAMPPROOFING OR WEATHERPROOFING	26. DOUBLE WINDOW HEADER	47. PLASTER FINISH
	27. CEILING JOIST	48. MANTEL
6. BACKFILL	28. DOUBLE PLATE	49. ASH DUMP
7. ANCHOR BOLT	29. STUD	50. BASE TOP MOULDING
8. SILL	30. RAFTERS	51. BASEBOARD
9. TERMITE SHIELD	31. COLLAR BEAM	52. SHOE MOULDING
10. FLOOR JOIST	32. GABLE END OF ROOF	53. FINISH MOULDING
11. BAND OR BOX SILL	33. RIDGE BOARD	54. BRIDGING
12. PLATE	34. CHIMNEY POTS	55. PIER
13. SUBFLOORING	35. CHIMNEY CAP	56. GIRDER
14. BUILDING PAPER	36. CHIMNEY	57. FOOTING
15. WALL STUD	37. CHIMNEY FLASHING	58. RISER
16. DOUBLE CORNER STUD	38. ROOFING SHINGLES	59. TREAD
17. INSULATION	39. ROOFING FELTS	60. STRINGER
18. BUILDING PAPER	40. ROOF SHEATHING	61. CLEANOUT DOOR
19. WALL SHEATHING	41. EVE TROUGH OR GUTTER	62. CONCRETE BASEMENT FLOOR
20. SIDING	42. FRIEZE BOARD	63. GRAVEL FILL
21. MULLION		

ers, you will know that the service has been modernized. But there is nothing wrong with an old-fashioned fuse system, if it is extensive enough and was carefully installed.

Plumbing

More expensive to remedy than inadequate wiring is faulty plumbing. You hope to find all the old galvanized pipes replaced with copper. Galvanized pipe suffers from corrosion and eventually deposits build up on the inside until they impede the flow of water. This happens first with the horizontal hot-water lines, so check by starting outward from the water heater.

What you don't want to see is a patch job, where putting a length of copper pipe into old galvanized tubing solved a single emergency. Such a joint signals a serious chemical reaction ahead. Eventually someone will have to rip out the whole line and replace it with copper, and that someone might be you.

If the house has updated kitchen and baths, it's likely that the whole plumbing system was also updated. If you're in doubt, ask.

If there is a well, you'll want proof of water quality and flow. If there is a septic system, ask questions about legal installation and past performance. (If sewers are available but not utilized, the FHA will refuse to insure a mortgage.)

Basement Water

In areas where basements are prevalent, buyers are understandably worried that flooding might develop during spring thaws or summer storms. One quick way to judge is to see how much junk people store directly on a basement floor. Piles of very old newspapers may mean a packrat style—and a dry basement.

To see if a basement has flooded, inspect the bottom of the furnace and the water heater. Rust or a newly painted neat strip across the bottom few inches calls for an explanation. If a one-time flood (which can happen in the best of families) occurred while the furnace was hot, the firebox may be cracked.

Small amounts of dampness on basement walls, though, are almost standard in some areas.

Pay little attention to the condition of the water heater. Even the most meticulous homeowner will use one down to the very end, so it isn't much of a clue to how the rest of the house has been maintained. It is more of an appliance than a structural part of the house. Replacing it would not be a drastic enough expense to influence your decision on whether or not to buy.

Insulation

If an older house in a cold climate hasn't been adequately insulated, you will certainly do it yourself immediately. The best place for insulation is under the attic floor or in the crawl space. Look for holes in the stair risers that were drilled for blown-in insulation and then plugged. Try to find out how many inches were installed. Some old jobs were very good indeed; others don't meet modern standards. Another simple installation with a fine payback is band insulation around the top of the basement wall, where the foundation meets the floor joists.

Different types of insulation have been used through the years and something can probably be said for each type. Whether made of Fiberglass or cellulose, applied blown or batted, insulation is usually easily replaced.

If a house in a colder climate doesn't have good storm windows and screens, it probably doesn't have much else; for this is one of the first comfort items people buy. You don't need fancy metal self-storing ones. A well-kept wooden set means that the place is owned by someone who doesn't mind climbing ladders to replace them spring and fall, and you'll have to do the same. Properly fitting old-fashioned wooden storm windows can be even better than newer metal ones.

If the house lacks insulation or storm windows, inquire, when you come to the time of the mortgage application, about whether you may include the cost of installing energy-savers in your mortgage.

Don't pay more just because an older house has wall insulation. It's nice, of course, but it doesn't have the payback of that thick layer under the attic floor.

Termites and Toxins

In some northern areas, termites are just about unheard of, but you might run into carpenter ants. Look for small piles of fine sawdust below ceiling beams. To check for soft spots, prod floor joists that are exposed in the cellar.

In other parts of the United States, a termite inspection may be required by lenders, and should certainly be demanded by astute homebuyers. Termite infestation has its best potential where wood meets dirt, such as at foundation levels for wood-built homes and decking. It is difficult to see the ravages of termites in some types of construction, like stucco. Call a local pest control company and get the scoop on what to look for. Any purchase contract can be written up to specify that a sale is contingent upon the satisfactory result of a pest inspection. The contract can also designate who will pay for any pest control treatments, based on those findings, negotiated at the time of purchase.

In some states, purchase contracts routinely disclose the possible existence of hazardous materials in the soil. Some of this may have come from groundwater contamination, some from mining, and some areas may have previously been used by the military and were cleaned up for residential use. Read over this verbiage ahead of time and discuss it with your agent.

High-voltage lines. Scientists are still debating the effect of electromagnetic radiation, particularly on children. Some early studies indicate increased rates of cancer in those who live close to high-voltage lines. There's not yet a dependable guideline in this matter; emissions are easily tested, however.

If a home you are considering is adjacent to or fairly close to power lines, it may be considered to be less desirable, affecting your ability to get your asking price if you decide to sell later on.

Radon. One toxic substance you can't see for yourself is radon, a colorless, odorless gas that seeps into houses from the earth itself. The Environmental Protection Agency (EPA) considers it second only to cigarette smoke as a cause of lung cancer. "It's like exposing your family to hundreds of chest X-rays a year," says the EPA. The agency estimates that one house in five has unacceptable levels of radon. Testing can be unreliable unless carefully done, best by a professional. Simply using a test kit can yield false results if windows are kept open during the test, which takes several days. Some areas are at higher risk than others.

Fortunately, curing a radon problem is relatively simple and inexpensive, usually with specific ventilation in foundation and basement.

Lead

High levels of lead in children have been shown to affect mental and physical development. Lead paint is no longer used, but the EPA requires that anyone considering a house built before 1978 receive a written information sheet about it. Chipping paint is particularly dangerous. As with asbestos, removing lead paint can release dangerous amounts of the substance; sometimes the best solution is to cover it. If it is to be removed, safety precautions must be taken.

Lead is also found in drinking water because of its use in soldering materials. Simple tests can be done, preferably on early-morning samples. Lead in water decreases when you let the tap run for a couple of minutes, especially if you haven't used the faucet for a few hours. For houses built before 1978, any buyer must be allowed a period of up to ten days in which to have lead testing done before a purchase contract may become binding.

Asbestos

This fireproof mineral was widely used before 1975 in all sorts of building materials, from insulation to floor tiles. Its tiny fibers can cause lung cancer. Where it is intact and not deteriorating, it poses little or no danger. The most common problem may be heavy insulation wrapped around heat ducts from an old-fashioned furnace. Removing it releases the fibers; sometimes encasing it best solves the problem.

Building Inspection Engineers

In some states, home inspectors are licensed. Elsewhere, licensed engineers may offer inspection service. (See your Yellow Pages under "Building Inspectors" or "Home Inspectors.") Those who belong to the American Society of Home Inspectors (ASHI) have met specific standards of education and experience.

You can hire an inspector before or after you make an offer on a house; the next chapter has information on how to make your purchase offer dependent upon a satisfactory report. You may be charged a few hundred dollars, depending on the inspector's travel time.

Try to accompany your inspector with a tape recorder or video camera. You'll learn many interesting things about the house that wouldn't be in a written report. The engineer can't tell you what the house is worth or give you advice on whether to buy it. Instead, you'll hear things like, "That roof looks as if it has another five years or so on it. If you had to replace it today, it might cost . . ." Making the final decision is up to you.

Ask specifically whether there are indications that the house needs a specialist's inspection for a toxic substance.

Some types of inspectors do structural inspections, and can give you reports on electrical and plumbing conditions of a home. More specialized types include roof and pool inspectors. You must decide just how many inspections are feasible for the home you are considering, and how much you are willing to spend for the assurance they may or may not provide.

Check Taxes

Make certain that you know the true tax figure, as explained in Chapter 5, for every house you are considering. Find out whether a tax assessment would be changed and how much taxes would be if you bought at a given figure.

Valiant efforts are made to keep taxes equitable, but the process is a constant challenge. Your agent can tell you what system is used in your community.

New homebuilders must disclose to buyers the existence of extra assessments, such as school bonds, lighting and landscaping maintenance in some communities, and infrastructure improvements. They should be able to provide information on the duration of these assessments, what your monthly outgo would be, how they are collected, and under what circumstances they may be escalated.

What Else?

Ask whether trash collection is included in the taxes or in a separate bill. Is it billed with water, sewer, and garbage, or is it a private matter? Inquire of owners about their heating and cooling costs. Ask to see past utility bills, or call the local utility company and ask for a recent street survey of bills.

Open Houses

One good way to start your house hunting is to visit open houses. Usually held on Saturday or Sunday afternoons, they are an invitation to the general public. You won't need any advance appointment or research; you can tour the neighborhoods that most interest you, stopping in at one house after another. It's a great way to get a feeling for prices.

Don't hesitate to visit even if you're not ready to buy. Brokers can be lonely, giving up a Sunday afternoon to sit in a house, and they will welcome you. Don't be worried if you're asked to sign in. If it were your house, wouldn't you want people to identify themselves before they came in? Be sure to wipe your feet, restrain your children, leave your food and drink in the car, and put out your cigarette before entering. If you are accompanied by your agent, he or she will leave a business card with the hosting agent.

Later, the seller's agent may call your agent for opinions as to what you both thought of the house, whether your agent believes it to be priced properly, or what should be done to encourage offers.

Community practices differ in the matter of open-house etiquette among brokers. If you are working with one agent, discuss frankly the best way to visit open houses on your own when your agent isn't available. Sometimes just offering your agent's card upon entering is enough to assure a seller's agent that you have engaged a buyer's broker. You don't want to find your dream house, only to discover that you've stepped into jurisdictional disputes. Some agents sit on open houses primarily to find buyer clients, so be prepared for questions and chitchat.

Stay in Touch with Your Agent

Of course, you'll read the ads avidly while you are house hunting. Particular real estate terms common to each area may puzzle you; don't hesitate to ask your agent to explain them.

If you want to work through a seller's agent who gives you good service, or if you have retained a buyer's broker, don't answer ads yourself. Phone the agent and mention the items that catch your eye. The broker can do a little investigating, particularly where the Multiple Listing Service is involved. Then you'll receive a call back: "That ad on page five was the house I showed you last week; it sure looks different on paper, doesn't it? The one on the bottom of the page is about $60,000 over your price range. But the one on page six was just listed yesterday, and it sounds as if you might like it. I arranged with the listing agent for us to view it this afternoon."

If you're working with your own buyer's agent, he or she will follow up on discount broker, FSBO, or Internet ads as well.

Looking at New Homes

Many weekend newspapers also include builder advertising, with displays naming their new home communities in various areas. When verbiage or pricing about homes catches your eye, ask your agent to call the community to find out more about it. The agent can see if there are bargains or inventory homes available, and set up a time when he or she can accompany and register you there for a stroll around their model homes. It is not uncommon for agents to combine tours of new home areas with surrounding resale showings, giving you a broader prospective and range of opportunities.

As mentioned earlier, always have your agent with you on the first visit to a new home community. You will be able to have the luxury of a liaison between you and the builder, helping you through the maze of tasks that need to be accomplished if you decide to buy. Some of these include helping to explain the builder's purchase agreement and addenda, gaining your loan pre-approval, or guiding you in your design center choices so that you don't overimprove the home.

It is not uncommon for some builders to refuse to entertain real estate brokers at a given community or with all of their homes, because they ultimately pay a cooperating commission in most cases. Brokers in a particular area generally know who these builders are and may avoid driving by new homes if they cannot gainfully represent you there. The good ones, however, will pick up on your desire (or lack of one) for a newly constructed home, and will tell you which builders are familiar to them and which deal only with buyers themselves.

It is indeed unfortunate that some builders dive into and out of cooperating with buyers' brokers, inviting them to participate only when it serves them, such as in a slower market or at closeout.

9

Buying Investment Property

Although the purpose of *The Homebuyer's Kit* is to explain the ins and outs of buying a home for you to occupy, this chapter will discuss the purchase of investment property. While any purchase of real estate can be looked on as a kind of investment, buying investment property usually means holding it for the production of income (kind of like buying stock), and not necessarily buying and selling for immediate profit. There is an entire science to the purchase of property for this purpose, but space permits only a brief review.

Real estate has been called not only the best way to build an estate but also the only way. Real estate investment, though, takes constant effort on your part. You can buy shares of stock and then limit your effort to checking every day on the Financial News Network. Not so with a duplex three blocks from your home. You must be ready for a phone call at 6 A.M. explaining that the water heater has burst, be ready to buy a replacement promptly, and arrange for someone to meet the plumber that very day.

Despite the plumbing problems, real estate investment is not liquid. You can take your money out of the stock market with a simple phone call to your stockbroker. When your capital is in real estate, you shouldn't count on taking it out under, say, six months' notice. When things (such as low employment levels) get bad in your community, it's possible that you can't get your money until the economic cycle changes. Certain economic factors locally can contribute to an unpredictable vacancy period, forcing you to *carry* your investment property when you may not be in a financial position to do so.

Getting Started

As an investor, you face three challenges—finding the right property, buying it right, and then managing it. You will need:

- A good real estate broker who is interested in helping you reach your goals
- A lawyer who specializes in real estate
- An accountant

Line up all three before you make your first purchase. You'll need them to locate and then analyze the proposed investment. To prepare, talk with brokers, read the papers, visit open houses, and develop some expertise so you'll recognize a bargain when you see it.

Read everything you can find—but don't send hundreds of dollars for home study courses advertised on cable TV infomercials. Those couples going from welfare to riches because of a course advertised there may just be as believable as the people who lose 50 lbs. in four months and keep it off for a lifetime. Materials on investing in real estate are available in local bookstores and for free in the public library. Take basic real estate courses at community colleges—the sort offered to rookie real estate salespersons. That will give you the vocabulary and some basic information, and your fellow students may eventually prove helpful.

Start Small

It's wise to start small for your first few transactions so that you're not risking too much capital or taking on too much liability while you learn. The old adage goes, "don't invest any more than you can realistically afford to lose," but it's also said that investment in real estate is one of the better risks in the big scheme of things. A one- to six-unit building or a small, low maintenance house in a familiar neighborhood near your own home is best. If the place needs fixing up, pay for a building engineer's inspection so that you'll know what you're getting into before your purchase offer becomes firm (the lawyer can help arrange that provision). Try for property that will appeal to the largest number of responsible prospective tenants.

Avoid Land

Forget about vacant land, condos, or building lots in resort areas. Land has to appreciate markedly before it pays off because it produces no income, ties up your money, and requires tax payments. Judging which areas will be in demand in years to come takes skill and expertise, and even long-time investors can get burned. Land is no investment for beginners; even seasoned veterans tend to shy away from land purchases because of their inherently uncertain prospects.

BUYER'S TIP

When you begin buying investment property:

- Start with small investments to minimize risk while you learn

- Get a building engineer's inspection

- Avoid vacant land or lots, on which you pay taxes but receive no income

- Get prequalified with a mortgage lender

How Leverage Works

Traditionally, real estate investors have used leverage (other people's money) to pyramid a small amount of capital. If, for example, you had $100,000 and bought one piece that went up 5 percent in the next year, you'd make $5,000 in appreciation. To use leverage, you find ten such parcels, putting $10,000 down on each and taking out $90,000 mortgages. If they went up 5 percent, you'd have appreciation totaling $50,000 in the same one year—and you'd control a million dollars' worth of real estate.

This traditional technique runs into problems, however, when local conditions change, employment drops, and it becomes difficult to find tenants who will pay enough to cover those ten mortgage payments. You may end up supporting the real estate by taking money out of your pocket each month—if you have enough money in your pocket. This is the vacancy factor referred to earlier.

Those cheery investors who give testimonials on cable TV may say, "Within a week I owned a million dollars' worth of real estate," but a more accurate statement would be, "Within a week I *owed* on a million dollars' worth of real estate."

Analyzing Your First Investment

An accountant can help analyze any purchase before you make it. You use annual figures, calculating first the gross rental income. If present rentals are below market average, it's permissible to estimate using the rentals you'd charge (just find out whether present figures are locked in with leases).

From the gross rental you subtract:

- An estimated allowance for vacancies and uncollected rents (in normal times, typically 5 percent of gross rental income)
- Utilities paid by the landlord
- Heat or air conditioning (if furnished)
- Property taxes
- Insurance
- Trash removal

- Water charges (if paid by the landlord)
- Any applicable association dues or homeowner's fees
- Estimate for repairs
- Janitor service, snow removal, lawn care, and the like
- A reserve for future large improvements (new roof, furnace)

An accountant can help estimate the proper amount for reserve, which might run, for example, 2 percent of the value of the property.

With projected expenses subtracted from gross rental, you have the *annual net operating income.* From that, you then subtract debt service (mortgage payments). The resulting figure is your cash flow—actual dollars you can expect to take out of the property each year. If you have a minus figure, you have negative cash flow and had better think hard and long before taking on the investment. The beginner needs positive cash flow. It might be small, but the good news is that it does not represent your total return.

To calculate your actual return, first figure your taxable income on the property. It should be less than cash flow, because of an artificial bookkeeping concept known as *depreciation* (cost recovery). You can charge as a so-called expense a portion of what you paid for the building (the lot is not depreciated). On residential property, divide the cost of the building by 27.5 to learn the amount you may charge each year for depreciation. (Commercial property is depreciated over 31.5 years.)

Subtract this depreciation amount from your net operating income to determine how much profit or loss you will declare on your federal income tax return. If it's a loss, discuss with an accountant whether you can take the loss against other sources of income. The rules are complex. If your total income is less than $100,000 and you actively manage the property, you may be able to claim up to $25,000 in losses against other types of income (salary, dividends, etc.).

With total income up to $150,000, part of a loss may be deducted. Otherwise, your paper loss can be taken only against other passive income (the category into which all rental income now falls for tax purposes). Any loss not deductible can be used eventually against capital gains when the property is finally sold.

If you can take any loss on your income tax return, the next step is to figure the income tax savings that result, depending on your tax bracket. This figure is one component in calculating the true return from the proposed investment, which consists of cash flow plus:

- Principal paid down the first year on mortgage (amortization)
- Estimated annual appreciation
- Income tax saving (if any)

The total annual return is then analyzed as a percentage of the cash you will invest. In order for the investment to fly, this should be considerably higher than the return available on, for example, certificates of deposit. Otherwise, there's no point in risking your capital and making an additional investment of your time and effort.

The one- to six-family residential buildings suitable for beginning investors will usually not support professional management and still show positive cash flow. In most cases, you'll have to manage the property yourself. It won't work if you have to pay someone else to change every faucet washer.

Financing Investment Property

An investment property purchase is an entirely different animal than the purchase of a principal residence. By the same token, qualifying for and obtaining financing for such a purchase is not the same.

Lenders generally charge higher interest rates for *non-owner-occupied* types of mortgages because their risk is higher as well. The lender worries that investment property may eventually be left in its hands if it sits vacant in tougher times. There is also the belief that landlords (and their tenants) don't take as much pride of ownership as they would in their own homes, making the lender view it as riskier.

The vacancy factor (sometimes 25 percent of the total monthly payment, depending on the area) will be taken into account in your qualifying ratios just like an extra debt every month, whether the property is occupied 100 percent of the time or not, to hedge against disaster. This is why it is more difficult to qualify for a non–owner-occupied type loan.

It's dangerous to try to claim that the property will serve as your own personal residence, or to attempt to convince the lender that you don't plan to rent it out. Even claiming that you will use the residence as a second personal home, when in fact you have other plans, can get you into hot water, and constitutes loan fraud.

Risk and Decision

Investments are risks. You must ultimately ask yourself what your reasons and your goals are for buying investment property, and analyze them carefully before going ahead with a purchase. Ask your attorney or real estate broker to give you an honest description of your duties as a landlord; what back-up plans you'll need to have in mind when unexpected issues arise, and whether the investment you're considering is a prudent one. If these experts can assure you that certain types of property, certain locations, or certain factors have already demonstrated a track record of success, and this property falls into those categories, it may be a move with less risk, making you feel a bit more secure in your decision.

All of this is the subject for another book, however. For now, let's return to making a home purchase.

10

Arriving at a Contract

When you've found your dream house—or your compromise house—or your investment property—what then? How do you reach a binding agreement with the seller?

The process resembles a tennis game. The homeowner makes the first serve, a public offer to sell the property at a given price. Now the ball is in your court.

Local customs differ, with some areas using a system of bids or offers and counteroffers. Final contracts can be written by attorneys, brokers, or even buyers themselves if no agents are involved (as in a FSBO situation). The key thing to remember here is that *everything* is negotiable: price, terms—you name it, it can be written into an offer to purchase and countered by the sellers. Depending on how creative you or your agent get, negotiating tactics will determine whether the sellers take you seriously.

In most locales, you start things off with an offer to buy, which includes not only a price but many other provisions. The document you present to the seller is a written *purchase offer;* when the seller accepts it exactly as you presented it, it becomes a *binding contract,* which may be known in your community as a deposit receipt, contract of sale, or agreement to buy and sell. Time frames for a response from the seller are usually written into your offer. If that time elapses and no answer from the seller is forthcoming, the deal is usually deemed dead or (silently) unaccepted in most areas.

All real estate contracts must be in writing in order to be enforceable. (Translation: "Oral agreements aren't worth the paper they're written on.") If, in front of 20 witnesses, a homeowner said she was willing to sell you the property for $225,000 cash and took your deposit check—you still could not legally hold her to it.

The written contract supersedes any oral agreements; if the sellers promise to leave the refrigerator, make sure that the contract specifies it, or you could be out of luck.

The Written Offer

Written is an arbitrary term in these days of computers and preloaded software, generating both purchase agreements and accompanying addenda. Computer-generated contracts are most popular in new home sales offices. Many agents, however, still fill in by hand the blanks on formatted real estate contracts endorsed either by their local board of REALTORS® or their brokerages. Depending on local custom, a broker or attorney usually helps draw up a written purchase offer detailing the terms under which you propose to buy. In some areas this is a full-fledged contract, needing only the seller's acceptance to be complete. Elsewhere, local custom may employ a preliminary memorandum, articles of agreement, binder, or deposit receipt.

Can you draw up the offer for yourself? Yes, and you could perform your own surgery, too. In either case, it would be fine unless you happened to make an amateurish mistake. There's no use copying someone else's contract as a model; yours will differ in many respects according to the needs of the parties involved, local custom, and state law. Brokers and lawyers must take courses, pass exams, and gain related experience before they're allowed to fill out these forms. Although in pure FSBO situations, you may not have a choice but to sit down with the seller and mire through an offer to purchase, it is best not to try to do it yourself when you don't have to. The least you'll want to invest in is a fee-for-service broker or an attorney to assist you in this task.

Ask the broker with whom you are working for a copy of a purchase offer common in your area, or obtain a copy of the contract generally used by your Multiple Listing System or bar association. Study it at leisure in advance, for when it comes time to fill one in and sign it, you'll be too nervous for quiet consideration.

If you are purchasing a home from a builder, the agent may be able to give you a generic copy of the builder's purchase offer to look over and take home. If asked, the builder may also furnish copies of any applicable preliminary property reports, neighborhood restrictions, tax assessments unique to the area, and homeowners association budgets to look over before you decide to buy.

First Decision: Purchase Price

Before you begin and before emotions take over, settle in your mind the top price you really would invest in the house—a figure you will not share with the agent, unless it is someone you specifically hired as your own broker.

Should you expect to pay full asking price, or is there a formula for the amount of bargaining built in by the sellers?

It all depends.

Homeowners who hate haggling may have listed their house at a rock-bottom price with no room for flexibility. Others may add a 5 percent cushion to what they'd really take.

The sellers' circumstances affect price. They may be under some of the pressures mentioned in the last chapter. Elderly homeowners, on the other hand, are often in no hurry to move. They may have emotional ties that make it difficult for them to view their property impartially.

If a house has been on the market a long time (more than five months), the buying public has voted that it isn't worth what the sellers are asking. In that case, don't offer full price.

On the other hand, don't fool around if you've stumbled on a hot listing, one that has just come on the market and is uniquely appealing or noticeably underpriced. If there is a possibility of several offers within the next day, consider coming in somewhere over asking price. This gives you an advantage against competition.

It sounds suspicious when a broker recommends such action; this is where it helps if you already know and trust the agent.

New home offers are usually negotiable only when the house is one the builder has a vested interest in unloading, such as standing inventory. Builders deal in volume, operating on a much smaller profit margin than resale sellers, so there is generally not as much bargaining power here. You may find a builder most negotiable on *soft costs* (those that have some built-in profit), such as design center options and upgrades. Contributions towards your closing costs if the lender is their in-house or preferred lender may also be a point for negotiation, instead of on sales price, which may affect future appraisals in a neighborhood just beginning to establish values.

Look for Comparables

When you conduct your house hunt extensively in a given area, you quickly become an expert on homes that fall within your price range. You can recognize a bargain when you see it appear on the market. You can also spot overpriced property. For a short time, you may know more than anyone else in the world about the proper price for a three-bedroom ranch in Milkwood.

In an unfamiliar area, ask the agent for sales prices, usually no older than six months, of comparables. These are similar homes in the neighborhood that have recently changed hands; they'll give you something to judge by. Comparables, in fact, are the principal tool brokers themselves use to appraise property for market value. Other considerations in making price comparisons include the condition of the house, size of the property, time of year, special financing available, and the general economic climate—whether it's a buyers' or sellers' market.

You may be curious about what the homeowners paid three years ago for the place you want to buy today, but that is not relevant. It tells you only what values were like in that neighborhood three years ago. Even if the owners got it at an incredible bargain, that doesn't affect what it would sell for now. No matter how much the house's market value was then or how many improvements the present owners have made, it doesn't factor into today's value.

How much money the sellers have invested in the property, and how much they need to get out of it are their own concerns, not yours. In the end, says the professional appraiser's maxim, "buyers make value." Willing buyers and willing sellers make the world go 'round. The selling price is set by the operation of supply and demand, in competition on the open market.

The reaction to your offering price will be affected by the terms under which you expect to buy. If the sellers have to wait around while you market your present home, they'll be less inclined to drop their price. The same applies if they must come up with a cash payment of points to your lender. By the same token, a clean offer with no contingencies is worth a price concession.

Allow for Contingencies

After price, the next big item in the contract is how you will finance your purchase. If you are going to assume a present loan or place your mortgage with the sellers themselves, these terms are detailed. You'll stipulate that the mortgage you are taking over must be current (paid up to date) at the time of transfer.

If you must obtain financing, as most people do, the details of your proposed mortgage are spelled out, along with a statement that the contract is "contingent upon" or "subject to" your obtaining the loan. If you cannot find financing at the specific interest rate you have stipulated in the offer, you cannot be required to go through with the purchase. The contract should state that in such a case your deposit is to be returned. This is usually spelled out in a part of the contract called (in most states) *liquidated damages*. Ask your agent to explain this vital part of your purchase offer.

There may be other contingencies (conditions of the sale that must be satisfied before the purchase is complete). You may need to sell your present home in order to have the necessary down payment money. You may make the deal contingent on landing the job you came to town to interview for, or you may not feel comfortable with proceeding fully until an inspector's report is acceptable to you. These conditions are inserted into the contract.

In a new home purchase, buyers can also request that contingencies be written into their purchase agreements, even though builders don't particularly like them. Making a new home purchase contingent upon the sale of an existing unsold home can be setting yourself up for heartbreak in a good real estate market, because the builder can continue to look for solid buyers without contingencies, guaranteeing them a sale. You may lose the home site for which you had heart palpitations and have to start all over again. If your present home already has a sales contract, however, making the deal contingent upon the close is usually a no-brainer for the builder.

New home purchasers are wise to list other types of contingencies, such as seeing the floor plan they are about to buy at drywall stage (for their approval) if there is no model home to use as an example.

Sellers will be nervous about contingent offers. They will be taking their house off the market on your behalf, without any guarantee that the sale will go through. So it's customary to set a time limit on contingencies. The contract might state that it is "contingent upon buyer's receiving a satisfactory inspector's report on the property within three days of acceptance of this offer" or "contingent upon approval by the buyer's husband when he arrives in town before next Saturday, September 11, by 6 P.M."

For longer contingencies, particularly those involving the sale of your present house, the sellers may envision waiting around forever. Instead of worrying about the sale of their home, they must now worry about yours, an element over which they have even less control. And if you accept a contingent offer on your own home, it can have a domino effect on the entire transaction, turning into a very complex and confusing prospect for everyone involved.

So it's only fair for sellers to insert an escape clause, or kickout. The wording may differ according to local practice, but the escape clause usually gives the seller the right to continue to show and market the house. If another good offer comes in, you may be required to remove the contingency and make your offer firm or else drop out.

If your contingency is called, you don't have to meet anyone else's offering price; your deal has been nailed down. But you would have to agree, for example, to buy the property whether or not you sell your present home if you wish to proceed further.

Make sure you can qualify for this ahead of time if you are applying for a mortgage loan. Otherwise, you would drop out of the entire deal and receive your deposit back.

Lead Paint Addendum

If the house was built before 1978, the EPA requires that you be given ten days in which to conduct an inspection for lead paint hazards before any contract can become binding. If you are willing, however, that time can be shortened or eliminated.

If lead paint hazards are found, the seller cannot be required to remedy the situation, but you need not go through with the purchase.

An addendum outlining the requirement, and acknowledging your receipt of a lead paint information booklet, should be part of the purchase contract.

Personal Property versus Real Estate

It is essential to spell out all the gray-area items (unattached carpeting, fireplace equipment, chandeliers, drapes, workshop, pool equipment, etc.) about which there may be disputes as to whether they stay with the property.

In general, personal property is that which can be picked up and moved by the seller without leaving any nail or screw holes. By contrast, real estate is the land and anything permanently attached (affixed) to it. The rules are complicated, though, and it's best to stipulate in the contract that "Stove and refrigerator are to remain" or "Seller may remove dining room chandelier."

Items like custom-sized area carpeting, wood stoves, play equipment, and satellite dishes are subject to occasional differences of opinion; head off trouble by detailing them in the written offer. If the listing agent did a proper job, the sellers will already have indicated which items they are taking or leaving. Ask the broker to do some delicate investigating about the sellers' plans for the aboveground pool or the tool shed. Garage cabinetry may or may not be bolted to the floors or walls, and your dreams of stashing your holiday decorations and kids' toys there can go up in smoke if you don't address the inclusion of them up front, in writing.

Don't get bogged down over small items. Just make sure that your offer specifies what you expect to remain. Don't discuss furniture or rugs that you might like to buy at this point; wait until you have a firm purchase contract.

What Else in Your Offer?

A walk-through or buyer inspection is usually written into purchase agreements. In a resale purchase, you'll usually inspect the premises within 24 hours before closing. In a new home purchase, the builder may cushion completion and buyer possession by a few days or a week to fine-tune and touch up the home after you tour it with the building superintendent. You will want to make sure that everything you and the seller agreed to include or remove has been tended to, and that the owner hasn't left the house in disarray or the builder has not left building materials there.

Clean is a matter of interpretation. You know that no two people view cleanliness identically, so be fair and broad-minded here. Most buyers reclean homes to their own tastes no matter how hard the previous owners may have worked to get ready for them.

Also necessary in the contract are a target date and place for transfer of title. Choose a date that allows for processing of your mortgage application; the agent will have suggestions.

What if that date comes and goes? You still have a binding contract. "Time is of the essence," included in some real estate agreements, can have stronger legal meanings in some states than others. Consult your own attorney if you want to take the risk of setting up a powerful legal deadline. In a new home purchase, many builders stipulate that buyers must close within five days of the certificate of completion of the home, so that they no longer have to carry the unit. In a resale purchase, however, factors on both sides figure into this equation.

Experience has taught agents and lawyers to provide for all sorts of complications that may not have occurred to you. Homebuilders have become masters at disclosing everything that has the potential to come back and bite them. What if the place burns down before closing? If the appraiser thinks it isn't worth the price

BUYER'S TIP

When you make an offer to purchase property:

- Keep in mind that oral agreements have no legal force

- Specify any and all contingencies

- List personal property to be left on the premises

- Include a target date for final settlement and transfer of property

you're paying? If taxes weren't paid last year? If the sellers can't prove they have clear title (ownership)?

Will you receive occupancy on the day you become the owners? What constitutes closing escrow or settlement in your state? In some states, signing and physical acceptance of the deed transfers ownership. In others, closing takes place when a confirmation call is received by an agent, builder, or buyer by the escrow or title company that the new deed is on record at the county recorder's office; then (and only then) can buyers receive keys. In a few areas, sellers are allowed to remain for up to a month; the contract should stipulate exactly to what you agree.

If you need, for some reason, to move in before closing, be prepared for some resistance on the part of the sellers, their attorney, and their agent. Lawyers, builders, and sellers' agents know that it is a risky arrangement, and a good one will write a contract nailing down all possible problems. It is difficult for anyone to be evicted from a house once they have taken occupancy. The liability involved could curl your hair. Sometimes an agreement can be reached in an emergency situation, such a garage rental, where the seller agrees to store your items in the home's locked garage until escrow officially closes. You would probably pay a daily rental fee and need to arrange for a binder to your homeowners insurance policy.

Your offer should have a time limit, and it should be a short one. A day or two is enough time for the sellers to consider your proposal. If you give them more time, they may be tempted to stall until after they see what next Sunday's open house might bring. They might also use your offer as an auction goad to bid up another prospective buyer. If the sellers are out of town, they should be available by phone, and could answer your offer by fax with a confirming letter to follow.

Earnest Money

An offer to buy is usually accompanied by a substantial deposit, variously known as *binder* or *earnest money*. This sum serves several purposes. It proves to the sellers that you mean business. They are, after all, going to take the place off the market on your behalf. The deposit also serves as a source of damages if you back out for no good reason a month down the line. The deposit is usually placed with a broker or attorney who puts it into a separate escrow, or trust, account. Avoid giving the deposit directly to the seller, especially in a FSBO situation. In this case, you and the seller are pretty much on your own to figure out how to keep these funds in a neutral, third party account if no agents are involved.

You may be told that 6 percent or 10 percent of the purchase price is necessary. If this is inconvenient, insist that you can come up with only a smaller amount. Remember, though, that the sellers are weighing your offer to see if it will result in a successful sale. Without much earnest money, it may not look convincing.

This earnest money, of course, counts toward the sum you'll need at closing. Your full deposit is credited toward the down payment or other settlement costs. The contract should clearly state under what circumstances it may be returned.

Legal Provisions

The contract provides that you will receive clear title, as well as full, unchallenged control and ownership, except for certain liens and easements that are spelled out. These are claims that third parties may have against the property. You agree to take it even though the telephone company has the right to run wires through the backyard, or the neighbor has the right to share the driveway; these are known as easements of record. You don't agree to be responsible for unknown liens (financial claims) that turn up later, like an unpaid roofing bill or an outstanding home-improvement loan.

Final Jitters

If this is your first homebuying experience, you will feel shaky when the time comes to sign the offer. You should receive an immediate duplicate of everything you sign; if it isn't offered, ask for it. You need not walk out wondering what you've just committed yourself to.

It's reassuring to take the contract to your lawyer or review it with a third party before you sign it. Many sales, though, are made after office hours and on weekends, and you may risk losing the right house by delay. You can write above your signature "subject to the approval of my attorney." This means that you can go ahead and make your offer, while reserving for your lawyer or someone else you trust the right to object later to any wording or provisions that don't protect your interests.

Negotiation—The Tennis Game

Although local customs vary, in most areas the broker will present your offer to the seller in your absence. You'll be advised to go home and wait by the phone. The agent, meanwhile, may contact the listing broker and the seller to arrange for presentation of the offer as soon as possible. Prompt forwarding of all offers is one of the broker's primary legal responsibilities. No broker has the right to refuse to convey a written offer, no matter how small.

The broker almost never reveals terms or price over the phone. The seller cannot accept over the phone and deserves the right to look over all the details of your proposal at leisure. Faxes for these purposes have become almost universally acceptable.

The tennis game is on, and the next move is the seller's. The response can be yes (acceptance), no (rejection), or maybe (counteroffer).

If it's yes, the seller accepts all your terms, and you have a binding contract (you can skip the rest of this chapter). If there is no response when the time limit has expired, the deal is usually dead.

If it's no, the homeowners cannot later change their minds and get your offer back (unless you agree).

Then there's maybe. Rather than a rejection, a good negotiator will bring you a counteroffer: "We accept all terms and conditions except that purchase price shall be $183,000, and we'll throw in the stove and refrigerator."

The seller is now bound by the counteroffer, which probably contains a time limit, while you are free to consider its terms. You may want to counter the counteroffer, perhaps split the difference.

Too many volleys, though, result in hard feelings and often kill the deal. People begin to say, "It's not the money, it's the principle of the thing." Instead of working together toward what is legally known as a *meeting of the minds,* buyer and seller start to see the negotiation as a war. They concentrate on winning and lose sight of their original goals.

Before you start, make up your mind that you will not lose the house you really want over the last thousand dollars. When you cannot make any further concessions on price, try to include some face-saving gesture toward the seller: "We can't go any higher, but we'll move the closing date for their convenience."

Make your first offer, certainly your second one, close to the top price you'd really pay. The idea is to tempt the sellers to wrap up the deal, even if it isn't quite what they had in mind.

At each stage, the person who made the last proposal is bound by it until it's withdrawn or answered. The game ends when one side accepts unconditionally the other's last offer.

Remember that if your proposal is accepted, you will have a binding legal contract (see Figure 10.1). Don't fool around with a purchase offer unless you really want to buy the property. It should be a thrill when you finally receive the notification of acceptance that is the final legal requirement to make a contract binding and your broker says, "Congratulations! Your offer is accepted!"

Buyer's Remorse

It's not at all unusual to experience a malady known as *buyer's remorse* within 24 hours to two weeks after your purchase offer was accepted. Symptoms include sleeplessness, second-guessing, feelings of inadequacy, and a sinking feeling in the pit of your stomach. You may have thoughts like, "What if I really can't afford this? "What if I don't get along with the neighbors?" What if my table doesn't fit in the dining room?" and so on and so forth.

Buyer's remorse is akin to the last minute jitters experienced by brides and grooms before the wedding. One consolation: If it's all a big mistake, selling a house is simpler than getting a divorce.

Rather than lose any more sleep, call the real estate broker the next day and ask if you can visit and tour the house again, preferably with the sellers absent. "Measuring for curtains" is a logical request, so as not to cause alarm at this point. You may even bring your video camera along, citing the need to send a video to your parents or family members. The least it will do is provide you with the ability to see the house over and over again while you are in escrow, waiting for occupancy.

In nearly every case, the buyer is pleasantly surprised during the return visit. You will probably find that all that hard work, the research, the exhausting house hunting did pay off; this was clearly the right choice for you.

If it happens that you are more depressed than ever after your return visit, it's time for a conference with your broker or attorney to determine your legal position if you back out now, and how much money you stand to forfeit.

FIGURE 10.1   Real Estate Sales Contract

PURCHASE AND SALE CONTRACT
FOR RESIDENTIAL PROPERTY

Plain English Form published by and only for use of members of the Greater Rochester Association of Realtors, Inc. and the Monroe County Bar Association.
COMMISSIONS OR FEES FOR THE REAL ESTATE SERVICES TO BE PROVIDED ARE NEGOTIABLE BETWEEN REALTOR AND CLIENT.
When Signed, This Document Becomes A Binding Contract. Buyer or Seller May Wish To Consult Their Own Attorney.

TO: _____ (Seller) FROM: _____ (Buyer)

OFFER TO PURCHASE

Buyer offers to purchase the property described below from Seller on the following terms:

1. PROPERTY DESCRIPTION.
Property known as No. _____ in the (Town) (City) (Village) of_____ State of New York, also
known as Tax No. _____ including all buildings and any other improvements and all rights which the Seller has in or with the property.
Approximate Lot Size: _____. (Check if applicable) [ ] As described in more detail in the attached description.

Description of Buildings on Property: _____

2. OTHER ITEMS INCLUDED IN PURCHASE. The following items, if any, now in or on the property are included in this purchase and sale. All heating, plumbing, septic and private water systems, lighting fixtures, flowers, shrubs, trees, window shades and blinds, curtain and traverse rods, storm windows, storm doors, screens, awnings, TV antennae, water softeners, sump pumps, window boxes, mail box, tool shed, fences, underground pet containment fencing with control devices, wall-to-wall carpeting and runners, exhaust fans, hoods, garbage disposal, electric garage door opener and remote control devices, intercom equipment, humidifier, security systems, smoke detectors, all fireplace screens and enclosures, swimming pool and all related equipment and accessories, and the following, if built-in: cabinets, mirrors, stoves, ovens, dishwashers, trash compactors, shelving and air conditioning (except window units). Buyer agrees to accept these items in their present conditions. Other items to be included in the purchase and sale are:

_____

[ ] Seller represents to the best of Seller's knowledge that any heating, plumbing, air conditioning, electrical systems and included appliances are presently in good working order, except for

_____

Items not included are:_____
Seller represents that he has good title to all of the above items to be transferred to Buyer, and will deliver a Bill of Sale for the same at closing.

3. PRICE: AMOUNT AND HOW IT WILL BE PAID: The purchase price is _____ Dollars
$ _____, Buyer shall receive credit at closing for any deposit made hereunder. The balance of the purchase price shall be paid as follows: (Check and complete applicable provisions.)

[ ] (a) Seller agrees to pay a loan fee of _____% of the mortgage amount.

[ ] (b) All in cash, or certified check at closing.

[ ] (c) By Buyer assuming and agreeing to pay according to its terms, the principal balance of the mortgage in the approximate amount of $ _____
held by_____, provided that the mortgage is assumable without the holder's approval. Buyer
understands that the mortgage bears interest at the rate of _____% per year and the monthly payments are $ _____ which includes principal,
interest, taxes and insurance (strike out any item not included in payment), with the last payment due on approximately _____ 19/20_____. Buyer agrees to pay the balance of the purchase price over the amount of the assumed mortgage in cash or certified check at closing. Buyer understands that principal balance may be lower at time of closing because of monthly payments made after this contract is signed. If the mortgage to be assumed provides for graduated or balloon payments, then a copy of the original bond and mortgage shall be furnished to Buyer's attorney for approval within ten days after acceptance of this offer.

[ ] (d) By Buyer delivering a purchase money bond and mortgage to Seller at closing. This purchase money bond and mortgage shall be in the amount of $ _____
shall be amortized over a term of _____ years and all due and payable in _____ years from the date of closing, shall bear interest at the rate of _____% per year, and shall
be paid in monthly installments of $_____, including principal and interest. The mortgage shall contain the statutory clauses as to payment, insurance, acceleration on default of thirty days, taxes, assessments, and water rates and also shall provide for late charges of 2% of any monthly payment which is not paid within 15 days after it is due and for recovery of reasonable attorney's fees if the mortgage is foreclosed.

The mortgage shall allow Buyer to prepay all or part of the mortgage without penalty at any time but shall also provide that the mortgage be paid in full if Buyer sells the property, unless Seller consents in writing to assumption of the mortgage debt. The balance of the purchase price will be paid at closing in cash, or certified check.

FIGURE 10.1   Real Estate Sales Contract (Continued)

4.   **CONTINGENCIES.** Buyer makes this offer subject to the following contingencies. If any of these contingencies is not satisfied by the dates specified, then either Buyer or Seller may cancel this contract by written notice to the other. (Check and complete applicable provisions.)

[ ] (a) **Mortgage Contingency.** This offer subject to Buyer obtaining and accepting a _____ mortgage loan commitment in an amount not to exceed _____ at an interest rate not to exceed _____%, for a term of _____ years. Buyer shall immediately apply for this loan and shall have until _____, 199____ to obtain and accept a written mortgage commitment. The conditions of any such mortgage commitment shall not be deemed contingencies of this contract but shall be the sole responsibility of Buyer. If the loan commitment requires repairs, replacements, or improvements to be made or painting to be done, before closing, then Seller shall do the work and install the materials and improvements needed or have the same done, at Seller's expense. However, if the cost of doing so exceeds $_____ Seller shall not be obligated to have such work done, and Buyer will be allowed either to receive credit at closing for the amount recited above and incur any necessary expenses to comply with the loan commitment requirements, or to cancel this contract by written notice to Seller, and any deposit shall be returned to Buyer. Issuance and acceptance by the Buyer of a written mortgage commitment shall be deemed a waiver and satisfaction of this contingency.

[ ] (b) **Mortgage Assumption Contingency.** This offer is subject to Buyer obtaining permission to assume the existing mortgage loan balance referred to above in (3c) by _____ 19_____ . If the mortgage holder requires that the interest rate be increased for such approval to be given, Buyer agrees to assume the mortgage at such rate as long as it does not exceed _____% at the time of the commitment. [ ]Buyer agrees to obtain a release of Seller's liability and to pay any assumption or release of liability fees.

[ ] (c) **Sale Contract Contingency.** This offer is subject to Buyer obtaining a contract for the sale of Buyer's property located at _____ no later than _____, 199____. Unless and until Buyer has removed this sale contingency in writing, if Seller receives another acceptable purchase offer, Seller may notify Buyer in writing that Seller wants to accept the other offer and Buyer will then have _____ days to remove this sale contingency by written notice to the Seller. If Buyer does not remove this sale contingency after receiving notice from Seller, Buyer's rights under this contract shall end, and Seller shall be free to accept the other purchase offer and Buyer's deposit shall be returned. Buyer may not remove this sale contingency if Buyer's mortgage loan commitment requires the sale and/or transfer of this property as a condition of the mortgage loan funding, unless Buyer has a contract for the sale of this property which is not then subject to any unsatisfied contingencies.

[ ] (d) **Transfer of Title Contingency.** This offer is contingent upon the transfer of title to Buyer's property located at _____ no later than _____, 199____. [ ] Buyer represents that Buyer has entered into a contract for sale of Buyer's property which is now subject to the following contingencies: [ ] None; [ ] Mortgage; [ ] Assumption of Mortgage; [ ] Sale of Property; [ ] Transfer of Title; [ ] Attorney Approval; and/or [ ] Other_____. Unless and until Buyer has obtained a contract for sale of Buyer's property which is not subject to any unsatisfied contingencies, and has so notified the Seller in writing, if Seller receives another acceptable purchase offer, Seller may notify Buyer in writing that Seller wants to accept the other offer and Buyer will then have _____ days to remove this transfer of title contingency by written notice to the Seller. If Buyer does not remove this transfer of title contingency after receiving notice from Seller, Buyer's rights under this contract shall end, and Seller shall be free to accept the other purchase offer and Buyer's deposit shall be returned. Buyer may not remove this transfer of title contingency if Buyer's mortgage loan commitment requires the sale and transfer of this property as a condition of the mortgage loan funding, unless Buyer has a contract for sale of this property which is not then subject to any unsatisfied contingencies.

[ ] (e) **Attorney Approval.** This contract is subject to the written approval of attorneys for Buyer and Seller within _____ days from date of acceptance (the ''Approval Period''). If either attorney makes written objection to the contract within the Approval Period, and such objection is not cured by written approval by both attorneys and all of the parties within the Approval Period, then either Buyer or Seller may cancel this contract by written notice to the other and any deposit shall be returned to the Buyer.

[ ] (f) **Waiver of Attorney Approval.** This offer is not subject to the Buyer's attorney approval.

[ ] (g) **Other Contingencies.** _____
_____

5. **Closing Date and Place.** Transfer of title shall take place at the _____ County Clerk's Office or at the offices of Buyer's lender on or before _____, 19_____ .

6. **Buyer's Possession of Property.**

[ ] Buyer shall have possession of the property on the day of closing, in broom clean condition, with all keys to the property delivered to Buyer at closing.

[ ] Seller shall have the right to retain possession for_____ days after closing at the cost of $_____ per day, plus utilities. At possession, the property shall be broom clean and all keys shall be delivered to Buyer.

7. **Title Documents.** Seller shall provide the following documents in connection with the sale:

A. **Deed.** Seller will deliver to Buyer at closing a properly signed and notarized Warranty Deed with lien covenant (or Executor's Deed, Administrator's Deed or Trustee's Deed, if Seller holds title as such).

GRAR 3/94   B. **Abstract, Bankruptcy and Tax Searches, and Instrument Survey Map.** Seller will furnish and pay for and deliver to Buyer or Buyer's attorney at least 15 days prior to the date of closing, fully guaranteed tax, title and United States Court Searches dated or redated after the date of this contract with a local tax certificate for Village, or City taxes, if any, and an instrument survey map dated or redated after the date of this contract. Seller will pay for the map or redated map and for continuing such searches to and including the day of closing. Any survey map shall be prepared or redated and certified to meet the standards and requirements of Buyer's mortgage lender and of the Monroe County Bar Association.

FIGURE 10.1   **Real Estate Sales Contract (Continued)**

8. Marketability of Title. The deed and other documents delivered by Seller shall be sufficient to convey good marketable title in fee simple, to the property free and clear of all liens and encumbrances. However, Buyer agrees to accept title to the property subject to restrictive covenants of record common to the tract or subdivision of which the property is a part, provided these restrictions have not been violated, or if they have been violated, that the time for anyone to complain of the violations has expired. Buyer also agrees to accept title to the property subject to public utility easements along lot lines as long as those easements do not interfere with any buildings now on the property or with any improvements Buyer may construct in compliance with all present restrictive covenants of record and zoning and building codes applicable to the Property. Seller agrees to furnish a smoke alarm affidavit at closing and to cooperate in executing any documents required by federal or state laws for transfer of title to residential property.

9. Objections to Title. If Buyer raises a valid written objection to Seller's title which means that the title to the property is unmarketable, Seller may cancel this contract by giving prompt written notice of cancellation to Buyer. Buyer's deposit shall be returned immediately, and if Buyer makes a written request for it, Seller shall reimburse Buyer for the reasonable cost of having the title examined. However, if Seller gives notice within 5 days that Seller will cure the problem prior to the closing date, or if the title objection is insurable and Buyer is willing to accept insurable title, then this contract shall continue in force until the closing date, subject to the Seller performing as promised and/or providing insurable title at Seller's expense. If Seller fails to cure the problem within such time, Buyer will not be obligated to purchase the property and Buyer's deposit shall be returned together with reimbursement for the reasonable cost of having the title examined.

10. Recording Costs, Mortgage Tax, Transfer Tax and Closing Adjustments. Seller will pay the real property transfer tax and special additional mortgage recording tax, if applicable. Buyer will pay mortgage assumption charges, if any, and will pay for recording the deed and the mortgage, and for mortgage tax. The following, as applicable, will be prorated and adjusted between Seller and Buyer as of the date of closing: current taxes computed on a fiscal year basis, excluding any delinquent items, interest and penalties; rent payments; fuel oil on the premises; water charges; pure water charges; sewer charges; mortgage interest; current common charges or assessments; prepaid F.H.A. Mortgage Insurance Premium (M.I.P.) of approximately $_____, with the exact amount to be calculated at closing in accordance with F.H.A. formulae. Any F.H.A. insurance premium which is not prepaid, but rather paid monthly, shall be adjusted at closing. If there is a water meter at the property, Seller shall furnish an actual reading to a date not more than thirty (30) days before the closing date set forth in this contract. At closing the water charges and any sewer rent shall be apportioned on the basis of such actual reading.

11. Zoning. Seller represents that the property is in full compliance with all zoning or building ordinances for use as a _____. If applicable laws require it, the Seller will furnish at or before closing, a Certificate of Occupancy for the property, dated within ninety (90) days of the closing, with Seller completing the work and installing the materials and improvements needed to obtain Certificate of Occupancy. However, if the cost of obtaining a Certificate of Occupancy exceeds $_____, Seller shall not be obligated to have such work done, and Buyer will be allowed either to receive credit at closing for the amount recited above, and incur the necessary expenses to obtain the Certificate of Occupancy, or to cancel this contract by written notice to Seller, and any deposit shall be returned to Buyer.

12. Risk of Loss. Risk of loss or damage to the property by fire or other casualty until transfer of title shall be assumed by the Seller. If damage to the property by fire or such other casualty occurs prior to transfer, Buyer may cancel this contract without any further liability to Seller and Buyer's deposit is to be returned. If Buyer does not cancel but elects to close, then Seller shall transfer to Buyer any insurance proceeds, or Seller's claim to insurance proceeds payable for such damage.

13. Condition of Property. Buyer agrees to purchase the property "as is" except as provided in paragraph 2, subject to reasonable use, wear, tear, and natural deterioration between now and the time of closing. However, this paragraph shall not relieve Seller from furnishing a Certificate of Occupancy as called for in paragraph 11, if applicable. Buyer shall have the right, after reasonable notice to Seller, to inspect the property within 48 hours before the time of closing.

14. Services. Seller represents that property is serviced by: _____ Public Water, _____ Public Sewers, _____ Septic System, _____ Private Well.

15. Deposit to Listing Broker. Buyer (has deposited) (will deposit upon acceptance) $_____ in the form of a _____ with _____ (Escrow Agent) at _____ (bank), which deposit is to become part of the purchase price or returned if not accepted or if Buyer's contract thereafter fails to close for any reason not the fault of the Buyer. If Buyer fails to complete Buyer's part of this contract, Seller is allowed to retain the deposit to be applied to Seller's damages, and may also pursue other legal rights Seller has against the Buyer, including a lawsuit for any real estate brokerage commission paid by the Seller.

16. Real Estate Broker.
[ ] The parties agree that _____ brought about this purchase and sale.
[ ] It is understood and agreed by both Buyer and Seller that no broker secured this contract.

17. Life of Offer. This offer shall expire on_____ , 19____ , at _____ m.

18. Responsibility of Persons Under This Contract; Assignability. If more than one person signs this contract as Buyer, each person and any party who takes over that person's legal position will be responsible for keeping the promises made by Buyer in this contract. If more than one person signs this contract as Seller, each person or any party who takes over that person's legal position, will be fully responsible for keeping the promises made by Seller. However, this contract is personal to the parties and may not be assigned by either without the other's consent.

19. Entire Contract. This contract when signed by both Buyer and Seller will be the record of the complete agreement between the Buyer and Seller concerning the purchase and sale of the property. No verbal agreements or promises will be binding.

20. Notices. All notices under this contract shall be deemed delivered upon receipt. Any notices relating to this contract may be given by the attorneys for the parties.

21. Addenda. The following Addenda are incorporated into this contract:
[ ] All Parties Agreement   [ ] Services   [ ] Engineer's Inspection   [ ] Mediation   [ ] Electric Availability   [ ] Utility Surcharge   [ ] Lead Warning   [ ] Other:_____

FIGURE 10.1 Real Estate Sales Contract (Continued)

Dated: _____   BUYER _____

Witness: _____   BUYER _____

[ ] ACCEPTANCE OF OFFER BY SELLER   [ ] COUNTER OFFER BY SELLER

Seller certifies that Seller owns the property and has the power to sell the property. Seller accepts the offer and agrees to sell on the terms and conditions above set forth.

[ ] Waiver of Seller's attorney approval. This offer is not subject to Seller's attorney approval.

Dated: _____   SELLER _____

Witness: _____   SELLER _____

─────────────── ADMINISTRATIVE INFORMATION ───────────────

Buyer:_____

Social Security Number: _____

Address:_____

_____ Zip:_____

Phone: (H) _____(B) _____

Attorney:_____

Address:_____

Phone:(B) _____(FAX) _____

Selling Broker: _____

Address:_____

Phone: _____ Broker Code: _____

Selling Agent: _____ Phone:(H) ____

Selling Agent I.D. #_____ FAX_____

Seller:_____

Social Security Number:_____

GRAR MLS # _____

Address:_____

_____ Zip:_____

Phone:(H) _____(B) _____

Attorney:_____

Address:_____

Phone:(B) _____(FAX) _____

Listing Broker: _____

Address:_____

Phone: _____ Broker Code: _____

Listing Agent: _____ Phone:(H) ___

Listing Agent I.D. #_____ FAX_____

11

Your Mortgage Application

Most homebuyers don't have a huge lump sum of cash lying around for a home purchase unless they have been recipients of a substantial inheritance or a winning lottery ticket. If you require a new mortgage to finance your purchase, the sales contract probably contains your promise to apply promptly at a lending institution. The real estate broker can often suggest the lender most favorable to your situation and the seller's. Or perhaps you have already checked out several and have a comfort level with a lender who has prequalified you for a certain loan amount. Some lenders are experts at extending loans to buyers of older homes, others specialize in manufactured housing, still others, like portfolio lenders, work especially well with self-employed buyers.

In some areas, the agent makes the appointment for you and even accompanies you to the application session. The application these days, however, may be as simple as a phone conversation with the loan officer (phone applications can be input into the lender's computer, printed out, and then mailed to you for your signature). Or it may be an application online with a disembodied loan officer prompting you through the cyber loan application.

If you are on your own, sit down with the Yellow Pages open to "Mortgages" and ask to speak with a mortgage counselor or loan officer. Or log onto one of the many lender Web sites and start shopping. If you are buying a new home and opt to use the builder's in-house or preferred lender, the sales consultant will probably set up the meeting with a loan consultant. Do your own research, using the charts in Chapter 7.

Come to the application session armed with as many facts as possible (see Figure 11.1). The lender will want to know a great deal about your financial situation, all aimed at not letting you get in debt over your head.

The lender's process of analyzing a mortgage application, looking over the loan package (appraisal and/or inspection of the property, verification of employment, credit report, etc.), and making a decision about furnishing the loan, is known as *underwriting*.

Factors that lenders consider in deciding whether to make the loan are your employment stability and prospects, present assets, credit history, past mortgage experience, and present debts. Most lenders will consider all kinds of circumstances that may help to tip the scales in your favor if you remember to furnish them, like future verifiable salary bonuses or the drop-off of child-support payments by a certain date. They call these *compensating factors* (very much like mitigating circumstances in a court case).

The lender judges two things: your ability to meet your obligations in the future and your willingness to do so, as evidenced in the past. Lenders will ask you to furnish a list of documents. Some types of loans and some lenders require more than others. Over the past few years, some lenders have streamlined the process by dispensing with employment verifications, using only buyer-furnished paycheck stubs and verified credit scores. (See the section on Credit History later in this chapter.)

Figure 11.1 is a general checklist for items borrowers should prepare themselves to hand over for a complete and helpful total picture of loan worthiness. Lenders vary in the number of months for each type of statement they require, so ask ahead of time. And make copies of everything for the lender; don't hand them your originals!

FIGURE 11.1
Checklist: Take to Your Mortgage Application

Some of these items, if not available, can be obtained later during the application process—VA eligibility certificate, for example, or legal description of property. To expedite your application, though, take as much as possible to your initial interview.

❑ Original purchase contract signed by all parties. It will be copied and returned to you.

❑ Cash or check for application fee, to cover appraisal of the property and credit report. Additional points or origination fee if required.

❑ Social Security numbers.

❑ List of all income.

❑ List of debts, credit cards, account numbers, payments, balances. Addresses of out-of-town creditors.

❑ List of two years' past employment and two years' past addresses.

❑ Seller's agreement to pay points (if not in contract).

❑ If self-employed, two years' signed income-tax returns. If on job less than two years, copies of previous W-2s.

❑ Expense and income statements on property presently rented out. Leases signed by tenants.

❑ Account numbers and balances on checking and saving accounts, branch addresses.

❑ Donor's name and address for gift letter.

❑ Explanation of any credit problems. Copies of bankruptcy papers.

❑ Certificate of Eligibility, if applying for VA loan.

❑ Legal description of property, survey (not required for all loans).

❑ List of stocks and bonds, current market value.

❑ List of other assets.

❑ True property tax figure on the projected purchase.

❑ Name and phone number of person who will give access to the lending institution's appraiser.

❑ Copy of divorce decree or separation agreement if paying child support or alimony; same documents if claiming them for income, along with proof that payments are being received.

Assets

You may not borrow elsewhere for the down payment (secondary financing) on most loans. You will be asked to prove that you already have enough on hand for a down payment and closing costs. Many institutions are skeptical about claims that your money is under the mattress, and will credit you with only a limited amount in cash—as little as $200, perhaps. They will also want an explanation for large sums of money that have suddenly turned up in your savings accounts within the past few months. (Maybe, they figure, you borrowed it somewhere, thus taking on too much debt.)

Bring in all details on your assets: numbers and balances on savings accounts (the lender will check with the bank to verify), list of stocks and bonds owned, income tax return if you anticipate a refund. Your earnest money deposit counts as an asset; the lender will verify it with the person holding it. You may have assets you've forgotten about: cash surrender value on your life insurance policy, valuable collections, jewelry, boats and RVs, IRA accounts, other real estate owned. If your loan agent says you are a borderline qualifier, ask if you should list your free-and-clear furniture, appliances, and automobiles.

A gift letter from a relative, promising to furnish some of the funds you need for closing with no repayment required or anticipated, can sometimes be used at mortgage application. Many lenders require the letter on their own form, and most want to verify that the relative does indeed have the funds in question.

Income to Qualify

The lending institution will analyze your income and will accept only figures that can be verified and are claimed on your tax returns. More than one borrower (husband and wife or unrelated buyers) may pool their incomes to qualify for the loan.

The usual rule of thumb is that two years' continuous employment in the same field indicates employment stability. Exceptions are made for recent college graduates or those who have just left the service. Lenders are nervous about those who jump often from one sort of job to another; employment changes that show upward movement within the same field are more acceptable.

Bonuses and overtime count toward qualification if your employer will verify them as dependable. Part-time and commission income count if they have been steady for the past year or two. Alimony and child support can be considered as income if you want to claim them, but you must be able to show that they are being paid dependably and are likely to continue for the next five years or so.

Older applicants will not be asked their ages, but they will be asked to prove dependable Social Security and pension income if they anticipate retirement within the next few years. Disability income counts if it is permanent.

Seasonal income may count if applicants can prove at least a two-year history of such a cycle, and they may even be able to count unemployment insurance in qualifying.

The self-employed will be asked to furnish income tax returns for two years past and, where appropriate, audited profit-and-loss statements.

Other sources of income might include dividends and interest, and net rental from other properties (leases signed by your tenants may be required). If you will have rental income from the house you are buying (a duplex, for example, with the other side to be rented out), half or even all of the anticipated rent may be counted as further income.

Debts

Lenders give careful consideration to your present liabilities. Depending on the type of loan for which you are applying, they may count any debt on which you must pay for more than 6, 10, or 12 months. Car loans are among the most common liabilities in this category.

Before you arrive for the mortgage application session, list your debts, including loan numbers, monthly payments, balances, and time left to run. Student loans are considered obligations if payments are presently due. Child support or alimony is considered an obligation; so is childcare if you are applying for a VA or FHA loan.

Credit History

It is essential to divulge information about past credit problems frankly during your interview. You should already have discussed judgments or bankruptcies with the real estate agent during your first meeting. Such problems won't necessarily prevent you from obtaining a mortgage, but if the lender's checking turns up any lies, you're in trouble.

To find out about your credit history, simply go to your local credit bureau and draw an inexpensive report on yourself or take advantage of online free credit reports offered through some firms on the World Wide Web. Do it early on. If any inaccuracies show up, the bureau will help you clear them up. Sometimes it takes up to 120 days to see the results of your credit clean-up in the credit report, so as a back up keep copies of all letters from creditors who are helping you.

Credit scoring is a relatively recent tool used by lenders. The first such scoring system, FICO (Fair Isaac & Company) and systems like it are used by Experian, Equifax, and Trans Union, the three major credit bureaus. On a scale of 365 to 840, a FICO score of, for instance, 585, carries with it more than 2 to 1 odds that an account would go delinquent. One reading 700 would tell the lender that the chances were only 1 in 288 that the something would go wrong.

Some of the things that affect your FICO score are:

- Delinquencies on credit accounts
- Too many accounts opened within the last 12 months
- Short credit history
- Balances on revolving credit near the maximum limits
- Public records, such as tax liens, judgments, or bankruptcies

Lower scores may qualify you for one sort of loan and not another. VA and FHA guidelines are generally more lenient, though banks making their own portfolio loans can be flexible within certain limits. FICO scores are now considered guidelines, and even though creditors and lenders that view your credit report do not get to see the actual scorecard, they will use the final scores. How lenders view FICO scores vary a little from lender to lender. Some scores will require a very basic review of the entire loan package; some will require more underwriting.

The lender may ask you for written explanations of slow payment history or any negative report. You will have to pay off any open judgments, even if they flow from an "I won't pay as a matter of principle" dispute.

Bankruptcy guidelines vary, depending on the type of bankruptcy and type of loan. In general, two to four years must have elapsed since the discharge of your bankruptcy, though each case is considered separately. Foreclosures must usually be at least three years old. If your problem was due to something beyond your control, and your previous credit history was excellent, exceptions can be made. Most important is your record of payments on any previous mortgage loan.

You'll be asked to sign a number of papers when you apply for the loan, many of them authorizing the release of information from your employer, savings institution, or credit bureau.

After the Application

While the lending institution completes all the paperwork (assembling the loan package), the real estate agent should keep in touch in case any hitches develop. You might check yourself from time to time to see if things are going smoothly. Usually, however, no news is good news.

Within three days of your application, the lending institution must send you a *good faith estimate* of your closing costs, and notification of your APR, the adjusted percentage rate. If you paid for the appraisal, you are entitled to receive a copy; if it isn't offered, request it in writing.

B U Y E R ' S   T I P

After you have applied for a mortgage loan:

- Check periodically on its progress

- Obtain an estimate of closing costs

- Don't incur any new debts

- Don't apply for any new credit

Keep the broker or your lawyer informed of any communication you receive from the lending institution, local government, or FHA. Above all, don't go out and put a major purchase on credit. This is not the time to incur additional debt or deplete your cash.

After the loan package has been assembled, your loan consultant will submit the package to the mortgage-underwriting department for review. This is now done electronically with most lenders, a process called *desktop underwriting*. The lender may then issue its findings either in the form of a commitment letter or a conditional commitment dependent, for example, on certain repairs to the property before closing or on your clearing up an outstanding judgment, or even a final appraisal, if the house is brand new. In any event, be sure to contact the broker, your lawyer, or closing agent as soon as you hear from the lender.

Once you have the commitment safely in hand, nothing remains but to find a time (within the number of days stipulated in the commitment letter) that suits everyone for arranging your walk-through and transferring the property. You are ready for closing.

12

Buying Your Home at Last

In Maine they *pass papers;* in California they *close escrow.* It's closing, settlement, transfer of title—the moment when the seller gets the money and you get legal ownership and the front-door keys. In few real estate matters does local custom vary so widely.

In your area, closing may be conducted by attorneys, title companies, an escrow service, a lending institution, even by real estate brokers. It may take place at the county courthouse, a bank, an attorney's office, or another location. Sometimes everyone sits around a big table; sometimes buyer and seller never meet.

Your purchase contract provides a blueprint for the final transfer. The seller's main responsibility is to prove title, to show that you are receiving clear and trouble-free ownership. Depending on the mortgagee's requirements and local custom, the seller may prove title by furnishing an abstract and lawyer's opinion, title insurance, or, in some states, a *Torrens certificate.*

Two types of *title insurance* are available. A fee policy, which may be required by your lender, protects the mortgagee—the lender—against loss if other parties challenge your ownership. If you need the policy for your mortgage loan, you may be asked to pay for it. The premium is a single payment; good for the whole time you own the property. For a relatively small additional fee, you can purchase at the same time an owner's policy, which protects you personally.

An abstract is a history of all transactions affecting the property, researched from the public records (see Figure 12.1). Typically, the seller must furnish an up-to-date abstract and forward it to you (better yet, to your attorney) for inspection before the closing, just to make sure no problems exist. Where escrow or title companies handle closings, many of the same procedures are followed within the company.

A third method of proving title, the *Torrens system*, is used in some states and provides a central, permanent registration of title to real property.

Forms of Joint Ownership

If two persons are buying together, the wording of the deed determines their respective shares of ownership, their legal rights and the disposition of the property on the death of one of them. Depending on state law, types of joint ownership include:

- *Tenancy in common.* Each owner has the right to leave his or her share to chosen heirs.
- *Joint tenancy with right of survivorship.* The survivor automatically becomes complete owner.
- *Tenancy by the entirety.* This is a special form of joint tenancy for married couples.

If the owners have unequal shares, tenancy in common is the usual form. Except with tenancy by the entirety, any owner would have the right to force a division or sale of the property (partition).

When there is more than one owner, it is important to check with an attorney or the title company and to make sure that the deed clearly states the desired form of ownership.

That Clod of Earth—The Deed

The *deed,* the bill of sale for real estate, is drawn up ahead of time so that it can be examined and approved. A full *warranty*

FIGURE 12.1   **Portion of an Abstract**

A B S T R A C T   O F   T I T L E

- T O -

#47   W e s t   s i d e   R o w l e y   S t r e e t ,   b e i n g

P a r t   o f   L o t s   #27   a n d   28   o f   t h e

B r o o k s   T r a c t   (N. P a r t)   i n   t h e

C i t y   o f   R o c h e s t e r

Maps: Liber 2 of Maps, page 120 and 138
Liber 3 of Maps, page 45
1935 Hopkins Atlas, Vol. 1, Plate 4

1   Ida May Hughey   Mortgage to secure $5000.00
-TO-   Dated   June 3, 1947
Rochester Savings Bank   same day
47 Main Street West   same day at 12:30 P. M.
Rochester, New York   Liber 1800 of Mortgages, page 344

(*) Conveys land in the City of Rochester, being on the

west side of Rowley Street in said City and being part of lots

Nos. 27 and 28 in the Brooks Tract as shown on a map of said

Tract made by M. D. Rowley, surveyor, May 15, 1869, and filed

in Monroe County Clerk's Office and <u>c</u>ounded and described as

follows:

Beginning at a point in the west line of Row<u>e</u>ly

Street 15 feet northerly from the southeast corner of said

lot #27; thence northerly on the west line of Rowley Street,

<u>forth</u> (40) feet; thence westerly on a line parallel with the

south line of said lot #27, 121 feet; thence southerly on a

line parallel with the west line of Rowley Street, 40 feet;

thence easterly 121 feet to the place of beginning.

FIGURE 12.1   **Portion of an Abstract (Continued)**

Being the same premises conveyed to the mortgagor by Liber 2258 of Deeds, page 178.

Subject to any restrictions and public utility easements of record.

- -

2   Ida May Hughey, Landlord   Lease

         -To-   Dated May 23, 1952
                            Ack.   same day

Michael Franco   Rec.   August 4, 1952
Mildred Franco,his wife,
Tenants, 17 Glendale Park,   Liber 2769 of Deeds, page 290
Rochester, N.Y.,(Second
parties not certified)

First party leases to second parties premises described as #47 Rowley Street, Rochester, New York, being a 12 room house for a term of 5 years commencing July 16, 1952 and ending July 15, 1957 on certain terms and conditions set forth herein.

Second parties shall have the right of renewal on the same terms and conditions as herein for an additional period of 5 years provided that written notice of intention to renew is served upon Landlord or her assigns at least 30 days prior to end of initial term hereof.

- -

3   Ida May Hughey,   Warranty Deed

        -To-   Dated Oct. 30, 1953
                            Ack. Same day

Michele Franco, Mildred   Rec. Same day at 10:50 A.M.
Franco, his wife, as
tenants by the entirety,   Liber 2861 of Deeds, page 411
#47 Rowley St., Rochester,
N.Y. (Second parties not
certified).

         Conveys same as #1.

         Subject to all covenants, easements and restrictions

deed contains legal guarantees; that the seller really owns the property, for example, and that no one will ever challenge your right to it. In some areas, the standard is a *bargain and sale deed with covenant,* or *special warranty deed,* which contains some guarantees but not as many. If you buy from an estate, you receive an executor's deed. A quitclaim deed completely transfers whatever ownership the grantor (person signing the deed) may have had, but makes no claim of ownership in the first place.

In feudal times, when few could read or write, transfer of ownership took place with buyer and seller first walking the boundaries of the land in question together. Often they would take along young boys who would be there to serve as witnesses after buyer and seller were long gone. (One account says the boys were urged along with switches, on the theory that one doesn't forget painful experiences—"beating the bounds.")

With the boundaries agreed upon, the seller would then dig up a clod of earth from the land being transferred and hand it to the buyer, who seized it and at that moment was the new owner, "seized of the land." The legal term *seisin* still refers to the claim of ownership.

Today, in a literate society, that clod of earth is replaced by a document, the deed, whose sole purpose is to transfer ownership. The beating of the bounds is replaced by the legal description in the deed. And you become owner at the exact moment when the deed is handed to you and accepted by you—physical transfer, just as it was with that clod of earth.

What to Do before Closing

You'll be alerted a few days before closing as to the exact amount of money needed. A cashier's check or wire transfer is usually required; no one wants to turn over so valuable an asset on a personal check. Except where you won't be in attendance (escrow closing), it's simplest to have a cashier's check made out to yourself or your attorney; you can always endorse it, and matters are simpler if anything goes wrong. Bring a supply of your personal checks as well. A photo ID, such as a driver's license is also required in some states.

FIGURE 12.2
Before-Closing Checklist

- ❏ Homeowners insurance
- ❏ Flood insurance (if required)
- ❏ Water meter reading
- ❏ Electric and gas service
- ❏ Fuel supplier
- ❏ Newspaper delivery

- ❏ Telephone, cable
- ❏ Packing
- ❏ Garage sale
- ❏ Moving companies
- ❏ Change-of-address cards
- ❏ Walk-through

You may be asked to bring proof that you are placing insurance on the property (see Figure 12.2). Real estate in a flood-prone area may be required to carry flood insurance. (A survey proving that the building is located above the 100-year flood mark may allow you to drop a flood insurance requirement.) You should have been told about the requirement for flood insurance long before this, however.

As closing approaches, make a last-minute walk-through of the property. If you see a window that was broken since you first inspected the house or a junked car in the backyard, don't talk directly with the seller. Instead, contact the agent and your lawyer immediately. If you see damage possibly caused by the move, point that out also.

Closing a New Home Purchase

Unless waived by the buyer, new homebuilders usually require buyers to attend a *new home orientation*, the fancier term for a walk-through, as a stipulation of the sale. The building superintendent or customer service representative will accompany you on the inspection of both the exterior and interior of the house.

This is a golden opportunity to bring a list of questions and discuss how to maintain your home, picking your builder's brain as you go. You may even want to bring your video camera along so that you don't miss a thing being said. The builder can give you advice on how to take care of the various systems in your new home, such as heating and air conditioning (and explain thermostat setbacks for more energy efficiency). If you have a new security system, installed fancy structured wiring for home office use, need advice on what to do if one of the newer low-flow toilets clog, or want to know how to protect shiny new surfaces and seal tile grout—you name it, the builder's representative should know (or be able to get) the answers. Before the orientation, builders generally inspect the new house and make notes (a punch list) of things that need to be fine-tuned, such as uneven paint or drywall, some sloppy trim here and there, or a missing knob on an appliance. If you are video-taping the process and the builder agrees that other things need attention, you've got proof.

Should you not maintain some items in your home or have your own (rather than the builder's) installations put into the house, your new home warranty may be voided in some instances. For example, installing your own garage-door opener after you close escrow can void the builder's warranty for your garage door, because the garage door can be damaged by a faulty owner-purchased installation. If the builder had sold you the garage door opener as an upgrade, then anything that happens to the garage door and the opener will be backed up my both the product manufacturer and the sub-contractor installing it, according to the terms of the original warranty.

Keep all your appliance warranties, brochures, and house-related instructions in one drawer or file, readily accessible if items covered by your new home warranty need attention during the first year or so. And don't forget to send in all the warranty cards right away. Many companies accept online warranty registrations, making it easy for you to have records of them and save you the postage as well.

If the home you are buying is fairly new (no more than ten years old), ask the current owner, through his or her agent, to leave behind any warranty paperwork, receipts for improvements, or operating instructions for newer installations of systems or appliances. They may come in handy if something does not perform as promised and can be replaced or repaired if the proper paperwork is in hand.

What Happens at Closing?

At closing, the seller gives you a deed to the property in return for the purchase money. But you can't give the seller the cash until the lender gives you the loan. You can't get the check for the loan until you sign the mortgage (or trust deed). And you can't sign a mortgage until you own the property.

You can see why it must all take place at once and in the right order. In some areas, buyer and seller sign all the documents ahead of time, and when everything is in order, an escrow agent, who holds all the papers, declares that the transfer has taken place.

If you are assuming a mortgage, you will receive a reduction certificate, the lender's statement that the principal has been paid down to a certain amount. You should receive proof that payments are current and property taxes paid up to date. A last-minute title search will reassure you that the seller did not borrow money against the property earlier that morning.

Long Distance Closings

If you are in Massachusetts and about to close on a house in Oregon, closing long distance can be arranged in a variety of ways. In some cases, when title companies are involved and have offices in both states, you may merely go to the nearest branch and sign paperwork there. Documents are now routinely being transferred electronically and printed in remote locations, or overnight courier services can be arranged. Agents on both ends must prepare themselves well ahead of time, helping to smooth the process and avoiding any last-minute hitches.

Holding Proceeds in Escrow

It's extremely important to have problems cleared up before you hand over your check or the lender's. Once transfer of title has taken place, many matters are merged into the closing—you have bought the problems along with the property. Don't rely, then, on promises that something will be taken care of "in the next few days." If it is impractical to solve the problem immediately, ask that part of the purchase price be held in escrow, to be turned over to the seller only after the matter is attended to.

In new home purchases, an escrow holdback of mortgage funds can occur if there is work to be done after the close. In other cases, there may have been work that was not permitted on the builder's land before the property became yours. A swimming pool is one such example, because a homebuilder may not have wanted to permit a huge hole to be dug in the back yard until after the property was passed to you.

If the seller is to remain in occupancy after closing, be sure that there is plenty of financial motivation to move out as promised; otherwise, you could find yourself stuck with a lengthy and expensive eviction. Daily rental should be set at a high figure, with the provision that it will be deducted from that part of the purchase price held in escrow until the seller leaves as agreed.

Adjustments and Prorations

Many small items must be adjusted fairly between you and the seller. Your state will assume that the owner on the day of closing is seller or buyer. Items adjusted as of the date of closing might include property taxes, interest in a mortgage being assumed, or unpaid water bills.

If the tenants in the attic apartment have paid rent for the present month, part of that rent may belong to you. You should receive the entire security deposit they paid, because some day you will need to return it.

When all items are listed on a balance sheet, you'll receive full credit for the earnest money deposit you placed with the real estate agent. If the lender requires a trust account, you'll be asked to place in escrow several months' property taxes and insurance costs, mortgage insurance, or other items.

Various sums charged to either buyer or seller may include recording fees (for the new deed and mortgage), attorney's fees, transfer tax (revenue stamps), notary fees, charges for document preparation, mortgage tax, and closing agent's fee.

The Real Estate Settlement Procedures Act (RESPA) requires a uniform statement to be furnished to you (see Figure 12.3). In addition, your attorney or escrow company handling the closing should furnish you with a simpler account of your expenses and credits (see Figure 12.4).

A Word about the Power of the Cyber World

Online, paperless closings are now possible. With the federal government approving the use of electronic signatures, everything that once required hard-copy attention can now be done in a secure, online environment. As this grows in popularity, agents, principals, and various companies, such as inspection services, escrow services, lenders, and appraisers (just use your imagination) will be arranged for without benefit of phone calls, overnight messenger services, or bulky mail; changing how real estate transactions are done all over the world.

Passing Papers

You'll find yourself signing two papers for the mortgage. One is the bond, or note, the personal promise to repay the loan. The other is the *mortgage* itself, the financial lien (claim) against the property, which gives the lender the right to foreclose if you default. Then the mortgagee gives you a check, probably the largest you'll ever see. You get to hold it just long enough to endorse it and turn it over to the seller.

The deed, which is usually signed only by the grantor (the seller), will be placed in your hands, then taken away to be recorded. It will probably be sent to you later. If no one is available to record the deed, go to the county recorder (usually the county

FIGURE 12.3   RESPA Uniform Settlement Statement

A. **Settlement Statement**

U.S. Department of Housing
and Urban Development

OMB Approval No. 2502-0265

B. Type of Loan

1. ☐ FHA 2. ☐ FmHA 3. ☐ Cony. Unins.	6. File Number:	7. Loan Number:	8. Mortgage Insurance Case Number:
4. ☐ VA 5. ☐ Conv. Ins.		

C. Note: This form is furnished to give you a statement of actual settlement costs. Amounts paid to and by the settlement agent are shown. Items marked "(p.o.c.)" were paid outside the closing; they are shown here for informational purposes and are not included in the totals.

D. Name & Address of Borrower:	E. Name & Address of Seller:	F. Name & Address of Lender:

G. Property Location:	H. Settlement Agent:	
	Place of Settlement:	I. Settlement Date:

J. Summary of Borrower's Transaction		K. Summary of Seller's Transaction	
100. Gross Amount Due From Borrower		**400. Gross Amount Due To Seller**	
101. Contract sales price		401. Contract sales price	
102. Personal property		402. Personal property	
103. Settlement charges to borrower (line 1400)		403.	
104.		404.	
105.		405.	
Adjustments for items paid by seller in advance		**Adjustments for items paid by seller in advance**	
106. City/town taxes to		406. City/town taxes to	
107. County taxes to		407. County taxes to	
108. Assessments to		408. Assessments to	
109.		409.	
110.		410.	
111.		411.	
112.		412.	
120. Gross Amount Due From Borrower		**420. Gross Amount Due To Seller**	

FIGURE 12.3   RESPA Uniform Settlement Statement (Continued)

200. Amounts Paid By Or In Behalf Of Borrower		500. Reductions In Amount Due To Seller	
201. Deposit or earnest money		501. Excess deposit (see instructions)	
202. Principal amount of new loan(s)		502. Settlement charges to seller (line 1400)	
203. Existing loan(s) taken subject to		503. Existing loan(s) taken subject to	
204.		504. Payoff of first mortgage loan	
205.		505. Payoff of second mortgage loan	
206.		506.	
207.		507.	
208.		508.	
209.		509.	
Adjustments for items unpaid by seller		**Adjustments for items unpaid by seller**	
210. City/town taxes to		510. City/town taxes to	
211. County taxes to		511. County taxes to	
212. Assessments to		512. Assessments to	
213.		513.	
214.		514.	
215.		515.	
216.		516.	
217.		517.	
218.		518.	
219.		519.	
220. Total Paid By/For Borrower		**520. Total Reduction Amount Due Seller**	
300. Cash At Settlement From/To Borrower		**600. Cash At Settlement To/From Seller**	
301. Gross Amount due from borrower (line 120)		601. Gross amount due to seller (line 420)	
302. Less amounts paid by/for borrower (line 220)	( )	602. Less reductions in amt. due seller (line 520)	( )
303. Cash ☐ From ☐ To Borrower		**603. Cash** ☐ To ☐ From Seller	

L. Settlement Charges

700. Total Sales/Broker's Commission based on price $ @ % =		Paid From Borrowers Funds at Settlement	Paid From Seller's Funds at Settlement
Division of Commission (line 700) as follows:			
701. $ to			
702. $ to			
703. Commission paid at Settlement			
704.			
800. Items Payable In Connection With Loan			
801. Loan Origination Fee %			
802. Loan Discount %			
803. Appraisal Fee to			
804. Credit Report to			
805. Lender's Inspection Fee			
806. Mortgage Insurance Application Fee to			
807. Assumption Fee			
808.			
809.			
810.			
811.			

FIGURE 12.3   RESPA Uniform Settlement Statement (Continued)

900.	Items Required By Lender To Be Paid In Advance				
901.	Interest from	to	@$	/day	
902.	Mortgage Insurance Premium for		months to		
903.	Hazard Insurance Premium for		years to		
904.			years to		
905.					
1000.	**Reserves Deposited With Lender**				
1001.	Hazard insurance	months@$	per month		
1002.	Mortgage insurance	months@$	per month		
1003.	City property taxes	months@$	per month		
1004.	County property taxes	months@$	per month		
1005.	Annual assessments	months@$	per month		
1006.		months@$	per month		
1007.		months@$	per month		
1008.		months@$	per month		
1100.	**Title Charges**				
1101.	Settlement or closing fee	to			
1102.	Abstract or title search	to			
1103.	Title examination	to			
1104.	Title insurance binder	to			
1105.	Document preparation	to			
1106.	Notary fees	to			
1107.	Attorney's fees	to			
	(includes above items numbers:			)	
1108.	Title insurance	to			
	(includes above items numbers:			)	
1109.	Lender's coverage	$			
1110.	Owner's coverage	$			
1111.					
1112.					
1113.					
1200.	**Government Recording and Transfer Charges**				
1201.	Recording fees: Deed $	; Mortgage $	; Releases $		
1202.	City/county tax/stamps: Deed $	; Mortgage $			
1203.	State tax/stamps: Deed $	; Mortgage $			
1204.					
1205.					
1300.	**Additional Settlement Charges**				
1301.	Survey	to			
1302.	Pest inspection to				
1303.					
1304.					
1305.					
1400.	**Total Settlement Charges (enter on lines 103, Section J and 502, Section K)**				

FIGURE 12.4   Buyers' Closing Statement

SELLER'S CREDITS

Sale Price _____ $ 89,500.00

ADJUSTMENT OF TAXES

School Tax	7/1 to 6/30	Amount $ 1,176.35	Adj. 10 mos. 18 days $ 1,039.16
City/School Tax	7/1 to 6/30	Amount $_____	Adj. ___ mos. ___ days $_____
County Tax	19____	Amount $ 309.06	Adj. 4 mos. 18 days $ 118.52
Village Tax	6/1 to 5/31	Amount $_____	Adj. ___ mos. ___ days $_____
City Tax Embellishments		Amount $_____	Adj. ___ mos. ___ days $_____

_____

_____

Total Seller's Credits $ 90,657.68

PURCHASER'S CREDITS

Deposit with ____Nothnagle_____ $ 500.00

~~(Assumed)~~ (New) Mortgage with Seller $480.07 p/m_____ $ 40,000.00

beg. 9-12   12% int., 15 yrs._____ $_____

_____ $_____

_____ $_____

Total Purchaser's Credits $ 40,500.00

Cash ~~(Rec'd)~~ (Paid) at Closing $ 50,157.68

EXPENSES OF PURCHASER

Mortgage Tax	$	275.00
Recording Mortgage	$	11.00
Recording Deed	$	12.00
ESCROWS:		
___ mos. insurance	$ _____	
___ mos. school tax	$ _____	
___ mos. county tax	$ _____	
___ mos. village tax	$ _____	
PMI FHA Insurance	$ _____	
Total:	$_____	
Bank Attorney Fee	$_____	
Points	$_____	
Title Insurance	$_____	
Interest	$_____	
....	$_____	
....	$_____	
Legal Fee	$	500.00
Total	$	798.00
Cash Paid to Seller:	$ 50,157.68	
Plus Purchaser's Expenses:	$	798.00
Total Disbursed:	$ 50,955.68	

EXPENSES OF SELLER

Title Search Fee	$_____
Transfer Tax on Deed	$_____
Filing of Gains Tax Affidavit	$_____
Discharge Recording Fee	$_____
Mortgage Tax	$_____
Surveyor's Fees	$_____
Points	$_____
Mortgage Payoff	$_____
Real Estate Commission	$_____
Water Escrow	$_____
....	$_____
....	$_____
....	$_____
....	$_____
Legal Fee	$_____
Total	$_____
Cash Received:	$_____
Less Seller's Expenses:	$_____
Net Proceeds:	$_____

*This statement, from the lawyer to the buyer, is relatively simple because no lending institution is involved. In this state, taxes are paid in advance.

clerk) and do it yourself immediately; this is of utmost importance. In some states title companies handle this task.

You may also receive those keys, the garage door opener, and security system codes. In some areas, these will come later, once the real recording of title has taken place. You'll walk out with a mass of papers and head for the nearest glass of champagne.

Congratulations! The journey may have seemed long and complicated, but you'll no doubt feel it was well worth it when you wake up in your new home for the first time. You have just become a part of the American Dream.

A

Monthly Payment Tables

Your monthly mortgage payment will include interest on the amount borrowed, plus a bit more intended to whittle down the principal still owed. As the loan is gradually paid, less interest is owed, and a larger portion of each payment can go toward principal.

The following tables cover loan terms of 1 to 40 years, with interest rates between 2 percent and 19 percent.

To find your mortgage payment:

1. Search the left-hand column until you find the interest rate on your loan.
2. Search the top line for the number of years you will be making payments.
3. Follow the percentage line across and the "number of years" column down until the two intersect. The figure indicated is the monthly dollar amount necessary to amortize (pay off) a loan of $1,000 in the given time, at the given rate of interest.

    Example: If a 10 percent loan has a term of 25 years, the two lines intersect at 9.0870. This means that $9.087 a month, for 25 years, would pay off a loan of $1,000 at 10 percent interest.

4. Multiply the figure indicated by the number of thousands being borrowed. This gives you the monthly payment necessary to amortize the entire loan.

Example: If, in the example above, the loan amount is $74,500, this represents 74.5 thousands. Multiplying $9.087 by 74.5 gives you $676.9816, which would be rounded off to a monthly payment of $676.98.

The figure you have found represents principal and interest only; if a lending institution requires escrow for taxes and insurance, one-twelfth of those costs must be added to arrive at the PITI payment.

MONTHLY PAYMENT TO AMORTIZE A LOAN OF $1,000

Term of Loan

Interest Rate	1 Year	2 Years	3 Years	4 Years	5 Years	6 Years	7 Years	8 Years
2.000%	84.2389	42.5403	28.6426	21.6951	17.5278	14.7504	12.7674	11.2809
2.125%	84.2956	42.5952	28.6972	21.7497	17.5825	14.8054	12.8226	11.3364
2.250%	84.3524	42.6502	28.7518	21.8044	17.6373	14.8605	12.8780	11.3920
2.375%	84.4093	42.7053	28.8066	21.8592	17.6923	14.9157	12.9335	11.4478
2.500%	84.4661	42.7604	28.8614	21.9140	17.7474	14.9710	12.9892	11.5038
2.625%	84.5230	42.8155	28.9162	21.9690	17.8025	15.0265	13.0450	11.5600
2.750%	84.5799	42.8707	28.9712	22.0240	17.8578	15.0821	13.1009	11.6164
2.875%	84.6368	42.9259	29.0262	22.0791	17.9132	15.1378	13.1570	11.6729
3.000%	84.6937	42.9812	29.0812	22.1343	17.9687	15.1937	13.2133	11.7296
3.125%	84.7506	43.0365	29.1363	22.1896	18.0243	15.2497	13.2697	11.7864
3.250%	84.8076	43.0919	29.1915	22.2450	18.0800	15.3058	13.3263	11.8435
3.375%	84.8646	43.1473	29.2468	22.3005	18.1358	15.3620	13.3830	11.9007
3.500%	84.9216	43.2027	29.3021	22.3560	18.1917	15.4184	13.4399	11.9581
3.625%	84.9787	43.2582	29.3575	22.4116	18.2478	15.4749	13.4969	12.0156
3.750%	85.0357	43.3137	29.4129	22.4674	18.3039	15.5315	13.5540	12.0733
3.875%	85.0928	43.3693	29.4684	22.5232	18.3602	15.5883	13.6113	12.1312
4.000%	85.1499	43.4249	29.5240	22.5791	18.4165	15.6452	13.6688	12.1893
4.125%	85.2070	43.4806	29.5796	22.6350	18.4730	15.7022	13.7264	12.2475
4.250%	85.2642	43.5363	29.6353	22.6911	18.5296	15.7593	13.7842	12.3059
4.375%	85.3213	43.5920	29.6911	22.7472	18.5862	15.8166	13.8421	12.3645
4.500%	85.3785	43.6478	29.7469	22.8035	18.6430	15.8740	13.9002	12.4232
4.625%	85.4357	43.7036	29.8028	22.8598	18.6999	15.9316	13.9584	12.4822
4.750%	85.4930	43.7595	29.8588	22.9162	18.7569	15.9892	14.0167	12.5412
4.875%	85.5502	43.8154	29.9148	22.9727	18.8140	16.0470	14.0752	12.6005
5.000%	85.6075	43.8714	29.9709	23.0293	18.8712	16.1049	14.1339	12.6599
5.125%	85.6648	43.9274	30.0271	23.0860	18.9286	16.1630	14.1927	12.7195
5.250%	85.7221	43.9834	30.0833	23.1427	18.9860	16.2212	14.2517	12.7793
5.375%	85.7794	44.0395	30.1396	23.1996	19.0435	16.2795	14.3108	12.8392
5.500%	85.8368	44.0957	30.1959	23.2565	19.1012	16.3379	14.3700	12.8993
5.625%	85.8942	44.1518	30.2523	23.3135	19.1589	16.3964	14.4294	12.9596
5.750%	85.9516	44.2080	30.3088	23.3706	19.2168	16.4551	14.4890	13.0200
5.875%	86.0090	44.2643	30.3653	23.4278	19.2747	16.5139	14.5487	13.0807
6.000%	86.0664	44.3206	30.4219	23.4850	19.3328	16.5729	14.6086	13.1414
6.125%	86.1239	44.3770	30.4786	23.5424	19.3910	16.6320	14.6686	13.2024
6.250%	86.1814	44.4333	30.5353	23.5998	19.4493	16.6912	14.7287	13.2635
6.375%	86.2389	44.4898	30.5921	23.6573	19.5077	16.7505	14.7890	13.3248
6.500%	86.2964	44.5463	30.6490	23.7150	19.5661	16.8099	14.8494	13.3862
6.625%	86.3540	44.6028	30.7059	23.7726	19.6248	16.8695	14.9100	13.4479
6.750%	86.4115	44.6593	30.7629	23.8304	19.6835	16.9292	14.9708	13.5096
6.875%	86.4691	44.7159	30.8200	23.8883	19.7423	16.9890	15.0316	13.5716

MONTHLY PAYMENT TO AMORTIZE A LOAN OF $1,000

Term of Loan

Interest Rate	9 Years	10 Years	11 Years	12 Years	13 Years	14 Years	15 Years	16 Years
2.000%	10.1253	9.2013	8.4459	7.8168	7.2850	6.8295	6.4351	6.0903
2.125%	10.1811	9.2574	8.5023	7.8736	7.3420	6.8869	6.4928	6.1484
2.250%	10.2370	9.3137	8.5590	7.9305	7.3994	6.9446	6.5508	6.2068
2.375%	10.2932	9.3703	8.6158	7.9878	7.4570	7.0025	6.6092	6.2655
2.500%	10.3496	9.4270	8.6729	8.0453	7.5149	7.0608	6.6679	6.3246
2.625%	10.4061	9.4839	8.7303	8.1031	7.5730	7.1194	6.7269	6.3840
2.750%	10.4629	9.5411	8.7879	8.1611	7.6315	7.1783	6.7862	6.4438
2.875%	10.5198	9.5985	8.8457	8.2193	7.6902	7.2375	6.8459	6.5039
3.000%	10.5769	9.6561	8.9038	8.2779	7.7492	7.2970	6.9058	6.5643
3.125%	10.6343	9.7139	8.9621	8.3367	7.8085	7.3567	6.9661	6.6251
3.250%	10.6918	9.7719	9.0206	8.3957	7.8680	7.4168	7.0267	6.6862
3.375%	10.7495	9.8301	9.0793	8.4550	7.9279	7.4772	7.0876	6.7477
3.500%	10.8074	9.8886	9.1383	8.5145	7.9880	7.5378	7.1488	6.8095
3.625%	10.8655	9.9472	9.1976	8.5743	8.0484	7.5988	7.2104	6.8716
3.750%	10.9238	10.0061	9.2570	8.6344	8.1090	7.6601	7.2722	6.9340
3.875%	10.9823	10.0652	9.3167	8.6947	8.1700	7.7216	7.3344	6.9968
4.000%	11.0410	10.1245	9.3767	8.7553	8.2312	7.7835	7.3969	7.0600
4.125%	11.0998	10.1840	9.4368	8.8161	8.2926	7.8456	7.4597	7.1234
4.250%	11.1589	10.2438	9.4972	8.8772	8.3544	7.9080	7.5228	7.1872
4.375%	11.2181	10.3037	9.5579	8.9385	8.4164	7.9707	7.5862	7.2513
4.500%	11.2776	10.3638	9.6187	9.0001	8.4787	8.0338	7.6499	7.3158
4.625%	11.3372	10.4242	9.6798	9.0619	8.5413	8.0971	7.7140	7.3805
4.750%	11.3971	10.4848	9.7411	9.1240	8.6041	8.1607	7.7783	7.4456
4.875%	11.4571	10.5456	9.8027	9.1863	8.6672	8.2245	7.8430	7.5111
5.000%	11.5173	10.6066	9.8645	9.2489	8.7306	8.2887	7.9079	7.5768
5.125%	11.5777	10.6678	9.9265	9.3117	8.7942	8.3532	7.9732	7.6429
5.250%	11.6383	10.7292	9.9888	9.3748	8.8582	8.4179	8.0388	7.7093
5.375%	11.6990	10.7908	10.0512	9.4381	8.9223	8.4829	8.1047	7.7760
5.500%	11.7600	10.8526	10.1139	9.5017	8.9868	8.5483	8.1708	7.8430
5.625%	11.8212	10.9147	10.1769	9.5655	9.0515	8.6139	8.2373	7.9104
5.750%	11.8825	10.9769	10.2400	9.6296	9.1165	8.6797	8.3041	7.9781
5.875%	11.9440	11.0394	10.3034	9.6939	9.1817	8.7459	8.3712	8.0461
6.000%	12.0057	11.1021	10.3670	9.7585	9.2472	8.8124	8.4386	8.1144
6.125%	12.0677	11.1649	10.4309	9.8233	9.3130	8.8791	8.5062	8.1830
6.250%	12.1298	11.2280	10.4949	9.8884	9.3790	8.9461	8.5742	8.2519
6.375%	12.1920	11.2913	10.5592	9.9537	9.4453	9.0134	8.6425	8.3212
6.500%	12.2545	11.3548	10.6238	10.0192	9.5119	9.0810	8.7111	8.3908
6.625%	12.3172	11.4185	10.6885	10.0850	9.5787	9.1488	8.7799	8.4606
6.750%	12.3800	11.4824	10.7535	10.1510	9.6458	9.2169	8.8491	8.5308
6.875%	12.4431	11.5465	10.8187	10.2173	9.7131	9.2853	8.9185	8.6013

MONTHLY PAYMENT TO AMORTIZE A LOAN OF $1,000

Term of Loan

Interest Rate	17 Years	18 Years	19 Years	20 Years	21 Years	22 Years	23 Years	24 Years
2.000%	5.7865	5.5167	5.2756	5.0588	4.8630	4.6852	4.5232	4.3748
2.125%	5.8449	5.5754	5.3346	5.1182	4.9228	4.7453	4.5836	4.4356
2.250%	5.9036	5.6345	5.3941	5.1781	4.9830	4.8059	4.6445	4.4969
2.375%	5.9627	5.6940	5.4540	5.2383	5.0436	4.8669	4.7059	4.5587
2.500%	6.0222	5.7539	5.5143	5.2990	5.1047	4.9284	4.7678	4.6209
2.625%	6.0821	5.8142	5.5750	5.3601	5.1662	4.9904	4.8302	4.6837
2.750%	6.1423	5.8748	5.6360	5.4217	5.2282	5.0528	4.8930	4.7470
2.875%	6.2028	5.9358	5.6975	5.4836	5.2906	5.1156	4.9564	4.8108
3.000%	6.2637	5.9972	5.7594	5.5460	5.3534	5.1790	5.0202	4.8751
3.125%	6.3250	6.0590	5.8217	5.6088	5.4167	5.2427	5.0844	4.9399
3.250%	6.3867	6.1212	5.8844	5.6720	5.4804	5.3070	5.1492	5.0051
3.375%	6.4487	6.1837	5.9474	5.7356	5.5446	5.3717	5.2144	5.0709
3.500%	6.5110	6.2466	6.0109	5.7996	5.6092	5.4368	5.2801	5.1371
3.625%	6.5737	6.3099	6.0748	5.8640	5.6742	5.5024	5.3463	5.2039
3.750%	6.6368	6.3736	6.1390	5.9289	5.7396	5.5684	5.4129	5.2711
3.875%	6.7002	6.4376	6.2037	5.9941	5.8055	5.6349	5.4800	5.3387
4.000%	6.7639	6.5020	6.2687	6.0598	5.8718	5.7018	5.5475	5.4069
4.125%	6.8280	6.5667	6.3341	6.1259	5.9385	5.7692	5.6155	5.4755
4.250%	6.8925	6.6319	6.3999	6.1923	6.0056	5.8370	5.6840	5.5446
4.375%	6.9573	6.6974	6.4661	6.2592	6.0732	5.9052	5.7529	5.6142
4.500%	7.0225	6.7632	6.5327	6.3265	6.1412	5.9739	5.8222	5.6842
4.625%	7.0880	6.8295	6.5996	6.3942	6.2096	6.0430	5.8920	5.7547
4.750%	7.1538	6.8961	6.6670	6.4622	6.2784	6.1125	5.9623	5.8257
4.875%	7.2200	6.9630	6.7347	6.5307	6.3476	6.1824	6.0329	5.8971
5.000%	7.2866	7.0303	6.8028	6.5996	6.4172	6.2528	6.1041	5.9690
5.125%	7.3534	7.0980	6.8712	6.6688	6.4872	6.3236	6.1756	6.0413
5.250%	7.4206	7.1660	6.9401	6.7384	6.5576	6.3948	6.2476	6.1140
5.375%	7.4882	7.2344	7.0093	6.8085	6.6285	6.4664	6.3200	6.1872
5.500%	7.5561	7.3032	7.0789	6.8789	6.6997	6.5385	6.3929	6.2609
5.625%	7.6243	7.3723	7.1488	6.9497	6.7713	6.6109	6.4661	6.3350
5.750%	7.6929	7.4417	7.2191	7.0208	6.8434	6.6838	6.5398	6.4095
5.875%	7.7618	7.5115	7.2898	7.0924	6.9158	6.7571	6.6139	6.4844
6.000%	7.8310	7.5816	7.3608	7.1643	6.9886	6.8307	6.6885	6.5598
6.125%	7.9006	7.6521	7.4322	7.2366	7.0618	6.9048	6.7634	6.6356
6.250%	7.9705	7.7229	7.5040	7.3093	7.1353	6.9793	6.8387	6.7118
6.375%	8.0407	7.7941	7.5761	7.3823	7.2093	7.0541	6.9145	6.7884
6.500%	8.1112	7.8656	7.6486	7.4557	7.2836	7.1294	6.9906	6.8654
6.625%	8.1821	7.9375	7.7214	7.5295	7.3583	7.2050	7.0672	6.9429
6.750%	8.2533	8.0096	7.7945	7.6036	7.4334	7.2811	7.1441	7.0207
6.875%	8.3248	8.0822	7.8681	7.6781	7.5089	7.3575	7.2215	7.0990

MONTHLY PAYMENT TO AMORTIZE A LOAN OF $1,000

Term of Loan

Interest Rate	25 Years	26 Years	27 Years	28 Years	29 Years	30 Years	35 Years	40 Years
2.000%	4.2385	4.1130	3.9969	3.8893	3.7893	3.6962	3.3126	3.0283
2.125%	4.2997	4.1744	4.0587	3.9515	3.8518	3.7590	3.3771	3.0944
2.250%	4.3613	4.2364	4.1211	4.0142	3.9149	3.8225	3.4424	3.1614
2.375%	4.4235	4.2990	4.1840	4.0775	3.9786	3.8865	3.5083	3.2292
2.500%	4.4862	4.3621	4.2475	4.1414	4.0429	3.9512	3.5750	3.2978
2.625%	4.5494	4.4257	4.3115	4.2058	4.1078	4.0165	3.6423	3.3671
2.750%	4.6131	4.4899	4.3761	4.2709	4.1732	4.0824	3.7103	3.4373
2.875%	4.6774	4.5546	4.4413	4.3365	4.2393	4.1489	3.7791	3.5082
3.000%	4.7421	4.6198	4.5070	4.4027	4.3059	4.2160	3.8485	3.5798
3.125%	4.8074	4.6856	4.5733	4.4694	4.3732	4.2838	3.9186	3.6523
3.250%	4.8732	4.7519	4.6401	4.5367	4.4410	4.3521	3.9894	3.7254
3.375%	4.9394	4.8187	4.7074	4.6046	4.5094	4.4210	4.0608	3.7993
3.500%	5.0062	4.8860	4.7753	4.6730	4.5783	4.4904	4.1329	3.8739
3.625%	5.0735	4.9539	4.8437	4.7420	4.6478	4.5605	4.2057	3.9492
3.750%	5.1413	5.0222	4.9126	4.8115	4.7179	4.6312	4.2791	4.0253
3.875%	5.2096	5.0911	4.9821	4.8815	4.7885	4.7024	4.3531	4.1020
4.000%	5.2784	5.1605	5.0521	4.9521	4.8597	4.7742	4.4277	4.1794
4.125%	5.3476	5.2304	5.1226	5.0233	4.9315	4.8465	4.5030	4.2575
4.250%	5.4174	5.3008	5.1936	5.0949	5.0038	4.9194	4.5789	4.3362
4.375%	5.4876	5.3717	5.2652	5.1671	5.0766	4.9929	4.6555	4.4156
4.500%	5.5583	5.4430	5.3372	5.2398	5.1499	5.0669	4.7326	4.4956
4.625%	5.6295	5.5149	5.4098	5.3130	5.2238	5.1414	4.8103	4.5763
4.750%	5.7012	5.5873	5.4828	5.3868	5.2982	5.2165	4.8886	4.6576
4.875%	5.7733	5.6601	5.5564	5.4610	5.3732	5.2921	4.9674	4.7395
5.000%	5.8459	5.7334	5.6304	5.5357	5.4486	5.3682	5.0469	4.8220
5.125%	5.9190	5.8072	5.7049	5.6110	5.5246	5.4449	5.1269	4.9050
5.250%	5.9925	5.8815	5.7799	5.6867	5.6010	5.5220	5.2074	4.9887
5.375%	6.0665	5.9562	5.8554	5.7629	5.6780	5.5997	5.2885	5.0729
5.500%	6.1409	6.0314	5.9314	5.8397	5.7554	5.6779	5.3702	5.1577
5.625%	6.2157	6.1071	6.0078	5.9168	5.8334	5.7566	5.4523	5.2430
5.750%	6.2911	6.1832	6.0847	5.9945	5.9118	5.8357	5.5350	5.3289
5.875%	6.3668	6.2598	6.1620	6.0726	5.9907	5.9154	5.6182	5.4153
6.000%	6.4430	6.3368	6.2399	6.1512	6.0700	5.9955	5.7019	5.5021
6.125%	6.5196	6.4142	6.3181	6.2303	6.1499	6.0761	5.7861	5.5895
6.250%	6.5967	6.4921	6.3968	6.3098	6.2302	6.1572	5.8708	5.6774
6.375%	6.6742	6.5704	6.4760	6.3898	6.3109	6.2387	5.9559	5.7657
6.500%	6.7521	6.6492	6.5555	6.4702	6.3921	6.3207	6.0415	5.8546
6.625%	6.8304	6.7284	6.6356	6.5510	6.4738	6.4031	6.1276	5.9438
6.750%	6.9091	6.8079	6.7160	6.6323	6.5558	6.4860	6.2142	6.0336
6.875%	6.9883	6.8880	6.7969	6.7140	6.6384	6.5693	6.3011	6.1237

MONTHLY PAYMENT TO AMORTIZE A LOAN OF $1,000

Term of Loan

Interest Rate	1 Year	2 Years	3 Years	4 Years	5 Years	6 Years	7 Years	8 Years
7.000%	86.5267	44.7726	30.8771	23.9462	19.8012	17.0490	15.0927	13.6337
7.125%	86.5844	44.8293	30.9343	24.0043	19.8602	17.1091	15.1539	13.6960
7.250%	86.6420	44.8860	30.9915	24.0624	19.9194	17.1693	15.2152	13.7585
7.375%	86.6997	44.9428	31.0488	24.1206	19.9786	17.2296	15.2767	13.8211
7.500%	86.7574	44.9996	31.1062	24.1789	20.0379	17.2901	15.3383	13.8839
7.625%	86.8151	45.0565	31.1637	24.2373	20.0974	17.3507	15.4000	13.9468
7.750%	86.8729	45.1134	31.2212	24.2957	20.1570	17.4114	15.4620	14.0099
7.875%	86.9306	45.1703	31.2787	24.3543	20.2166	17.4723	15.5240	14.0732
8.000%	86.9884	45.2273	31.3364	24.4129	20.2764	17.5332	15.5862	14.1367
8.125%	87.0462	45.2843	31.3941	24.4716	20.3363	17.5943	15.6486	14.2003
8.250%	87.1041	45.3414	31.4518	24.5304	20.3963	17.6556	15.7111	14.2641
8.375%	87.1619	45.3985	31.5096	24.5893	20.4563	17.7169	15.7737	14.3280
8.500%	87.2198	45.4557	31.5675	24.6483	20.5165	17.7784	15.8365	14.3921
8.625%	87.2777	45.5129	31.6255	24.7074	20.5768	17.8400	15.8994	14.4564
8.750%	87.3356	45.5701	31.6835	24.7665	20.6372	17.9017	15.9625	14.5208
8.875%	87.3935	45.6274	31.7416	24.8257	20.6977	17.9636	16.0257	14.5854
9.000%	87.4515	45.6847	31.7997	24.8850	20.7584	18.0255	16.0891	14.6502
9.125%	87.5095	45.7421	31.8579	24.9444	20.8191	18.0876	16.1526	14.7151
9.250%	87.5675	45.7995	31.9162	25.0039	20.8799	18.1499	16.2162	14.7802
9.375%	87.6255	45.8570	31.9745	25.0635	20.9408	18.2122	16.2800	14.8455
9.500%	87.6835	45.9145	32.0329	25.1231	21.0019	18.2747	16.3440	14.9109
9.625%	87.7416	45.9720	32.0914	25.1829	21.0630	18.3373	16.4081	14.9765
9.750%	87.7997	46.0296	32.1499	25.2427	21.1242	18.4000	16.4723	15.0422
9.875%	87.8578	46.0873	32.2085	25.3026	21.1856	18.4629	16.5367	15.1081
10.000%	87.9159	46.1449	32.2672	25.3626	21.2470	18.5258	16.6012	15.1742
10.125%	87.9740	46.2026	32.3259	25.4227	21.3086	18.5889	16.6658	15.2404
10.250%	88.0322	46.2604	32.3847	25.4828	21.3703	18.6522	16.7306	15.3068
10.375%	88.0904	46.3182	32.4435	25.5431	21.4320	18.7155	16.7956	15.3733
10.500%	88.1486	46.3760	32.5024	25.6034	21.4939	18.7790	16.8607	15.4400
10.625%	88.2068	46.4339	32.5614	25.6638	21.5559	18.8426	16.9259	15.5069
10.750%	88.2651	46.4919	32.6205	25.7243	21.6180	18.9063	16.9913	15.5739
10.875%	88.3234	46.5498	32.6796	25.7849	21.6801	18.9701	17.0568	15.6411
11.000%	88.3817	46.6078	32.7387	25.8455	21.7424	19.0341	17.1224	15.7084
11.125%	88.4400	46.6659	32.7979	25.9063	21.8048	19.0982	17.1882	15.7759
11.250%	88.4983	46.7240	32.8572	25.9671	21.8673	19.1624	17.2542	15.8436
11.375%	88.5567	46.7821	32.9166	26.0280	21.9299	19.2267	17.3202	15.9114
11.500%	88.6151	46.8403	32.9760	26.0890	21.9926	19.2912	17.3865	15.9794
11.625%	88.6735	46.8985	33.0355	26.1501	22.0554	19.3557	17.4528	16.0475
11.750%	88.7319	46.9568	33.0950	26.2113	22.1183	19.4204	17.5193	16.1158
11.875%	88.7903	47.0151	33.1546	26.2725	22.1813	19.4853	17.5860	16.1842

MONTHLY PAYMENT TO AMORTIZE A LOAN OF $1,000

Term of Loan

Interest Rate	9 Years	10 Years	11 Years	12 Years	13 Years	14 Years	15 Years	16 Years
7.000%	12.5063	11.6108	10.8841	10.2838	9.7807	9.3540	8.9883	8.6721
7.125%	12.5697	11.6754	10.9497	10.3506	9.8486	9.4230	9.0583	8.7432
7.250%	12.6333	11.7401	11.0156	10.4176	9.9167	9.4922	9.1286	8.8146
7.375%	12.6971	11.8050	11.0817	10.4848	9.9851	9.5617	9.1992	8.8863
7.500%	12.7610	11.8702	11.1480	10.5523	10.0537	9.6314	9.2701	8.9583
7.625%	12.8252	11.9355	11.2145	10.6200	10.1226	9.7015	9.3413	9.0306
7.750%	12.8895	12.0011	11.2813	10.6879	10.1917	9.7718	9.4128	9.1032
7.875%	12.9540	12.0668	11.3483	10.7561	10.2611	9.8423	9.4845	9.1761
8.000%	13.0187	12.1328	11.4154	10.8245	10.3307	9.9132	9.5565	9.2493
8.125%	13.0836	12.1989	11.4829	10.8932	10.4006	9.9843	9.6288	9.3227
8.250%	13.1487	12.2653	11.5505	10.9621	10.4708	10.0557	9.7014	9.3965
8.375%	13.2139	12.3318	11.6183	11.0312	10.5412	10.1273	9.7743	9.4706
8.500%	13.2794	12.3986	11.6864	11.1006	10.6118	10.1992	9.8474	9.5449
8.625%	13.3450	12.4655	11.7547	11.1701	10.6827	10.2713	9.9208	9.6195
8.750%	13.4108	12.5327	11.8232	11.2400	10.7538	10.3438	9.9945	9.6945
8.875%	13.4767	12.6000	11.8919	11.3100	10.8252	10.4164	10.0684	9.7697
9.000%	13.5429	12.6676	11.9608	11.3803	10.8968	10.4894	10.1427	9.8452
9.125%	13.6093	12.7353	12.0299	11.4508	10.9687	10.5626	10.2172	9.9209
9.250%	13.6758	12.8033	12.0993	11.5216	11.0408	10.6360	10.2919	9.9970
9.375%	13.7425	12.8714	12.1689	11.5925	11.1131	10.7097	10.3670	10.0733
9.500%	13.8094	12.9398	12.2386	11.6637	11.1857	10.7837	10.4422	10.1499
9.625%	13.8764	13.0083	12.3086	11.7352	11.2586	10.8579	10.5178	10.2268
9.750%	13.9437	13.0770	12.3788	11.8068	11.3316	10.9324	10.5936	10.3039
9.875%	14.0111	13.1460	12.4493	11.8787	11.4049	11.0071	10.6697	10.3813
10.000%	14.0787	13.2151	12.5199	11.9508	11.4785	11.0820	10.7461	10.4590
10.125%	14.1465	13.2844	12.5907	12.0231	11.5523	11.1572	10.8227	10.5370
10.250%	14.2144	13.3539	12.6618	12.0957	11.6263	11.2327	10.8995	10.6152
10.375%	14.2826	13.4236	12.7330	12.1684	11.7005	11.3084	10.9766	10.6937
10.500%	14.3509	13.4935	12.8045	12.2414	11.7750	11.3843	11.0540	10.7724
10.625%	14.4193	13.5636	12.8761	12.3146	11.8497	11.4605	11.1316	10.8514
10.750%	14.4880	13.6339	12.9480	12.3880	11.9247	11.5370	11.2095	10.9307
10.875%	14.5568	13.7043	13.0201	12.4617	11.9999	11.6136	11.2876	11.0102
11.000%	14.6259	13.7750	13.0923	12.5356	12.0753	11.6905	11.3660	11.0900
11.125%	14.6950	13.8459	13.1648	12.6096	12.1509	11.7677	11.4446	11.1700
11.250%	14.7644	13.9169	13.2375	12.6839	12.2268	11.8451	11.5234	11.2503
11.375%	14.8339	13.9881	13.3104	12.7584	12.3029	11.9227	11.6026	11.3309
11.500%	14.9037	14.0595	13.3835	12.8332	12.3792	12.0006	11.6819	11.4116
11.625%	14.9735	14.1312	13.4568	12.9081	12.4557	12.0786	11.7615	11.4927
11.750%	15.0436	14.2029	13.5303	12.9833	12.5325	12.1570	11.8413	11.5740
11.875%	15.1138	14.2749	13.6040	13.0586	12.6095	12.2355	11.9214	11.6555

MONTHLY PAYMENT TO AMORTIZE A LOAN OF $1,000

Term of Loan

Interest Rate	17 Years	18 Years	19 Years	20 Years	21 Years	22 Years	23 Years	24 Years
7.000%	8.3966	8.1550	7.9419	7.7530	7.5847	7.4342	7.2992	7.1776
7.125%	8.4688	8.2282	8.0161	7.8282	7.6609	7.5114	7.3773	7.2566
7.250%	8.5412	8.3017	8.0907	7.9038	7.7375	7.5889	7.4558	7.3361
7.375%	8.6140	8.3756	8.1656	7.9797	7.8144	7.6668	7.5347	7.4159
7.500%	8.6871	8.4497	8.2408	8.0559	7.8917	7.7451	7.6139	7.4960
7.625%	8.7605	8.5242	8.3163	8.1325	7.9693	7.8237	7.6935	7.5766
7.750%	8.8342	8.5990	8.3922	8.2095	8.0473	7.9027	7.7735	7.6576
7.875%	8.9082	8.6742	8.4685	8.2868	8.1256	7.9821	7.8538	7.7389
8.000%	8.9826	8.7496	8.5450	8.3644	8.2043	8.0618	7.9345	7.8205
8.125%	9.0572	8.8254	8.6219	8.4424	8.2833	8.1418	8.0156	7.9026
8.250%	9.1321	8.9015	8.6991	8.5207	8.3627	8.2222	8.0970	7.9850
8.375%	9.2074	8.9779	8.7766	8.5993	8.4424	8.3030	8.1788	8.0677
8.500%	9.2829	9.0546	8.8545	8.6782	8.5224	8.3841	8.2609	8.1508
8.625%	9.3588	9.1316	8.9326	8.7575	8.6028	8.4655	8.3433	8.2343
8.750%	9.4349	9.2089	9.0111	8.8371	8.6834	8.5472	8.4261	8.3181
8.875%	9.5113	9.2865	9.0899	8.9170	8.7645	8.6293	8.5092	8.4022
9.000%	9.5880	9.3644	9.1690	8.9973	8.8458	8.7117	8.5927	8.4866
9.125%	9.6650	9.4427	9.2484	9.0778	8.9275	8.7945	8.6765	8.5714
9.250%	9.7423	9.5212	9.3281	9.1587	9.0094	8.8775	8.7606	8.6566
9.375%	9.8199	9.6000	9.4081	9.2398	9.0917	8.9609	8.8450	8.7420
9.500%	9.8978	9.6791	9.4884	9.3213	9.1743	9.0446	8.9297	8.8277
9.625%	9.9760	9.7585	9.5690	9.4031	9.2573	9.1286	9.0148	8.9138
9.750%	10.0544	9.8382	9.6499	9.4852	9.3405	9.2129	9.1002	9.0002
9.875%	10.1331	9.9182	9.7311	9.5675	9.4240	9.2975	9.1858	9.0869
10.000%	10.2121	9.9984	9.8126	9.6502	9.5078	9.3825	9.2718	9.1739
10.125%	10.2914	10.0790	9.8944	9.7332	9.5919	9.4677	9.3581	9.2612
10.250%	10.3709	10.1598	9.9764	9.8164	9.6763	9.5532	9.4447	9.3488
10.375%	10.4507	10.2409	10.0588	9.9000	9.7610	9.6390	9.5315	9.4366
10.500%	10.5308	10.3223	10.1414	9.9838	9.8460	9.7251	9.6187	9.5248
10.625%	10.6112	10.4039	10.2243	10.0679	9.9312	9.8114	9.7061	9.6133
10.750%	10.6918	10.4858	10.3075	10.1523	10.0168	9.8981	9.7938	9.7020
10.875%	10.7727	10.5680	10.3909	10.2370	10.1026	9.9850	9.8818	9.7910
11.000%	10.8538	10.6505	10.4746	10.3219	10.1887	10.0722	9.9701	9.8803
11.125%	10.9352	10.7332	10.5586	10.4071	10.2751	10.1597	10.0586	9.9698
11.250%	11.0169	10.8162	10.6429	10.4926	10.3617	10.2475	10.1474	10.0596
11.375%	11.0988	10.8994	10.7274	10.5783	10.4486	10.3355	10.2365	10.1497
11.500%	11.1810	10.9830	10.8122	10.6643	10.5358	10.4237	10.3258	10.2400
11.625%	11.2634	11.0667	10.8972	10.7506	10.6232	10.5123	10.4154	10.3306
11.750%	11.3461	11.1507	10.9825	10.8371	10.7109	10.6011	10.5052	10.4214
11.875%	11.4290	11.2350	11.0681	10.9238	10.7988	10.6901	10.5953	10.5125

MONTHLY PAYMENT TO AMORTIZE A LOAN OF $1,000

Term of Loan

Interest Rate	25 Years	26 Years	27 Years	28 Years	29 Years	30 Years	35 Years	40 Years
7.000%	7.0678	6.9684	6.8781	6.7961	6.7213	6.6530	6.3886	6.2143
7.125%	7.1477	7.0492	6.9598	6.8786	6.8047	6.7372	6.4764	6.3053
7.250%	7.2281	7.1304	7.0419	6.9616	6.8884	6.8218	6.5647	6.3967
7.375%	7.3088	7.2121	7.1244	7.0449	6.9726	6.9068	6.6533	6.4885
7.500%	7.3899	7.2941	7.2073	7.1287	7.0572	6.9921	6.7424	6.5807
7.625%	7.4714	7.3765	7.2906	7.2128	7.1422	7.0779	6.8319	6.6733
7.750%	7.5533	7.4593	7.3743	7.2974	7.2276	7.1641	6.9218	6.7662
7.875%	7.6355	7.5424	7.4584	7.3823	7.3133	7.2507	7.0120	6.8595
8.000%	7.7182	7.6260	7.5428	7.4676	7.3995	7.3376	7.1026	6.9531
8.125%	7.8012	7.7099	7.6276	7.5533	7.4860	7.4250	7.1936	7.0471
8.250%	7.8845	7.7942	7.7128	7.6393	7.5729	7.5127	7.2849	7.1414
8.375%	7.9682	7.8788	7.7983	7.7257	7.6601	7.6007	7.3766	7.2360
8.500%	8.0523	7.9638	7.8842	7.8125	7.7477	7.6891	7.4686	7.3309
8.625%	8.1367	8.0491	7.9705	7.8996	7.8357	7.7779	7.5610	7.4262
8.750%	8.2214	8.1348	8.0570	7.9871	7.9240	7.8670	7.6536	7.5217
8.875%	8.3065	8.2209	8.1440	8.0749	8.0126	7.9564	7.7466	7.6175
9.000%	8.3920	8.3072	8.2313	8.1630	8.1016	8.0462	7.8399	7.7136
9.125%	8.4777	8.3939	8.3189	8.2515	8.1909	8.1363	7.9335	7.8100
9.250%	8.5638	8.4810	8.4068	8.3403	8.2805	8.2268	8.0274	7.9066
9.375%	8.6502	8.5683	8.4950	8.4294	8.3705	8.3175	8.1216	8.0035
9.500%	8.7370	8.6560	8.5836	8.5188	8.4607	8.4085	8.2161	8.1006
9.625%	8.8240	8.7440	8.6725	8.6086	8.5513	8.4999	8.3109	8.1980
9.750%	8.9114	8.8323	8.7617	8.6986	8.6421	8.5915	8.4059	8.2956
9.875%	8.9990	8.9209	8.8512	8.7890	8.7333	8.6835	8.5012	8.3934
10.000%	9.0870	9.0098	8.9410	8.8796	8.8248	8.7757	8.5967	8.4915
10.125%	9.1753	9.0990	9.0311	8.9705	8.9165	8.8682	8.6925	8.5897
10.250%	9.2638	9.1885	9.1214	9.0618	9.0085	8.9610	8.7886	8.6882
10.375%	9.3527	9.2782	9.2121	9.1533	9.1008	9.0541	8.8848	8.7868
10.500%	9.4418	9.3683	9.3030	9.2450	9.1934	9.1474	8.9813	8.8857
10.625%	9.5312	9.4586	9.3943	9.3371	9.2862	9.2410	9.0781	8.9847
10.750%	9.6209	9.5492	9.4857	9.4294	9.3793	9.3348	9.1750	9.0840
10.875%	9.7109	9.6401	9.5775	9.5220	9.4727	9.4289	9.2722	9.1834
11.000%	9.8011	9.7313	9.6695	9.6148	9.5663	9.5232	9.3696	9.2829
11.125%	9.8916	9.8227	9.7618	9.7079	9.6601	9.6178	9.4672	9.3827
11.250%	9.9824	9.9143	9.8543	9.8012	9.7542	9.7126	9.5649	9.4826
11.375%	10.0734	10.0063	9.9471	9.8948	9.8486	9.8077	9.6629	9.5826
11.500%	10.1647	10.0984	10.0401	9.9886	9.9431	9.9029	9.7611	9.6828
11.625%	10.2562	10.1909	10.1333	10.0826	10.0379	9.9984	9.8594	9.7832
11.750%	10.3480	10.2835	10.2268	10.1769	10.1329	10.0941	9.9579	9.8836
11.875%	10.4400	10.3764	10.3205	10.2714	10.2281	10.1900	10.0566	9.9843

MONTHLY PAYMENT TO AMORTIZE A LOAN OF $1,000

Term of Loan

Interest Rate	1 Year	2 Years	3 Years	4 Years	5 Years	6 Years	7 Years	8 Years
12.000%	88.8488	47.0735	33.2143	26.3338	22.2444	19.5502	17.6527	16.2528
12.125%	88.9073	47.1319	33.2740	26.3953	22.3077	19.6153	17.7197	16.3216
12.250%	88.9658	47.1903	33.3338	26.4568	22.3710	19.6804	17.7867	16.3905
12.375%	89.0243	47.2488	33.3937	26.5183	22.4344	19.7457	17.8539	16.4596
12.500%	89.0829	47.3073	33.4536	26.5800	22.4979	19.8112	17.9212	16.5288
12.625%	89.1414	47.3659	33.5136	26.6417	22.5616	19.8767	17.9887	16.5982
12.750%	89.2000	47.4245	33.5737	26.7036	22.6253	19.9424	18.0563	16.6677
12.875%	89.2586	47.4831	33.6338	26.7655	22.6891	20.0082	18.1241	16.7374
13.000%	89.3173	47.5418	33.6940	26.8275	22.7531	20.0741	18.1920	16.8073
13.125%	89.3759	47.6006	33.7542	26.8896	22.8171	20.1401	18.2600	16.8773
13.250%	89.4346	47.6593	33.8145	26.9517	22.8813	20.2063	18.3282	16.9474
13.375%	89.4933	47.7182	33.8749	27.0140	22.9455	20.2726	18.3965	17.0177
13.500%	89.5520	47.7770	33.9353	27.0763	23.0098	20.3390	18.4649	17.0882
13.625%	89.6108	47.8359	33.9958	27.1387	23.0743	20.4055	18.5335	17.1588
13.750%	89.6695	47.8949	34.0563	27.2012	23.1388	20.4721	18.6022	17.2295
13.875%	89.7283	47.9539	34.1169	27.2638	23.2035	20.5389	18.6710	17.3004
14.000%	89.7871	48.0129	34.1776	27.3265	23.2683	20.6057	18.7400	17.3715
14.125%	89.8459	48.0720	34.2384	27.3892	23.3331	20.6727	18.8091	17.4427
14.250%	89.9048	48.1311	34.2992	27.4520	23.3981	20.7398	18.8784	17.5141
14.375%	89.9637	48.1902	34.3600	27.5150	23.4631	20.8071	18.9478	17.5856
14.500%	90.0225	48.2494	34.4210	27.5780	23.5283	20.8744	19.0173	17.6573
14.625%	90.0815	48.3087	34.4820	27.6410	23.5935	20.9419	19.0870	17.7291
14.750%	90.1404	48.3680	34.5430	27.7042	23.6589	21.0095	19.1568	17.8010
14.875%	90.1993	48.4273	34.6041	27.7674	23.7244	21.0772	19.2267	17.8731
15.000%	90.2583	48.4866	34.6653	27.8307	23.7899	21.1450	19.2968	17.9454
15.125%	90.3173	48.5461	34.7266	27.8942	23.8556	21.2130	19.3670	18.0178
15.250%	90.3763	48.6055	34.7879	27.9576	23.9214	21.2810	19.4373	18.0904
15.375%	90.4354	48.6650	34.8492	28.0212	23.9872	21.3492	19.5077	18.1631
15.500%	90.4944	48.7245	34.9107	28.0849	24.0532	21.4175	19.5783	18.2359
15.625%	90.5535	48.7841	34.9722	28.1486	24.1193	21.4859	19.6491	18.3089
15.750%	90.6126	48.8437	35.0337	28.2124	24.1854	21.5544	19.7199	18.3821
15.875%	90.6717	48.9034	35.0954	28.2763	24.2517	21.6231	19.7909	18.4554
16.000%	90.7309	48.9631	35.1570	28.3403	24.3181	21.6918	19.8621	18.5288
16.125%	90.7900	49.0229	35.2188	28.4043	24.3845	21.7607	19.9333	18.6024
16.250%	90.8492	49.0826	35.2806	28.4685	24.4511	21.8297	20.0047	18.6761
16.375%	90.9084	49.1425	35.3425	28.5327	24.5178	21.8988	20.0762	18.7500
16.500%	90.9676	49.2024	35.4044	28.5970	24.5845	21.9681	20.1479	18.8240
16.625%	91.0269	49.2623	35.4664	28.6614	24.6514	22.0374	20.2197	18.8981
16.750%	91.0862	49.3222	35.5284	28.7259	24.7184	22.1069	20.2916	18.9724
16.875%	91.1454	49.3822	35.5905	28.7904	24.7854	22.1764	20.3636	19.0469

MONTHLY PAYMENT TO AMORTIZE A LOAN OF $1,000

Term of Loan

Interest Rate	9 Years	10 Years	11 Years	12 Years	13 Years	14 Years	15 Years	16 Years
12.000%	15.1842	14.3471	13.6779	13.1342	12.6867	12.3143	12.0017	11.7373
12.125%	15.2548	14.4194	13.7520	13.2100	12.7641	12.3933	12.0822	11.8193
12.250%	15.3256	14.4920	13.8263	13.2860	12.8417	12.4725	12.1630	11.9015
12.375%	15.3965	14.5647	13.9007	13.3622	12.9196	12.5520	12.2440	11.9840
12.500%	15.4676	14.6376	13.9754	13.4386	12.9977	12.6317	12.3252	12.0667
12.625%	15.5388	14.7107	14.0503	13.5152	13.0760	12.7116	12.4067	12.1496
12.750%	15.6102	14.7840	14.1254	13.5920	13.1545	12.7917	12.4884	12.2328
12.875%	15.6818	14.8574	14.2006	13.6690	13.2332	12.8721	12.5703	12.3162
13.000%	15.7536	14.9311	14.2761	13.7463	13.3121	12.9526	12.6524	12.3999
13.125%	15.8255	15.0049	14.3518	13.8237	13.3912	13.0334	12.7348	12.4837
13.250%	15.8976	15.0789	14.4276	13.9013	13.4706	13.1144	12.8174	12.5678
13.375%	15.9699	15.1531	14.5036	13.9791	13.5502	13.1956	12.9002	12.6521
13.500%	16.0423	15.2274	14.5799	14.0572	13.6299	13.2771	12.9832	12.7367
13.625%	16.1149	15.3020	14.6563	14.1354	13.7099	13.3587	13.0664	12.8214
13.750%	16.1877	15.3767	14.7329	14.2138	13.7901	13.4406	13.1499	12.9064
13.875%	16.2606	15.4516	14.8097	14.2925	13.8704	13.5226	13.2335	12.9916
14.000%	16.3337	15.5266	14.8867	14.3713	13.9510	13.6049	13.3174	13.0770
14.125%	16.4070	15.6019	14.9638	14.4503	14.0318	13.6874	13.4015	13.1626
14.250%	16.4804	15.6773	15.0412	14.5295	14.1128	13.7701	13.4858	13.2484
14.375%	16.5540	15.7529	15.1187	14.6089	14.1940	13.8529	13.5703	13.3345
14.500%	16.6277	15.8287	15.1964	14.6885	14.2754	13.9360	13.6550	13.4207
14.625%	16.7016	15.9046	15.2743	14.7683	14.3570	14.0193	13.7399	13.5071
14.750%	16.7757	15.9807	15.3524	14.8483	14.4387	14.1028	13.8250	13.5938
14.875%	16.8499	16.0570	15.4307	14.9284	14.5207	14.1865	13.9104	13.6806
15.000%	16.9243	16.1335	15.5091	15.0088	14.6029	14.2704	13.9959	13.7677
15.125%	16.9989	16.2101	15.5878	15.0893	14.6852	14.3545	14.0816	13.8549
15.250%	17.0736	16.2869	15.6666	15.1700	14.7678	14.4388	14.1675	13.9424
15.375%	17.1485	16.3639	15.7456	15.2509	14.8505	14.5232	14.2536	14.0300
15.500%	17.2235	16.4411	15.8247	15.3320	14.9335	14.6079	14.3399	14.1179
15.625%	17.2987	16.5184	15.9041	15.4133	15.0166	14.6928	14.4264	14.2059
15.750%	17.3741	16.5958	15.9836	15.4948	15.0999	14.7778	14.5131	14.2941
15.875%	17.4496	16.6735	16.0633	15.5764	15.1834	14.8630	14.5999	14.3825
16.000%	17.5253	16.7513	16.1432	15.6583	15.2670	14.9485	14.6870	14.4711
16.125%	17.6011	16.8293	16.2232	15.7403	15.3509	15.0341	14.7743	14.5599
16.250%	17.6771	16.9074	16.3034	15.8224	15.4349	15.1199	14.8617	14.6488
16.375%	17.7532	16.9858	16.3838	15.9048	15.5192	15.2058	14.9493	14.7380
16.500%	17.8295	17.0642	16.4644	15.9873	15.6036	15.2920	15.0371	14.8273
16.625%	17.9059	17.1429	16.5451	16.0700	15.6881	15.3783	15.1251	14.9168
16.750%	17.9825	17.2217	16.6260	16.1529	15.7729	15.4648	15.2132	15.0065
16.875%	18.0593	17.3006	16.7071	16.2360	15.8578	15.5515	15.3015	15.0963

MONTHLY PAYMENT TO AMORTIZE A LOAN OF $1,000

Term of Loan

Interest Rate	17 Years	18 Years	19 Years	20 Years	21 Years	22 Years	23 Years	24 Years
12.000%	11.5122	11.3195	11.1539	11.0109	10.8870	10.7794	10.6856	10.6038
12.125%	11.5956	11.4043	11.2399	11.0981	10.9754	10.8689	10.7762	10.6954
12.250%	11.6792	11.4893	11.3262	11.1856	11.0641	10.9587	10.8670	10.7872
12.375%	11.7631	11.5745	11.4127	11.2734	11.1530	11.0487	10.9581	10.8792
12.500%	11.8473	11.6600	11.4995	11.3614	11.2422	11.1390	11.0494	10.9714
12.625%	11.9316	11.7457	11.5865	11.4496	11.3316	11.2294	11.1409	11.0639
12.750%	12.0162	11.8317	11.6738	11.5381	11.4212	11.3202	11.2326	11.1566
12.875%	12.1011	11.9179	11.7613	11.6268	11.5111	11.4111	11.3246	11.2495
13.000%	12.1861	12.0043	11.8490	11.7158	11.6011	11.5023	11.4168	11.3427
13.125%	12.2714	12.0910	11.9369	11.8049	11.6915	11.5937	11.5092	11.4360
13.250%	12.3570	12.1779	12.0251	11.8943	11.7820	11.6853	11.6018	11.5296
13.375%	12.4427	12.2650	12.1135	11.9839	11.8727	11.7771	11.6946	11.6233
13.500%	12.5287	12.3523	12.2021	12.0737	11.9637	11.8691	11.7876	11.7173
13.625%	12.6149	12.4399	12.2910	12.1638	12.0549	11.9613	11.8808	11.8114
13.750%	12.7013	12.5276	12.3800	12.2541	12.1463	12.0538	11.9743	11.9058
13.875%	12.7879	12.6156	12.4693	12.3445	12.2379	12.1464	12.0679	12.0003
14.000%	12.8748	12.7038	12.5588	12.4352	12.3297	12.2393	12.1617	12.0950
14.125%	12.9618	12.7922	12.6485	12.5261	12.4217	12.3323	12.2557	12.1900
14.250%	13.0491	12.8809	12.7384	12.6172	12.5139	12.4256	12.3500	12.2851
14.375%	13.1366	12.9697	12.8285	12.7085	12.6063	12.5190	12.4443	12.3803
14.500%	13.2242	13.0587	12.9188	12.8000	12.6989	12.6126	12.5389	12.4758
14.625%	13.3121	13.1480	13.0093	12.8917	12.7917	12.7065	12.6337	12.5714
14.750%	13.4002	13.2374	13.1000	12.9836	12.8847	12.8004	12.7286	12.6672
14.875%	13.4885	13.3271	13.1909	13.0756	12.9778	12.8946	12.8237	12.7632
15.000%	13.5770	13.4169	13.2820	13.1679	13.0712	12.9890	12.9190	12.8593
15.125%	13.6657	13.5069	13.3733	13.2603	13.1647	13.0835	13.0144	12.9556
15.250%	13.7546	13.5972	13.4647	13.3530	13.2584	13.1782	13.1100	13.0520
15.375%	13.8437	13.6876	13.5564	13.4458	13.3523	13.2731	13.2058	13.1486
15.500%	13.9329	13.7782	13.6483	13.5388	13.4464	13.3681	13.3018	13.2454
15.625%	14.0224	13.8690	13.7403	13.6320	13.5406	13.4633	13.3979	13.3423
15.750%	14.1120	13.9600	13.8325	13.7253	13.6350	13.5587	13.4941	13.4394
15.875%	14.2019	14.0511	13.9249	13.8189	13.7296	13.6542	13.5905	13.5366
16.000%	14.2919	14.1425	14.0175	13.9126	13.8243	13.7499	13.6871	13.6339
16.125%	14.3821	14.2340	14.1102	14.0064	13.9192	13.8457	13.7838	13.7314
16.250%	14.4725	14.3257	14.2031	14.1005	14.0143	13.9417	13.8806	13.8290
16.375%	14.5630	14.4176	14.2962	14.1946	14.1095	14.0379	13.9776	13.9268
16.500%	14.6538	14.5096	14.3894	14.2890	14.2048	14.1342	14.0747	14.0247
16.625%	14.7447	14.6018	14.4829	14.3835	14.3004	14.2306	14.1720	14.1227
16.750%	14.8358	14.6942	14.5764	14.4782	14.3960	14.3272	14.2694	14.2208
16.875%	14.9270	14.7868	14.6702	14.5730	14.4919	14.4239	14.3669	14.3191

MONTHLY PAYMENT TO AMORTIZE A LOAN OF $1,000

Term of Loan

Interest Rate	25 Years	26 Years	27 Years	28 Years	29 Years	30 Years	35 Years	40 Years
12.000%	10.5322	10.4695	10.4145	10.3661	10.3236	10.2861	10.1555	10.0850
12.125%	10.6247	10.5629	10.5087	10.4611	10.4192	10.3824	10.2545	10.1859
12.250%	10.7174	10.6565	10.6030	10.5562	10.5151	10.4790	10.3537	10.2869
12.375%	10.8104	10.7503	10.6977	10.6516	10.6112	10.5757	10.4531	10.3880
12.500%	10.9035	10.8443	10.7925	10.7471	10.7074	10.6726	10.5525	10.4892
12.625%	10.9969	10.9385	10.8875	10.8429	10.8039	10.7697	10.6522	10.5905
12.750%	11.0905	11.0329	10.9827	10.9388	10.9005	10.8669	10.7520	10.6920
12.875%	11.1843	11.1276	11.0781	11.0350	10.9973	10.9644	10.8519	10.7935
13.000%	11.2784	11.2224	11.1738	11.1313	11.0943	11.0620	10.9519	10.8951
13.125%	11.3726	11.3175	11.2696	11.2279	11.1915	11.1598	11.0521	10.9969
13.250%	11.4670	11.4127	11.3656	11.3246	11.2888	11.2577	11.1524	11.0987
13.375%	11.5616	11.5082	11.4618	11.4214	11.3864	11.3558	11.2529	11.2006
13.500%	11.6564	11.6038	11.5581	11.5185	11.4841	11.4541	11.3534	11.3026
13.625%	11.7515	11.6996	11.6547	11.6157	11.5819	11.5525	11.4541	11.4047
13.750%	11.8467	11.7956	11.7514	11.7131	11.6799	11.6511	11.5549	11.5069
13.875%	11.9420	11.8917	11.8483	11.8107	11.7781	11.7498	11.6557	11.6091
14.000%	12.0376	11.9881	11.9453	11.9084	11.8764	11.8487	11.7567	11.7114
14.125%	12.1334	12.0846	12.0425	12.0062	11.9749	11.9477	11.8578	11.8138
14.250%	12.2293	12.1813	12.1399	12.1043	12.0735	12.0469	11.9590	11.9162
14.375%	12.3254	12.2781	12.2375	12.2024	12.1722	12.1461	12.0603	12.0187
14.500%	12.4216	12.3751	12.3351	12.3007	12.2711	12.2456	12.1617	12.1213
14.625%	12.5181	12.4723	12.4330	12.3992	12.3701	12.3451	12.2632	12.2240
14.750%	12.6146	12.5696	12.5310	12.4978	12.4693	12.4448	12.3647	12.3267
14.875%	12.7114	12.6671	12.6291	12.5965	12.5686	12.5445	12.4664	12.4294
15.000%	12.8083	12.7647	12.7274	12.6954	12.6680	12.6444	12.5681	12.5322
15.125%	12.9054	12.8625	12.8258	12.7944	12.7675	12.7445	12.6699	12.6351
15.250%	13.0026	12.9604	12.9243	12.8935	12.8672	12.8446	12.7718	12.7380
15.375%	13.0999	13.0584	13.0230	12.9928	12.9669	12.9448	12.8738	12.8410
15.500%	13.1975	13.1566	13.1218	13.0922	13.0668	13.0452	12.9758	12.9440
15.625%	13.2951	13.2550	13.2208	13.1916	13.1668	13.1456	13.0780	13.0471
15.750%	13.3929	13.3534	13.3198	13.2913	13.2669	13.2462	13.1801	13.1502
15.875%	13.4908	13.4520	13.4190	13.3910	13.3671	13.3468	13.2824	13.2533
16.000%	13.5889	13.5507	13.5183	13.4908	13.4674	13.4476	13.3847	13.3565
16.125%	13.6871	13.6496	13.6178	13.5908	13.5679	13.5484	13.4871	13.4597
16.250%	13.7854	13.7485	13.7173	13.6908	13.6684	13.6493	13.5895	13.5630
16.375%	13.8839	13.8476	13.8169	13.7910	13.7690	13.7504	13.6920	13.6663
16.500%	13.9824	13.9468	13.9167	13.8912	13.8697	13.8515	13.7945	13.7696
16.625%	14.0811	14.0461	14.0166	13.9916	13.9705	13.9527	13.8971	13.8730
16.750%	14.1800	14.1456	14.1165	14.0921	14.0714	14.0540	13.9998	13.9764
16.875%	14.2789	14.2451	14.2166	14.1926	14.1724	14.1553	14.1025	14.0798

MONTHLY PAYMENT TO AMORTIZE A LOAN OF $1,000

Term of Loan

Interest Rate	1 Year	2 Years	3 Years	4 Years	5 Years	6 Years	7 Years	8 Years
17.000%	91.2048	49.4423	35.6527	28.8550	24.8526	22.2461	20.4358	19.1215
17.125%	91.2641	49.5023	35.7150	28.9198	24.9198	22.3159	20.5081	19.1962
17.250%	91.3234	49.5625	35.7773	28.9845	24.9872	22.3859	20.5805	19.2710
17.375%	91.3828	49.6226	35.8396	29.0494	25.0547	22.4559	20.6531	19.3461
17.500%	91.4422	49.6828	35.9021	29.1144	25.1222	22.5260	20.7258	19.4212
17.625%	91.5016	49.7431	35.9646	29.1794	25.1899	22.5963	20.7986	19.4965
17.750%	91.5611	49.8034	36.0271	29.2445	25.2576	22.6667	20.8716	19.5719
17.875%	91.6205	49.8637	36.0897	29.3097	25.3255	22.7372	20.9446	19.6475
18.000%	91.6800	49.9241	36.1524	29.3750	25.3934	22.8078	21.0178	19.7232
18.125%	91.7395	49.9845	36.2151	29.4404	25.4615	22.8785	21.0912	19.7991
18.250%	91.7990	50.0450	36.2779	29.5058	25.5296	22.9493	21.1646	19.8751
18.375%	91.8586	50.1055	36.3408	29.5713	25.5979	23.0203	21.2382	19.9512
18.500%	91.9181	50.1660	36.4037	29.6369	25.6662	23.0914	21.3119	20.0274
18.625%	91.9777	50.2266	36.4667	29.7026	25.7346	23.1625	21.3858	20.1038
18.750%	92.0373	50.2872	36.5297	29.7684	25.8032	23.2338	21.4597	20.1804
18.875%	92.0969	50.3479	36.5929	29.8342	25.8718	23.3052	21.5338	20.2571
19.000%	92.1566	50.4086	36.6560	29.9001	25.9406	23.3767	21.6080	20.3339

Term of Loan

Interest Rate	9 Years	10 Years	11 Years	12 Years	13 Years	14 Years	15 Years	16 Years
17.000%	18.1362	17.3798	16.7883	16.3192	15.9430	15.6384	15.3900	15.1863
17.125%	18.2132	17.4591	16.8697	16.4026	16.0282	15.7254	15.4787	15.2765
17.250%	18.2905	17.5385	16.9513	16.4862	16.1137	15.8126	15.5676	15.3669
17.375%	18.3678	17.6181	17.0330	16.5700	16.1993	15.9000	15.6566	15.4574
17.500%	18.4453	17.6979	17.1149	16.6539	16.2851	15.9876	15.7458	15.5481
17.625%	18.5230	17.7778	17.1970	16.7380	16.3711	16.0753	15.8351	15.6390
17.750%	18.6008	17.8579	17.2792	16.8222	16.4572	16.1632	15.9247	15.7300
17.875%	18.6788	17.9381	17.3616	16.9066	16.5435	16.2513	16.0144	15.8212
18.000%	18.7569	18.0185	17.4442	16.9912	16.6300	16.3395	16.1042	15.9126
18.125%	18.8351	18.0991	17.5269	17.0759	16.7166	16.4279	16.1942	16.0041
18.250%	18.9136	18.1798	17.6098	17.1608	16.8034	16.5165	16.2844	16.0957
18.375%	18.9921	18.2606	17.6928	17.2459	16.8904	16.6052	16.3747	16.1875
18.500%	19.0708	18.3417	17.7760	17.3311	16.9775	16.6941	16.4652	16.2795
18.625%	19.1497	18.4228	17.8593	17.4165	17.0648	16.7831	16.5559	16.3716
18.750%	19.2287	18.5041	17.9428	17.5021	17.1523	16.8723	16.6467	16.4639
18.875%	19.3078	18.5856	18.0265	17.5878	17.2399	16.9616	16.7376	16.5564
19.000%	19.3871	18.6672	18.1103	17.6736	17.3276	17.0511	16.8288	16.6489

MONTHLY PAYMENT TO AMORTIZE A LOAN OF $1,000

Term of Loan

Interest Rate	17 Years	18 Years	19 Years	20 Years	21 Years	22 Years	23 Years	24 Years
17.000%	15.0184	14.8795	14.7641	14.6680	14.5878	14.5208	14.4646	14.4175
17.125%	15.1100	14.9724	14.8581	14.7631	14.6839	14.6178	14.5624	14.5160
17.250%	15.2018	15.0654	14.9524	14.8584	14.7802	14.7149	14.6603	14.6147
17.375%	15.2937	15.1586	15.0467	14.9538	14.8766	14.8122	14.7584	14.7134
17.500%	15.3858	15.2519	15.1412	15.0494	14.9731	14.9095	14.8565	14.8123
17.625%	15.4780	15.3455	15.2359	15.1451	15.0698	15.0071	14.9548	14.9113
17.750%	15.5704	15.4391	15.3307	15.2410	15.1666	15.1047	15.0532	15.0104
17.875%	15.6630	15.5329	15.4257	15.3370	15.2635	15.2025	15.1518	15.1096
18.000%	15.7557	15.6269	15.5208	15.4331	15.3605	15.3004	15.2504	15.2089
18.125%	15.8486	15.7210	15.6160	15.5294	15.4577	15.3984	15.3492	15.3083
18.250%	15.9416	15.8153	15.7114	15.6258	15.5550	15.4965	15.4480	15.4078
18.375%	16.0348	15.9097	15.8069	15.7223	15.6525	15.5948	15.5470	15.5074
18.500%	16.1281	16.0042	15.9026	15.8190	15.7500	15.6931	15.6461	15.6071
18.625%	16.2216	16.0989	15.9984	15.9158	15.8477	15.7916	15.7452	15.7069
18.750%	16.3152	16.1938	16.0943	16.0127	15.9455	15.8902	15.8445	15.8068
18.875%	16.4090	16.2887	16.1904	16.1097	16.0434	15.9889	15.9439	15.9068
19.000%	16.5029	16.3838	16.2866	16.2068	16.1414	16.0876	16.0434	16.0069

Term of Loan

Interest Rate	25 Years	26 Years	27 Years	28 Years	29 Years	30 Years	35 Years	40 Years
17.000%	14.3780	14.3447	14.3168	14.2933	14.2734	14.2568	14.2053	14.1832
17.125%	14.4771	14.4445	14.4171	14.3940	14.3746	14.3583	14.3081	14.2867
17.250%	14.5764	14.5443	14.5174	14.4948	14.4758	14.4599	14.4109	14.3902
17.375%	14.6758	14.6443	14.6179	14.5957	14.5771	14.5615	14.5138	14.4938
17.500%	14.7753	14.7443	14.7184	14.6967	14.6785	14.6633	14.6168	14.5973
17.625%	14.8749	14.8445	14.8191	14.7978	14.7800	14.7651	14.7197	14.7009
17.750%	14.9746	14.9447	14.9198	14.8989	14.8815	14.8669	14.8228	14.8045
17.875%	15.0744	15.0451	15.0206	15.0002	14.9831	14.9689	14.9258	14.9082
18.000%	15.1743	15.1455	15.1215	15.1015	15.0848	15.0709	15.0289	15.0118
18.125%	15.2743	15.2460	15.2225	15.2029	15.1865	15.1729	15.1321	15.1155
18.250%	15.3744	15.3466	15.3235	15.3043	15.2883	15.2750	15.2352	15.2192
18.375%	15.4746	15.4473	15.4247	15.4059	15.3902	15.3772	15.3384	15.3229
18.500%	15.5748	15.5481	15.5259	15.5075	15.4922	15.4794	15.4417	15.4266
18.625%	15.6752	15.6489	15.6272	15.6091	15.5942	15.5817	15.5449	15.5304
18.750%	15.7757	15.7499	15.7285	15.7109	15.6962	15.6841	15.6483	15.6342
18.875%	15.8762	15.8509	15.8300	15.8127	15.7983	15.7865	15.7516	15.7379
19.000%	15.9768	15.9520	15.9315	15.9145	15.9005	15.8889	15.8549	15.8417

B

Remaining Principal Balance

If you arrange a balloon mortgage, monthly payments will be set on a long-term schedule. At some point during the life of the loan, though, the entire remaining balance will suddenly become due and payable.

How much will that final (balloon) payment be? In the early years of a loan, interest charges absorb most of the monthly payment, and little is left to reduce the principal. It is not unusual for the final payment to be almost as much as the original debt.

To calculate the amount:

1. Find the table with the interest rate on your mortgage.
2. Follow across the top line until you find the original term of the loan (the number of years used to calculate the monthly payment).
3. Go down the left-hand column until you find the number of years the loan will actually last (the age of the loan when you will make that balloon payment).
4. Find the spot where the two lines intersect.

   Example: On the chart for 10 percent loans, with an original term of 25 years, a ten-year balloon has a factor of .846. Almost 85 percent of the original loan is still due.

5. Multiply the original loan amount by the factor.

   Example: A loan of $74,500 × .846 (84.6%) = $63,027. This represents the remaining balance after ten years' payments have been made, and it represents the final balloon payment.

Remaining Principal Balance Factors

For Mortgages with an Interest Rate of 6.00% and an Original Term of:

Age of Loan in Years	5 Years	6 Years	7 Years	8 Years	9 Years	10 Years	11 Years	12 Years	15 Years	20 Years	25 Years	30 Years	35 Years	40 Years
1	0.823	0.857	0.881	0.900	0.914	0.925	0.934	0.941	0.958	0.973	0.982	0.988	0.991	0.994
2	0.635	0.706	0.756	0.793	0.822	0.845	0.864	0.879	0.913	0.945	0.963	0.975	0.982	0.987
3	0.436	0.545	0.622	0.680	0.724	0.760	0.789	0.813	0.865	0.915	0.943	0.961	0.972	0.980
4	0.225	0.374	0.480	0.560	0.621	0.670	0.710	0.743	0.814	0.883	0.922	0.946	0.962	0.973
5	0.000	0.193	0.330	0.432	0.511	0.574	0.626	0.668	0.760	0.849	0.899	0.931	0.951	0.965
6		0.000	0.170	0.297	0.395	0.473	0.536	0.589	0.703	0.813	0.875	0.914	0.939	0.957
7			0.000	0.153	0.271	0.365	0.441	0.505	0.642	0.775	0.850	0.896	0.927	0.948
8				0.000	0.139	0.250	0.341	0.416	0.578	0.734	0.823	0.878	0.914	0.938
9					0.000	0.129	0.234	0.321	0.509	0.691	0.794	0.858	0.900	0.928
10						0.000	0.120	0.220	0.436	0.645	0.764	0.837	0.885	0.918
11							0.000	0.113	0.359	0.597	0.731	0.815	0.869	0.906
12								0.000	0.277	0.545	0.697	0.791	0.852	0.894
15									0.000	0.371	0.580	0.710	0.796	0.854
20										0.000	0.333	0.540	0.676	0.768
25											0.000	0.310	0.514	0.652
30												0.000	0.295	0.496
35													0.000	0.285
40														0.000

For Mortgages with an Interest Rate of 6.25% and an Original Term of:

Age of Loan in Years	5 Years	6 Years	7 Years	8 Years	9 Years	10 Years	11 Years	12 Years	15 Years	20 Years	25 Years	30 Years	35 Years	40 Years
1	0.824	0.858	0.882	0.901	0.915	0.926	0.935	0.942	0.958	0.974	0.983	0.988	0.992	0.994
2	0.637	0.707	0.757	0.795	0.824	0.847	0.865	0.881	0.914	0.946	0.965	0.976	0.983	0.988
3	0.438	0.547	0.624	0.682	0.727	0.762	0.791	0.815	0.867	0.917	0.945	0.963	0.974	0.981
4	0.226	0.376	0.482	0.562	0.624	0.673	0.713	0.746	0.817	0.886	0.925	0.948	0.964	0.974
5	0.000	0.194	0.331	0.434	0.514	0.577	0.629	0.671	0.764	0.852	0.903	0.933	0.953	0.967
6		0.000	0.171	0.299	0.397	0.476	0.540	0.592	0.707	0.817	0.879	0.917	0.942	0.959
7			0.000	0.154	0.273	0.368	0.445	0.508	0.646	0.779	0.854	0.900	0.930	0.951
8				0.000	0.141	0.253	0.344	0.419	0.582	0.739	0.828	0.882	0.918	0.942
9					0.000	0.130	0.236	0.324	0.514	0.696	0.799	0.863	0.904	0.932
10						0.000	0.122	0.223	0.441	0.651	0.769	0.842	0.890	0.922
11							0.000	0.115	0.363	0.603	0.737	0.821	0.875	0.911
12								0.000	0.281	0.551	0.703	0.797	0.858	0.900
15									0.000	0.376	0.588	0.718	0.803	0.861
20										0.000	0.339	0.548	0.685	0.777
25											0.000	0.317	0.523	0.662
30												0.000	0.302	0.506
35													0.000	0.292
40														0.000

Remaining Principal Balance Factors

For Mortgages with an Interest Rate of 6.50% and an Original Term of:

Age of Loan in Years	5 Years	6 Years	7 Years	8 Years	9 Years	10 Years	11 Years	12 Years	15 Years	20 Years	25 Years	30 Years	35 Years	40 Years
1	0.825	0.859	0.883	0.901	0.915	0.927	0.936	0.943	0.959	0.975	0.983	0.989	0.992	0.995
2	0.638	0.709	0.759	0.796	0.825	0.848	0.867	0.882	0.916	0.948	0.966	0.977	0.984	0.989
3	0.439	0.548	0.626	0.684	0.729	0.765	0.794	0.818	0.869	0.919	0.947	0.964	0.975	0.983
4	0.227	0.377	0.484	0.564	0.626	0.675	0.715	0.748	0.820	0.889	0.927	0.951	0.966	0.976
5	0.000	0.195	0.333	0.437	0.517	0.580	0.632	0.675	0.767	0.856	0.906	0.936	0.956	0.969
6		0.000	0.172	0.301	0.400	0.479	0.543	0.596	0.711	0.821	0.883	0.921	0.945	0.962
7			0.000	0.155	0.275	0.370	0.448	0.512	0.651	0.784	0.858	0.904	0.934	0.954
8				0.000	0.142	0.255	0.347	0.422	0.587	0.744	0.832	0.887	0.922	0.945
9					0.000	0.132	0.238	0.327	0.518	0.702	0.805	0.868	0.909	0.936
10						0.000	0.123	0.225	0.445	0.657	0.775	0.848	0.895	0.926
11							0.000	0.116	0.367	0.608	0.744	0.826	0.880	0.916
12								0.000	0.284	0.557	0.710	0.804	0.864	0.905
15									0.000	0.381	0.595	0.726	0.810	0.867
20										0.000	0.345	0.557	0.694	0.785
25											0.000	0.323	0.532	0.672
30												0.000	0.309	0.516
35													0.000	0.299
40														0.000

For Mortgages with an Interest Rate of 6.75% and an Original Term of:

Age of Loan in Years	5 Years	6 Years	7 Years	8 Years	9 Years	10 Years	11 Years	12 Years	15 Years	20 Years	25 Years	30 Years	35 Years	40 Years
1	0.826	0.860	0.884	0.902	0.916	0.927	0.937	0.944	0.960	0.976	0.984	0.989	0.993	0.995
2	0.640	0.710	0.761	0.798	0.827	0.850	0.869	0.884	0.917	0.949	0.967	0.978	0.985	0.990
3	0.441	0.550	0.628	0.686	0.731	0.767	0.796	0.820	0.872	0.921	0.949	0.966	0.977	0.984
4	0.228	0.379	0.487	0.567	0.629	0.678	0.718	0.751	0.823	0.891	0.929	0.953	0.968	0.978
5	0.000	0.196	0.335	0.439	0.520	0.583	0.635	0.678	0.771	0.859	0.909	0.939	0.958	0.971
6		0.000	0.173	0.303	0.402	0.482	0.546	0.600	0.715	0.825	0.886	0.924	0.948	0.964
7			0.000	0.156	0.277	0.373	0.451	0.516	0.655	0.788	0.863	0.908	0.937	0.956
8				0.000	0.143	0.257	0.350	0.426	0.591	0.749	0.837	0.891	0.925	0.948
9					0.000	0.133	0.241	0.330	0.523	0.707	0.810	0.873	0.913	0.940
10						0.000	0.124	0.227	0.450	0.662	0.781	0.853	0.899	0.930
11							0.000	0.117	0.371	0.614	0.750	0.832	0.885	0.920
12								0.000	0.288	0.563	0.716	0.810	0.870	0.910
15									0.000	0.386	0.602	0.733	0.817	0.873
20										0.000	0.351	0.565	0.702	0.794
25											0.000	0.330	0.541	0.682
30												0.000	0.316	0.525
35													0.000	0.307
40														0.000

Remaining Principal Balance Factors

For Mortgages with an Interest Rate of 7.00% and an Original Term Of:

Age of Loan in Years	5 Years	6 Years	7 Years	8 Years	9 Years	10 Years	11 Years	12 Years	15 Years	20 Years	25 Years	30 Years	35 Years	40 Years
1	0.827	0.861	0.885	0.903	0.917	0.928	0.937	0.945	0.961	0.976	0.985	0.990	0.993	0.995
2	0.641	0.712	0.762	0.800	0.829	0.852	0.870	0.886	0.919	0.951	0.968	0.979	0.986	0.990
3	0.442	0.552	0.630	0.689	0.734	0.769	0.798	0.822	0.874	0.923	0.951	0.967	0.978	0.985
4	0.229	0.381	0.489	0.569	0.632	0.681	0.721	0.754	0.826	0.894	0.932	0.955	0.969	0.979
5	0.000	0.197	0.337	0.442	0.522	0.586	0.638	0.681	0.774	0.863	0.912	0.941	0.960	0.973
6		0.000	0.174	0.305	0.405	0.485	0.550	0.603	0.719	0.829	0.890	0.927	0.950	0.966
7			0.000	0.158	0.279	0.376	0.455	0.519	0.659	0.793	0.867	0.911	0.940	0.959
8				0.000	0.145	0.259	0.352	0.429	0.596	0.754	0.842	0.895	0.929	0.951
9					0.000	0.134	0.243	0.333	0.527	0.712	0.815	0.877	0.917	0.943
10						0.000	0.126	0.230	0.454	0.668	0.786	0.858	0.904	0.934
11							0.000	0.119	0.375	0.620	0.756	0.838	0.890	0.925
12								0.000	0.291	0.569	0.723	0.816	0.875	0.914
15									0.000	0.392	0.609	0.740	0.824	0.879
20										0.000	0.357	0.573	0.711	0.802
25											0.000	0.336	0.550	0.691
30												0.000	0.323	0.535
35													0.000	0.314
40														0.000

For Mortgages with an Interest Rate of 7.25% and an Original Term of:

Age of Loan in Years	5 Years	6 Years	7 Years	8 Years	9 Years	10 Years	11 Years	12 Years	15 Years	20 Years	25 Years	30 Years	35 Years	40 Years
1	0.828	0.862	0.886	0.904	0.918	0:929	0.938	0.946	0.962	0.977	0.985	0.990	0.994	0.996
2	0.643	0.714	0.764	0.801	0.830	0.853	0.872	0.887	0.921	0.952	0.969	0.980	0.987	0.991
3	0.444	0.554	0.632	0.691	0.736	0.772	0.801	0.825	0.876	0.925	0.952	0.969	0.979	0.986
4	0.230	0.383	0.491	0.572	0.634	0.684	0.724	0.757	0.829	0.897	0.934	0.957	0.971	0.980
5	0.000	0.198	0.339	0.444	0.525	0.589	0.642	0.685	0.778	0.866	0.915	0.944	0.962	0.974
6		0.000	0.176	0.307	0.408	0.488	0.553	0.607	0.723	0.833	0.893	0.930	0.953	0.968
7			0.000	0.159	0.281	0.379	0.458	0.523	0.663	0.797	0.871	0.915	0.943	0.961
8				0.000	0.146	0.262	0.355	0.433	0.600	0.759	0.846	0.899	0.932	0.954
9					0.000	0.136	0.245	0.336	0.532	0.718	0.820	0.882	0.921	0.946
10						0.000	0.127	0.232	0.458	0.673	0.792	0.863	0.908	0.938
11							0.000	0.120	0.379	0.626	0.761	0.843	0.895	0.929
12								0.000	0.295	0.574	0.729	0.822	0.880	0.919
15									0.000	0.397	0.616	0.747	0.831	0.885
20										0.000	0.363	0.581	0.719	0.809
25											0.000	0.342	0.559	0.701
30												0.000	0.330	0.545
35													0.000	0.321
40														0.000

Remaining Principal Balance Factors

For Mortgages with an Interest Rate of 7.50% and an Original Term of:

Age of Loan in Years	5 Years	6 Years	7 Years	8 Years	9 Years	10 Years	11 Years	12 Years	15 Years	20 Years	25 Years	30 Years	35 Years	40 Years
1	0.829	0.863	0.887	0.905	0.919	0.930	0.939	0.947	0.962	0.978	0.986	0.991	0.994	0.996
2	0.644	0.715	0.765	0.803	0.832	0.855	0.874	0.889	0.922	0.953	0.971	0.981	0.987	0.991
3	0.445	0.556	0.634	0.693	0.738	0.774	0.803	0.827	0.878	0.927	0.954	0.970	0.980	0.987
4	0.231	0.384	0.493	0.574	0.637	0.687	0.727	0.760	0.832	0.899	0.936	0.959	0.973	0.982
5	0.000	0.199	0.341	0.446	0.528	0.592	0.645	0.688	0.781	0.869	0.917	0.946	0.964	0.976
6		0.000	0.177	0.309	0.410	0.491	0.556	0.610	0.726	0.836	0.897	0.933	0.955	0.970
7			0.000	0.160	0.284	0.382	0.461	0.527	0.668	0.801	0.875	0.918	0.946	0.964
8				0.000	0.147	0.264	0.358	0.436	0.604	0.763	0.851	0.903	0.935	0.957
9					0.000	0.137	0.248	0.339	0.536	0.723	0.825	0.886	0.924	0.949
10						0.000	0.128	0.234	0.463	0.679	0.797	0.868	0.912	0.941
11							0.000	0.122	0.383	0.631	0.767	0.848	0.899	0.932
12								0.000	0.298	0.580	0.735	0.827	0.886	0.923
15									0.000	0.402	0.623	0.754	0.837	0.890
20										0.000	0.369	0.589	0.727	0.817
25											0.000	0.349	0.568	0.710
30												0.000	0.336	0.554
35													0.000	0.328
40														0.000

For Mortgages with an Interest Rate of 7.75% and an Original Term of:

Age of Loan in Years	5 Years	6 Years	7 Years	8 Years	9 Years	10 Years	11 Years	12 Years	15 Years	20 Years	25 Years	30 Years	35 Years	40 Years
1	0.830	0.864	0.888	0.906	0.920	0.931	0.940	0.947	0.963	0.978	0.986	0.991	0.994	0.996
2	0.646	0.717	0.767	0.805	0.834	0.857	0.875	0.891	0.924	0.955	0.972	0.982	0.988	0.992
3	0.447	0.558	0.636	0.695	0.740	0.776	0.805	0.829	0.881	0.929	0.956	0.971	0.981	0.988
4	0.232	0.386	0.495	0.577	0.639	0.689	0.730	0.763	0.834	0.902	0.939	0.960	0.974	0.983
5	0.000	0.200	0.343	0.449	0.531	0.595	0.648	0.691	0.784	0.872	0.920	0.948	0.966	0.978
6		0.000	0.178	0.311	0.413	0.494	0.560	0.614	0.730	0.840	0.900	0.936	0.958	0.972
7			0.000	0.161	0.286	0.384	0.464	0.530	0.672	0.806	0.878	0.922	0.949	0.966
8				0.000	0.148	0.266	0.361	0.440	0.609	0.768	0.855	0.907	0.939	0.959
9					0.000	0.138	0.250	0.342	0.541	0.728	0.830	0.890	0.928	0.952
10						0.000	0.130	0.237	0.467	0.684	0.802	0.873	0.916	0.944
11							0.000	0.123	0.387	0.637	0.773	0.854	0.904	0.936
12								0.000	0.301	0.586	0.741	0.833	0.890	0.927
15									0.000	0.407	0.629	0.761	0.843	0.896
20										0.000	0.375	0.597	0.735	0.824
25											0.000	0.355	0.577	0.719
30												0.000	0.343	0.564
35													0.000	0.336
40														0.000

Remaining Principal Balance Factors

For Mortgages with an Interest Rate of 8.00% and an Original Term of:

Age of Loan in Years	5 Years	6 Years	7 Years	8 Years	9 Years	10 Years	11 Years	12 Years	15 Years	20 Years	25 Years	30 Years	35 Years	40 Years
1	0.831	0.865	0.889	0.907	0.921	0.932	0.941	0.948	0.964	0.979	0.987	0.992	0.995	0.996
2	0.647	0.718	0.769	0.806	0.835	0.858	0.877	0.892	0.925	0.956	0.973	0.983	0.989	0.993
3	0.448	0.560	0.638	0.697	0.743	0.778	0.808	0.831	0.883	0.931	0.957	0.973	0.982	0.988
4	0.233	0.388	0.497	0.579	0.642	0.692	0.732	0.766	0.837	0.904	0.941	0.962	0.975	0.984
5	0.000	0.202	0.345	0.451	0.533	0.598	0.651	0.694	0.788	0.875	0.923	0.951	0.968	0.979
6		0.000	0.179	0.313	0.415	0.497	0.563	0.617	0.734	0.844	0.903	0.938	0.960	0.974
7			0.000	0.163	0.288	0.387	0.468	0.534	0.676	0.810	0.882	0.925	0.951	0.968
8				0.000	0.150	0.268	0.364	0.443	0.613	0.773	0.859	0.910	0.942	0.962
9					0.000	0.139	0.252	0.345	0.545	0.733	0.834	0.894	0.931	0.955
10						0.000	0.131	0.239	0.471	0.689	0.808	0.877	0.920	0.948
11							0.000	0.124	0.391	0.642	0.779	0.859	0.908	0.940
12								0.000	0.305	0.592	0.747	0.839	0.895	0.931
15									0.000	0.413	0.636	0.768	0.849	0.901
20										0.000	0.381	0.605	0.743	0.831
25											0.000	0.362	0.585	0.728
30												0.000	0.350	0.573
35													0.000	0.343
40														0.000

For Mortgages with an Interest Rate of 8.25% and an Original Term of:

Age of Loan in Years	5 Years	6 Years	7 Years	8 Years	9 Years	10 Years	11 Years	12 Years	15 Years	20 Years	25 Years	30 Years	35 Years	40 Years
1	0.831	0.866	0.890	0.908	0.922	0.933	0.942	0.949	0.965	0.979	0.987	0.992	0.995	0.997
2	0.648	0.720	0.770	0.808	0.837	0.860	0.878	0.894	0.927	0.957	0.974	0.983	0.989	0.993
3	0.450	0.561	0.640	0.699	0.745	0.781	0.810	0.834	0.885	0.933	0.959	0.974	0.983	0.989
4	0.234	0.389	0.500	0.581	0.645	0.695	0.735	0.769	0.840	0.907	0.943	0.964	0.977	0.985
5	0.000	0.203	0.347	0.454	0.536	0.601	0.654	0.698	0.791	0.878	0.925	0.953	0.970	0.980
6		0.000	0.180	0.315	0.418	0.500	0.566	0.621	0.738	0.847	0.906	0.941	0.962	0.975
7			0.000	0.164	0.290	0.390	0.471	0.537	0.680	0.814	0.886	0.928	0.954	0.970
8				0.000	0.151	0.271	0.367	0.447	0.617	0.777	0.863	0.914	0.945	0.964
9					0.000	0.141	0.255	0.349	0.549	0.738	0.839	0.898	0.935	0.958
10						0.000	0.133	0.242	0.476	0.695	0.813	0.882	0.924	0.951
11							0.000	0.126	0.395	0.648	0.784	0.864	0.912	0.943
12								0.000	0.308	0.597	0.753	0.844	0.900	0.935
15									0.000	0.418	0.643	0.774	0.855	0.906
20										0.000	0.387	0.613	0.751	0.838
25											0.000	0.368	0.594	0.736
30												0.000	0.357	0.582
35													0.000	0.250
40														0.000

Remaining Principal Balance Factors

For Mortgages with an Interest Rate of 8.50% and an Original Term of:

Age of Loan in Years	5 Years	6 Years	7 Years	8 Years	9 Years	10 Years	11 Years	12 Years	15 Years	20 Years	25 Years	30 Years	35 Years	40 Years
1	0.832	0.867	0.891	0.909	0.923	0.934	0.943	0.950	0.966	0.980	0.988	0.992	0.995	0.997
2	0.650	0.721	0.772	0.810	0.839	0.861	0.880	0.895	0.928	0.958	0.975	0.984	0.990	0.994
3	0.451	0.563	0.642	0.701	0.747	0.783	0.812	0.836	0.887	0.935	0.960	0.975	0.984	0.990
4	0.235	0.391	0.502	0.584	0.647	0.697	0.738	0.771	0.843	0.909	0.945	0.966	0.978	0.986
5	0.000	0.204	0.348	0.456	0.539	0.604	0.657	0.701	0.794	0.881	0.928	0.955	0.971	0.982
6		0.000	0.182	0.317	0.421	0.503	0.570	0.624	0.742	0.851	0.909	0.943	0.964	0.977
7			0.000	0.165	0.292	0.393	0.474	0.541	0.684	0.818	0.889	0.931	0.956	0.972
8				0.000	0.152	0.273	0.370	0.450	0.622	0.782	0.867	0.917	0.947	0.966
9					0.000	0.142	0.257	0.352	0.554	0.743	0.844	0.902	0.938	0.960
10						0.000	0.134	0.244	0.480	0.700	0.818	0.886	0.928	0.953
11							0.000	0.127	0.400	0.654	0.790	0.868	0.916	0.946
12								0.000	0.312	0.603	0.759	0.849	0.904	0.938
15									0.000	0.423	0.649	0.781	0.861	0.910
20										0.000	0.392	0.620	0.758	0.845
25											0.000	0.375	0.602	0.744
30												0.000	0.364	0.591
35													0.000	0.357
40														0.000

For Mortgages with an Interest Rate of 8.75% and an Original Term of:

Age of Loan in Years	5 Years	6 Years	7 Years	8 Years	9 Years	10 Years	11 Years	12 Years	15 Years	20 Years	25 Years	30 Years	35 Years	40 Years
1	0.833	0.867	0.892	0.910	0.924	0.935	0.943	0.951	0.966	0.981	0.988	0.993	0.995	0.997
2	0.651	0.723	0.773	0.811	0.840	0.863	0.882	0.897	0.929	0.960	0.976	0.985	0.991	0.994
3	0.453	0.565	0.645	0.704	0.749	0.785	0.814	0.838	0.889	0.937	0.962	0.976	0.985	0.991
4	0.236	0.393	0.504	0.586	0.650	0.700	0.741	0.774	0.845	0.912	0.947	0.967	0.979	0.987
5	0.000	0.205	0.350	0.458	0.541	0.607	0.660	0.704	0.797	0.884	0.930	0.957	0.973	0.983
6		0.000	0.183	0.319	0.423	0.506	0.573	0.628	0.745	0.854	0.912	0.946	0.966	0.978
7			0.000	0.166	0.294	0.396	0.477	0.545	0.688	0.822	0.893	0.934	0.958	0.973
8				0.000	0.154	0.275	0.373	0.454	0.626	0.786	0.871	0.920	0.950	0.968
9					0.000	0.144	0.259	0.355	0.558	0.747	0.848	0.906	0.941	0.962
10						0.000	0.135	0.247	0.484	0.705	0.823	0.890	0.931	0.956
11							0.000	0.129	0.404	0.659	0.795	0.873	0.920	0.949
12								0.000	0.315	0.609	0.765	0.854	0.908	0.942
15									0.000	0.428	0.656	0.787	0.866	0.915
20										0.000	0.398	0.628	0.766	0.851
25											0.000	0.381	0.611	0.753
30												0.000	0.371	0.600
35													0.000	0.364
40														0.000

Remaining Principal Balance Factors

For Mortgages with an Interest Rate of 9.00% and an Original Term of:

Age of Loan in Years	5 Years	6 Years	7 Years	8 Years	9 Years	10 Years	11 Years	12 Years	15 Years	20 Years	25 Years	30 Years	35 Years	40 Years
1	0.834	0.868	0.893	0.911	0.924	0.935	0.944	0.951	0.967	0.981	0.989	0.993	0.996	0.997
2	0.653	0.724	0.775	0.813	0.842	0.865	0.883	0.898	0.931	0.961	0.977	0.986	0.991	0.994
3	0.454	0.567	0.647	0.706	0.751	0.787	0.816	0.840	0.891	0.938	0.963	0.978	0.986	0.991
4	0.237	0.395	0.506	0.589	0.652	0.703	0.743	0.777	0.848	0.914	0.949	0.969	0.980	0.988
5	0.000	0.206	0.352	0.461	0.544	0.610	0.664	0.707	0.801	0.887	0.933	0.959	0.974	0.984
6		0.000	0.184	0.321	0.426	0.509	0.576	0.631	0.749	0.858	0.915	0.948	0.968	0.980
7			0.000	0.168	0.296	0.398	0.481	0.548	0.692	0.826	0.896	0.936	0.960	0.975
8				0.000	0.155	0.277	0.376	0.457	0.630	0.791	0.875	0.924	0.952	0.970
9					0.000	0.145	0.262	0.358	0.563	0.752	0.852	0.910	0.944	0.965
10						0.000	0.137	0.249	0.489	0.710	0.827	0.894	0.934	0.959
11							0.000	0.130	0.408	0.664	0.800	0.878	0.924	0.952
12								0.000	0.319	0.614	0.770	0.859	0.912	0.945
15									0.000	0.433	0.662	0.793	0.871	0.919
20										0.000	0.404	0.635	0.773	0.857
25											0.000	0.388	0.619	0.761
30												0.000	0.378	0.609
35													0.000	0.372
40														0.000

For Mortgages with an Interest Rate of 9.25% and an Original Term of:

Age of Loan in Years	5 Years	6 Years	7 Years	8 Years	9 Years	10 Years	11 Years	12 Years	15 Years	20 Years	25 Years	30 Years	35 Years	40 Years
1	0.835	0.869	0.893	0.911	0.925	0.936	0.945	0.952	0.968	0.982	0.989	0.994	0.996	0.998
2	0.654	0.726	0.777	0.814	0.843	0.866	0.885	0.900	0.932	0.962	0.978	0.986	0.992	0.995
3	0.456	0.569	0.649	0.708	0.753	0.790	0.819	0.842	0.893	0.940	0.965	0.979	0.987	0.992
4	0.238	0.396	0.508	0.591	0.655	0.705	0.746	0.780	0.851	0.916	0.951	0.970	0.982	0.989
5	0.000	0.207	0.354	0.463	0.547	0.613	0.667	0.710	0.804	0.890	0.935	0.961	0.976	0.985
6		0.000	0.185	0.323	0.428	0.512	0.579	0.635	0.753	0.861	0.918	0.950	0.969	0.981
7			0.000	0.169	0.299	0.401	0.484	0.552	0.696	0.830	0.899	0.939	0.962	0.977
8				0.000	0.156	0.280	0.379	0.461	0.635	0.795	0.879	0.927	0.955	0.972
9					0.000	0.146	0.264	0.361	0.567	0.757	0.857	0.913	0.947	0.967
10						0.000	0.138	0.252	0.493	0.715	0.832	0.898	0.937	0.961
11							0.000	0.132	0.412	0.670	0.805	0.882	0.927	0.955
12								0.000	0.322	0.620	0.776	0.864	0.916	0.948
15									0.000	0.439	0.669	0.799	0.876	0.923
20										0.000	0.410	0.643	0.780	0.863
25											0.000	0.394	0.627	0.768
30												0.000	0.384	0.618
35													0.000	0.379
40														0.000

Remaining Principal Balance Factors

For Mortgages with an Interest Rate of 9.50% and an Original Term of:

Age of Loan in Years	5 Years	6 Years	7 Years	8 Years	9 Years	10 Years	11 Years	12 Years	15 Years	20 Years	25 Years	30 Years	35 Years	40 Years
1	0.836	0.870	0.894	0.912	0.926	0.937	0.946	0.953	0.968	0.982	0.990	0.994	0.996	0.998
2	0.656	0.727	0.778	0.816	0.845	0.868	0.886	0.901	0.934	0.963	0.978	0.987	0.992	0.995
3	0.457	0.570	0.651	0.710	0.756	0.792	0.821	0.845	0.895	0.942	0.966	0.980	0.988	0.992
4	0.240	0.398	0.510	0.594	0.658	0.708	0.749	0.782	0.853	0.918	0.952	0.971	0.983	0.989
5	0.000	0.208	0.356	0.465	0.550	0.616	0.670	0.714	0.807	0.893	0.937	0.962	0.977	0.986
6		0.000	0.186	0.325	0.431	0.515	0.583	0.638	0.756	0.864	0.921	0.953	0.971	0.982
7			0.000	0.170	0.301	0.404	0.487	0.555	0.700	0.833	0.903	0.942	0.964	0.978
8				0.000	0.157	0.282	0.382	0.464	0.639	0.799	0.883	0.930	0.957	0.974
9					0.000	0.148	0.267	0.364	0.571	0.762	0.861	0.917	0.949	0.969
10						0.000	0.140	0.254	0.497	0.720	0.837	0.902	0.940	0.963
11							0.000	0.133	0.416	0.675	0.810	0.886	0.931	0.957
12								0.000	0.326	0.625	0.781	0.869	0.920	0.951
15									0.000	0.444	0.675	0.805	0.881	0.927
20										0.000	0.416	0.650	0.787	0.869
25											0.000	0.400	0.635	0.776
30												0.000	0.391	0.626
35													0.000	0.386
40														0.000

For Mortgages with an Interest Rate of 9.75% and an Original Term of:

Age of Loan in Years	5 Years	6 Years	7 Years	8 Years	9 Years	10 Years	11 Years	12 Years	15 Years	20 Years	25 Years	30 Years	35 Years	40 Years
1	0.837	0.871	0.895	0.913	0.927	0.938	0.947	0.954	0.969	0.983	0.990	0.994	0.996	0.998
2	0.657	0.729	0.780	0.818	0.846	0.869	0.888	0.903	0.935	0.964	0.979	0.988	0.993	0.995
3	0.459	0.572	0.653	0.712	0.758	0.794	0.823	0.847	0.897	0.943	0.967	0.981	0.988	0.993
4	0.241	0.400	0.512	0.596	0.660	0.711	0.751	0.785	0.856	0.921	0.954	0.973	0.984	0.990
5	0.000	0.210	0.358	0.468	0.552	0.619	0.673	0.717	0.810	0.895	0.940	0.964	0.978	0.987
6		0.000	0.188	0.327	0.434	0.518	0.586	0.642	0.760	0.868	0.923	0.955	0.973	0.983
7			0.000	0.171	0.303	0.407	0.490	0.559	0.704	0.837	0.906	0.944	0.966	0.980
8				0.000	0.159	0.284	0.385	0.468	0.643	0.803	0.886	0.933	0.959	0.975
9					0.000	0.149	0.269	0.367	0.576	0.766	0.865	0.920	0.952	0.971
10						0.000	0.141	0.257	0.501	0.725	0.841	0.906	0.943	0.966
11							0.000	0.134	0.420	0.680	0.815	0.890	0.934	0.960
12								0.000	0.330	0.631	0.786	0.873	0.924	0.954
15									0.000	0.449	0.681	0.811	0.886	0.931
20										0.000	0.422	0.657	0.793	0.875
25											0.000	0.407	0.643	0.783
30												0.000	0.398	0.634
35													0.000	0.393
40														0.000

Remaining Principal Balance Factors

For Mortgages with an Interest Rate of 10.00% and an Original Term of:

Age of Loan in Years	5 Years	6 Years	7 Years	8 Years	9 Years	10 Years	11 Years	12 Years	15 Years	20 Years	25 Years	30 Years	35 Years	40 Years
1	0.838	0.872	0.896	0.914	0.928	0.939	0.947	0.955	0.970	0.983	0.991	0.994	0.997	0.998
2	0.658	0.730	0.781	0.819	0.848	0.871	0.889	0.904	0.936	0.965	0.980	0.988	0.993	0.996
3	0.460	0.574	0.655	0.714	0.760	0.796	0.825	0.849	0.899	0.945	0.969	0.982	0.989	0.993
4	0.242	0.401	0.514	0.598	0.663	0.713	0.754	0.788	0.858	0.923	0.956	0.974	0.985	0.991
5	0.000	0.211	0.360	0.470	0.555	0.622	0.676	0.720	0.813	0.898	0.942	0.966	0.980	0.988
6		0.000	0.189	0.329	0.436	0.521	0.589	0.645	0.763	0.871	0.926	0.957	0.974	0.984
7			0.000	0.173	0.305	-0.410	0.494	0.562	0.708	0.841	0.909	0.946	0.968	0.981
8				0.000	0.160	0.286	0.388	0.471	0.647	0.807	0.890	0.935	0.961	0.977
9					0.000	0.150	0.271	0.370	0.580	0.771	0.869	0.923	0.954	0.972
10						0.000	0.142	0.259	0.506	0.730	0.846	0.909	0.946	0.968
11							0.000	0.136	0.424	0.685	0.820	0.894	0.937	0.962
12								0.000	0.333	0.636	0.792	0.878	0.927	0.956
15									0.000	0.454	0.688	0.817	0.891	0.934
20										0.000	0.428	0.664	0.800	0.880
25											0.000	0.413	0.651	0.790
30												0.000	0.405	0.643
35													0.000	0.400
40														0.000

For Mortgages with an Interest Rate of 10.25% and an Original Term of:

Age of Loan in Years	5 Years	6 Years	7 Years	8 Years	9 Years	10 Years	11 Years	12 Years	15 Years	20 Years	25 Years	30 Years	35 Years	40 Years
1	0.839	0.873	0.897	0.915	0.929	0.939	0.948	0.955	0.970	0.984	0.991	0.995	0.997	0.998
2	0.660	0.732	0.783	0.821	0.850	0.872	0.891	0.906	0.937	0.966	0.981	0.989	0.993	0.996
3	0.462	0.576	0.657	0.716	0.762	0.798	0.827	0.851	0.901	0.947	0.970	0.982	0.990	0.994
4	0.243	0.403	0.517	0.601	0.665	0.716	0.757	0.790	0.861	0.925	0.957	0.975	0.985	0.991
5	0.000	0.212	0.362	0.473	0.558	0.625	0.679	0.723	0.816	0.901	0.944	0.967	0.981	0.989
6		0.000	0.190	0.331	0.439	0.524	0.592	0.648	0.767	0.874	0.929	0.959	0.976	0.986
7			0.000	0.174	0.307	0.412	0.497	0.566	0.712	0.844	0.912	0.949	0.970	0.982
8				0.000	0.161	0.289	0.391	0.475	0.651	0.812	0.893	0.938	0.964	0.978
9					0.000	0.152	0.274	0.373	0.584	0.775	0.873	0.926	0.956	0.974
10						0.000	0.144	0.261	0.510	0.735	0.850	0.913	0.949	0.970
11							0.000	0.137	0.428	0.691	0.825	0.898	0.940	0.964
12								0.000	0.337	0.641	0.797	0.882	0.931	0.959
15									0.000	0.459	0.694	0.822	0.895	0.938
20										0.000	0.433	0.671	0.806	0.885
25											0.000	0.419	0.658	0.797
30												0.000	0.411	0.651
35													0.000	0.407
40														0.000

Remaining Principal Balance Factors

For Mortgages with an Interest Rate of 10.50% and an Original Term of:

Age of Loan in Years	5 Years	6 Years	7 Years	8 Years	9 Years	10 Years	11 Years	12 Years	15 Years	20 Years	25 Years	30 Years	35 Years	40 Years
1	0.839	0.874	0.898	0.916	0.929	0.940	0.949	0.956	0.971	0.984	0.991	0.995	0.997	0.998
2	0.661	0.733	0.784	0.822	0.851	0.874	0.892	0.907	0.939	0.967	0.982	0.989	0.994	0.996
3	0.463	0.578	0.659	0.718	0.764	0.800	0.829	0.853	0.903	0.948	0.971	0.983	0.990	0.994
4	0.244	0.405	0.519	0.603	0.668	0.719	0.759	0.793	0.863	0.927	0.959	0.976	0.986	0.992
5	0.000	0.213	0.364	0.475	0.561	0.628	0.682	0.726	0.819	0.903	0.946	0.969	0.982	0.989
6		0.000	0.191	0.333	0.442	0.527	0.596	0.652	0.770	0.877	0.931	0.960	0.977	0.986
7			0.000	0.175	0.309	0.415	0.500	0.570	0.716	0.848	0.915	0.951	0.971	0.983
8				0.000	0.163	0.291	0.394	0.478	0.656	0.816	0.897	0.941	0.965	0.980
9					0.000	0.153	0.276	0.377	0.589	0.780	0.876	0.929	0.959	0.976
10						0.000	0.145	0.264	0.514	0.740	0.854	0.916	0.951	0.971
11							0.000	0.139	0.432	0.696	0.829	0.902	0.943	0.967
12								0.000	0.340	0.647	0.802	0.886	0.934	0.961
15									0.000	0.464	0.700	0.828	0.900	0.941
20										0.000	0.439	0.678	0.812	0.890
25											0.000	0.426	0.666	0.804
30												0.000	0.418	0.659
35													0.000	0.413
40														0.000

For Mortgages with an Interest Rate of 10.75% and an Original Term of:

Age of Loan in Years	5 Years	6 Years	7 Years	8 Years	9 Years	10 Years	11 Years	12 Years	15 Years	20 Years	25 Years	30 Years	35 Years	40 Years
1	0.840	0.875	0.899	0.917	0.930	0.941	0.950	0.957	0.972	0.985	0.992	0.995	0.997	0.998
2	0.663	0.735	0.786	0.824	0.853	0.875	0.894	0.909	0.940	0.968	0.982	0.990	0.994	0.997
3	0.465	0.580	0.661	0.720	0.766	0.802	0.831	0.855	0.905	0.950	0.972	0.984	0.991	0.995
4	0.245	0.407	0.521	0.605	0.670	0.721	0.762	0.795	0.866	0.929	0.960	0.978	0.987	0.993
5	0.000	0.214	0.365	0.477	0.563	0.631	0.685	0.729	0.822	0.906	0.948	0.970	0.983	0.990
6		0.000	0.193	0.335	0.444	0.530	0.599	0.655	0.774	0.880	0.933	0.962	0.978	0.987
7			0.000	0.176	0.312	0.418	0.503	0.573	0.720	0.851	0.918	0.953	0.973	0.984
8				0.000	0.164	0.293	0.397	0.482	0.660	0.820	0.900	0.943	0.967	0.981
9					0.000	0.154	0.279	0.380	0.593	0.784	0.880	0.932	0.961	0.977
10						0.000	0.147	0.266	0.519	0.745	0.858	0.919	0.954	0.973
11							0.000	0.140	0.436	0.701	0.834	0.906	0.946	0.969
12								0.000	0.344	0.652	0.807	0.890	0.937	0.963
15									0.000	0.470	0.706	0.833	0.904	0.944
20										0.000	0.445	0.685	0.819	0.895
25											0.000	0.432	0.673	0.810
30												0.000	0.424	0.666
35													0.000	0.420
40														0.000

Remaining Principal Balance Factors

For Mortgages with an Interest Rate of 11.00% and an Original Term of:

Age of Loan in Years	5 Years	6 Years	7 Years	8 Years	9 Years	10 Years	11 Years	12 Years	15 Years	20 Years	25 Years	30 Years	35 Years	40 Years
1	0.841	0.875	0.900	0.917	0.931	0.942	0.950	0.957	0.972	0.985	0.992	0.995	0.997	0.999
2	0.664	0.736	0.788	0.825	0.854	0.877	0.895	0.910	0.941	0.969	0.983	0.990	0.995	0.997
3	0.466	0.581	0.662	0.722	0.768	0.805	0.833	0.857	0.907	0.951	0.973	0.985	0.991	0.995
4	0.246	0.408	0.523	0.608	0.673	0.724	0.765	0.798	0.868	0.931	0.962	0.979	0.988	0.993
5	0.000	0.215	0.367	0.480	0.566	0.634	0.688	0.732	0.825	0.908	0.950	0.972	0.984	0.991
6		0.000	0.194	0.337	0.447	0.533	0.602	0.659	0.777	0.883	0.936	0.964	0.979	0.988
7			0.000	0.178	0.314	0.421	0.507	0.577	0.724	0.855	0.920	0.955	0.974	0.985
8				0.000	0.165	0.296	0.400	0.485	0.664	0.823	0.903	0.945	0.969	0.982
9					0.000	0.156	0.281	0.383	0.597	0.788	0.884	0.935	0.963	0.979
10						0.000	0.148	0.269	0.523	0.749	0.862	0.923	0.956	0.975
11							0.000	0.142	0.440	0.706	0.838	0.909	0.948	0.970
12								0.000	0.347	0.657	0.812	0.894	0.940	0.965
15									0.000	0.475	0.712	0.838	0.908	0.947
20										0.000	0.451	0.691	0.824	0.899
25											0.000	0.438	0.680	0.817
30												0.000	0.431	0.674
35													0.000	0.427
40														0.000

For Mortgages with an Interest Rate of 11.25% and an Original Term of:

Age of Loan in Years	5 Years	6 Years	7 Years	8 Years	9 Years	10 Years	11 Years	12 Years	15 Years	20 Years	25 Years	30 Years	35 Years	40 Years
1	0.842	0.876	0.900	0.918	0.932	0.943	0.951	0.958	0.973	0.986	0.992	0.996	0.998	0.999
2	0.666	0.738	0.789	0.827	0.856	0.878	0.897	0.911	0.942	0.970	0.984	0.991	0.995	0.997
3	0.468	0.583	0.664	0.725	0.770	0.807	0.836	0.859	0.909	0.952	0.974	0.986	0.992	0.995
4	0.247	0.410	0.525	0.610	0.675	0.726	0.767	0.801	0.871	0.933	0.963	0.980	0.989	0.994
5	0.000	0.217	0.369	0.482	0.569	0.636	0.691	0.735	0.828	0.911	0.951	0.973	0.985	0.991
6		0.000	0.195	0.339	0.449	0.536	0.605	0.662	0.780	0.886	0.938	0.966	0.981	0.989
7			0.000	0.179	0.316	0.424	0.510	0.580	0.727	0.858	0.923	0.957	0.976	0.986
8				0.000	0.167	0.298	0.403	0.488	0.668	0.827	0.906	0.948	0.971	0.983
9					0.000	0.157	0.283	0.386	0.601	0.793	0.887	0.937	0.965	0.980
10						0.000	0.150	0.271	0.527	0.754	0.866	0.926	0.958	0.976
11							0.000	0.143	0.444	0.711	0.843	0.913	0.951	0.972
12								0.000	0.351	0.662	0.816	0.898	0.943	0.967
15									0.000	0.480	0.717	0.843	0.912	0.950
20										0.000	0.456	0.698	0.830	0.904
25											0.000	0.444	0.687	0.823
30												0.000	0.437	0.681
35													0.000	0.434
40														0.000

Remaining Principal Balance Factors

For Mortgages with an Interest Rate of 11.50% and an Original Term of:

Age of Loan in Years	5 Years	6 Years	7 Years	8 Years	9 Years	10 Years	11 Years	12 Years	15 Years	20 Years	25 Years	30 Years	35 Years	40 Years
1	0.843	0.877	0.901	0.919	0.933	0.943	0.952	0.959	0.973	0.986	0.993	0.996	0.998	0.999
2	0.667	0.739	0.791	0.828	0.857	0.880	0.898	0.913	0.944	0.971	0.984	0.991	0.995	0.997
3	0.470	0.585	0.666	0.727	0.773	0.809	0.838	0.861	0.910	0.954	0.975	0.986	0.992	0.996
4	0.248	0.412	0.527	0.612	0.678	0.729	0.770	0.803	0.873	0.935	0.965	0.981	0.989	0.994
5	0.000	0.218	0.371	0.485	0.571	0.639	0.694	0.738	0.831	0.913	0.953	0.974	0.986	0.992
6		0.000	0.196	0.341	0.452	0.539	0.609	0.665	0.784	0.889	0.940	0.967	0.982	0.990
7			0.000	0.180	0.318	0.426	0.513	0.584	0.731	0.861	0.925	0.959	0.977	0.987
8				0.000	0.168	0.300	0.406	0.492	0.672	0.831	0.909	0.950	0.972	0.984
9					0.000	0.159	0.286	0.389	0.606	0.797	0.891	0.940	0.967	0.981
10						0.000	0.151	0.274	0.531	0.759	0.870	0.929	0.960	0.978
11							0.000	0.145	0.448	0.716	0.847	0.916	0.953	0.974
12								0.000	0.354	0.667	0.821	0.902	0.945	0.969
15									0.000	0.485	0.723	0.848	0.915	0.953
20										0.000	0.462	0.704	0.836	0.908
25											0.000	0.450	0.694	0.829
30												0.000	0.444	0.689
35													0.000	0.440
40														0.000

For Mortgages with an Interest Rate of 11.75% and an Original Term of:

Age of Loan in Years	5 Years	6 Years	7 Years	8 Years	9 Years	10 Years	11 Years	12 Years	15 Years	20 Years	25 Years	30 Years	35 Years	40 Years
1	0.844	0.878	0.902	0.920	0.933	0.944	0.953	0.960	0.974	0.987	0.993	0.996	0.998	0.999
2	0.668	0.741	0.792	0.830	0.859	0.881	0.899	0.914	0.945	0.972	0.985	0.992	0.996	0.998
3	0.471	0.587	0.668	0.729	0.775	0.811	0.840	0.863	0.912	0.955	0.976	0.987	0.993	0.996
4	0.249	0.414	0.529	0.615	0.680	0.731	0.772	0.806	0.875	0.936	0.966	0.982	0.990	0.994
5	0.000	0.219	0.373	0.487	0.574	0.642	0.697	0.741	0.834	0.915	0.955	0.975	0.987	0.993
6		0.000	0.197	0.343	0.455	0.542	0.612	0.669	0.787	0.891	0.942	0.969	0.983	0.990
7			0.000	0.182	0.320	0.429	0.516	0.587	0.735	0.865	0.928	0.961	0.978	0.988
8				0.000	0.170	0.302	0.409	0.495	0.676	0.835	0.912	0.952	0.974	0.985
9					0.000	0.160	0.288	0.392	0.610	0.801	0.894	0.942	0.968	0.982
10						0.000	0.152	0.276	0.535	0.763	0.874	0.931	0.962	0.979
11							0.000	0.146	0.452	0.720	0.851	0.919	0.956	0.975
12								0.000	0.358	0.672	0.826	0.905	0.948	0.971
15									0.000	0.490	0.729	0.852	0.919	0.955
20										0.000	0.468	0.711	0.841	0.912
25											0.000	0.456	0.701	0.835
30												0.000	0.450	0.696
35													0.000	0.447
40														0.000

Remaining Principal Balance Factors

For Mortgages with an Interest Rate of 12.00% and an Original Term of:

Age of Loan in Years	5 Years	6 Years	7 Years	8 Years	9 Years	10 Years	11 Years	12 Years	15 Years	20 Years	25 Years	30 Years	35 Years	40 Years
1	0.845	0.879	0.903	0.921	0.934	0.945	0.953	0.960	0.975	0.987	0.993	0.996	0.998	0.999
2	0.670	0.742	0.794	0.831	0.860	0.883	0.901	0.915	0.946	0.973	0.986	0.992	0.996	0.998
3	0.473	0.589	0.670	0.731	0.777	0.813	0.842	0.865	0.914	0.956	0.977	0.988	0.993	0.996
4	0.250	0.415	0.531	0.617	0.683	0.734	0.775	0.808	0.877	0.938	0.967	0.982	0.990	0.995
5	0.000	0.220	0.375	0.489	0.577	0.645	0.700	0.744	0.837	0.917	0.957	0.977	0.987	0.993
6		0.000	0.199	0.345	0.457	0.545	0.615	0.672	0.790	0.894	0.944	0.970	0.984	0.991
7			0.000	0.183	0.323	0.432	0.519	0.590	0.738	0.868	0.930	0.963	0.980	0.989
8				0.000	0.171	0.305	0.412	0.499	0.680	0.838	0.915	0.954	0.975	0.986
9					0.000	0.161	0.291	0.395	0.614	0.805	0.897	0.945	0.970	0.984
10						0.000	0.154	0.279	0.540	0.767	0.878	0.934	0.964	0.980
11							0.000	0.148	0.456	0.725	0.855	0.922	0.958	0.977
12								0.000	0.361	0.677	0.830	0.909	0.950	0.973
15									0.000	0.495	0.734	0.857	0.922	0.958
20										0.000	0.473	0.717	0.846	0.916
25											0.000	0.462	0.708	0.840
30												0.000	0.457	0.703
35													0.000	0.453
40														0.000

APPENDIX

C

EPA Lead Paint Disclosure Brochure

Protect Your Family From Lead in Your Home

🔆EPA
United States
Enviromental Protection
Agency

United States Consumer
Product Safety Commission

U.S. EPA Washington DC 20460
U.S. CPSC Washington DC 20207

EPA747-K-94-001
May 1995

Are You Planning To Buy, Rent, or Renovate a Home Built Before 1978?

Many houses and apartments built before 1978 have paint that contains lead (called lead-based paint). Lead from paint, chips, and dust can pose serious health hazards if not taken care of properly.

By 1996, federal law will require that individuals receive certain information before renting, buying, or renovating pre-1978 housing:

LANDLORDS will have to disclose known information on lead-based paint hazards before leases take effect. Leases will include a federal form about lead-based paint.

SELLERS will have to disclose known information on lead-based paint hazards before selling a house. Sales contracts will include a federal form about lead-based paint in the building. Buyers will have up to 10 days to check for lead hazards.

RENOVATORS will have to give you this pamphlet before starting work.

IF YOU WANT MORE INFORMATION on these requirements, call the National Lead Information Clearinghouse at **1-800-424-LEAD**.

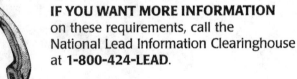

IMPORTANT!

Lead From Paint, Dust, and Soil Can Be Dangerous If Not Managed Properly

FACT: Lead exposure can harm young children and babies even before they are born.

FACT: Even children that seem healthy can have high levels of lead in their bodies.

FACT: People can get lead in their bodies by breathing or swallowing lead dust, or by eating soil or paint chips with lead in them.

FACT: People have many options for reducing lead hazards. In most cases, lead-based paint that is in good condition is not a hazard.

FACT: Removing lead-based paint improperly can increase the danger to your family.

If you think your home might have lead hazards, read this pamphlet to learn some simple steps to protect your family.

Lead Gets in the Body in Many Ways

1 out of every 11 children in the United States has dangerous levels of lead in the bloodstream.

Even children who appear healthy can have dangerous levels of lead.

People can get lead in their body if they:

◆ Put their hands or other objects covered with lead dust in their mouths.

◆ Eat paint chips or soil that contains lead.

◆ Breathe in lead dust (especially during renovations that disturb painted surfaces).

Lead is even more dangerous to children than adults because:

◆ Babies and young children often put their hands and other objects in their mouths. These objects can have lead dust on them.

◆ Children's growing bodies absorb more lead.

◆ Children's brains and nervous systems are more sensitive to the damaging effects of lead.

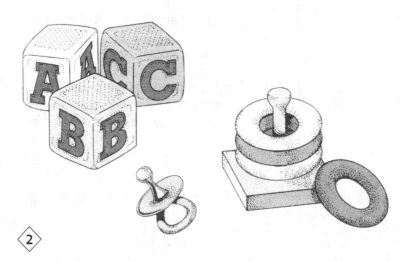

2

Lead's Effects

If not detected early, children with high levels of lead in their bodies can suffer from:

- Damage to the brain and nervous system
- Behavior and learning problems (such as hyperactivity)
- Slowed growth
- Hearing problems
- Headaches

Lead is also harmful to adults. Adults can suffer from:

- Difficulties during pregnancy
- Other reproductive problems (in both men and women)
- High blood pressure
- Digestive problems
- Nerve disorders
- Memory and concentration problems
- Muscle and joint pain

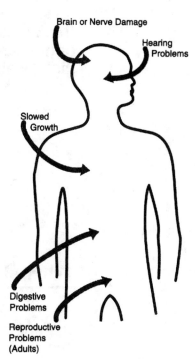

Lead affects the body in many ways.

Checking Your Family for Lead

Get your children tested if you think your home has high levels of lead.

A simple blood test can detect high levels of lead. Blood tests are important for:

◆ Children who are 6 months to 1 year old (6 months if you live in an older home with cracking or peeling paint).

◆ Family members that you think might have high levels of lead.

If your child is older than 1 year, talk to your doctor about whether your child needs testing.

Your doctor or health center can do blood tests. They are inexpensive and sometimes free. Your doctor will explain what the test results mean. *Treatment can range from changes in your diet to medication or a hospital stay.*

Where Lead-Based Paint Is Found

In general, the older your home, the more likely it has lead-based paint.

Many homes built before 1978 have lead-based paint. The federal government banned lead-based paint from housing in 1978. Some states stopped its use even earlier. Lead can be found:

◆ In homes in the city, country, or suburbs.

◆ In apartments, single-family homes, and both private and public housing.

◆ Inside *and* outside of the house.

◆ In soil around a home. (Soil can pick up lead from exterior paint, or other sources such as past use of leaded gas in cars.)

Where Lead Is Likely To Be a Hazard

Lead-based paint that is in good condition is usually not a hazard.

Peeling, chipping, chalking, or cracking lead-based paint is a hazard and needs immediate attention.

Lead-based paint may also be a hazard when found on surfaces that children can chew or that get a lot of wear-and-tear. These areas include:

◆ Windows and window sills.

◆ Doors and door frames.

◆ Stairs, railings, and banisters.

◆ Porches and fences.

Lead dust can form when lead-based paint is dry scraped, dry sanded, or heated. Dust also forms when painted surfaces bump or rub together. Lead chips and dust can get on surfaces and objects that people touch. Settled lead dust can reenter the air when people vacuum, sweep, or walk through it.

Lead in soil can be a hazard when children play in bare soil or when people bring soil into the house on their shoes. Call your state agency (see page 12) to find out about soil testing for lead.

Lead from paint chips, which you can see, and lead dust, which you can't always see, can both be serious hazards

⟨5⟩

Checking Your Home for Lead Hazards

Just knowing that a home has lead-based paint may not tell you if there is a hazard.

You can get your home checked for lead hazards in one of two ways, or both:

◆ A paint **inspection** tells you the lead content of every painted surface in your home. It won't tell you whether the paint is a hazard or how you should deal with it.

◆ A **risk assessment** tells you if there are any sources of serious lead exposure (such as peeling paint and lead dust). It also tells you what actions to take to address these hazards.

Have qualified professionals do the work. *The federal government is writing standards for inspectors and risk assessors. Some states might already have standards in place.* Call your state agency for help with locating qualified professionals in your area (see page 12).

Trained professionals use a range of methods when checking your home, including:

◆ Visual inspection of paint condition and location.

◆ Lab tests of paint samples.

◆ Surface dust tests.

◆ A portable x-ray fluorescence machine.

Home test kits for lead are available, but recent studies suggest that they are not always accurate. Consumers should not rely on these tests before doing renovations or to assure safety.

6

What You Can Do Now To Protect Your Family

If you suspect that your house has lead hazards, you can take some immediate steps to reduce your family's risk:

- ◆ **If you rent, notify your landlord of peeling or chipping paint.**

- ◆ **Clean up paint chips immediately.**

- ◆ **Clean floors, window frames, window sills, and other surfaces weekly.** Use a mop or sponge with warm water and a general all-purpose cleaner or a cleaner made specifically for lead. REMEMBER: NEVER MIX AMMONIA AND BLEACH PRODUCTS TOGETHER SINCE THEY CAN FORM A DANGEROUS GAS.

- ◆ **Thoroughly rinse sponges and mop heads after cleaning dirty or dusty areas.**

- ◆ **Wash children's hands often, especially before they eat and before nap time and bed time.**

- ◆ **Keep play areas clean.** Wash bottles, pacifiers, toys, and stuffed animals regularly.

- ◆ **Keep children from chewing window sills or other painted surfaces.**

- ◆ **Clean or remove shoes before entering your home to avoid tracking in lead from soil.**

- ◆ **Make sure children eat nutritious, low-fat meals high in iron and calcium,** such as spinach and low-fat dairy products. Children with good diets absorb less lead.

⑦

How To Significantly Reduce Lead Hazards

Removing lead improperly can increase the hazard to your family by spreading even more lead dust around the house.

Always use a professional who is trained to remove lead hazards safely.

In addition to day-to-day cleaning and good nutrition:

◆ You can **temporarily** reduce lead hazards by taking actions such as repairing damaged painted surfaces and planting grass to cover soil with high lead levels. These actions (called "interim controls") are not permanent solutions and will need ongoing attention.

◆ To **permanently** remove lead hazards, you must hire a lead "abatement" contractor. Abatement (or permanent hazard elimination) methods include removing, sealing, or enclosing lead-based paint with special materials. Just painting over the hazard with regular paint is not enough.

Always hire a person with special training for correcting lead problems—someone who knows how to do this work safely and has the proper equipment to clean up thoroughly. If possible, hire a certified lead abatement contractor. Certified contractors will employ qualified workers and follow strict safety rules as set by their state or by the federal government.

Call your state agency (see page 12) for help with locating qualified contractors in your area and to see if financial assistance is available.

Remodeling or Renovating a Home With Lead-Based Paint

Take precautions before you begin remodeling or renovations that disturb painted surfaces (such as scraping off paint or tearing out walls):

◆ **Have the area tested for lead-based paint.**

◆ **Do not use a dry scraper, belt-sander, propane torch, or heat gun** to remove lead-based paint. These actions create large amounts of lead dust and fumes. Lead dust can remain in your home long after the work is done.

◆ **Temporarily move your family** (especially children and pregnant women) out of the apartment or house until the work is done and the area is properly cleaned. If you can't move your family, at least completely seal off the work area.

◆ **Follow other safety measures to reduce lead hazards.** You can find out about other safety measures by calling 1-800-424-LEAD. Ask for the brochure "Reducing Lead Hazards When Remodeling Your Home." This brochure explains what to do before, during, and after renovations.

If you have already completed renovations or remodeling that could have released lead-based paint or dust, get your young children tested and follow the steps outlined on page 7 of this brochure.

If not conducted properly, certain types of renovations can release lead from paint and dust into the air.

Other Sources of Lead

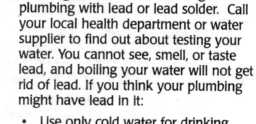

While paint, dust, and soil are the most common lead hazards, other lead sources also exist.

◆ **Drinking water.** Your home might have plumbing with lead or lead solder. Call your local health department or water supplier to find out about testing your water. You cannot see, smell, or taste lead, and boiling your water will not get rid of lead. If you think your plumbing might have lead in it:

- Use only cold water for drinking and cooking.

- Run water for 15 to 30 seconds before drinking it, especially if you have not used your water for a few hours.

◆ **The job.** If you work with lead, you could bring it home on your hands or clothes. Shower and change clothes before coming home. Launder your clothes separately from the rest of your family's.

◆ Old painted **toys** and **furniture.**

◆ Food and liquids stored in **lead crystal** or **lead-glazed pottery or porcelain.**

◆ **Lead smelters** or other industries that release lead into the air.

◆ **Hobbies** that use lead, such as making pottery or stained glass, or refinishing furniture.

◆ **Folk remedies** that contain lead, such as "greta" and "azarcon" used to treat an upset stomach.

For More Information

The National Lead Information Center

Call **1-800-LEAD-FYI** to learn how to protect children from lead poisoning.

For other information on lead hazards, call the center's clearinghouse at **1-800-424-LEAD.** For the hearing impaired, call, **TDD 1-800-526-5456** (FAX: **202-659-1192,** Internet: **EHC@CAIS.COM**).

EPA's Safe Drinking Water Hotline

Call **1-800-426-4791** for information about lead in drinking water.

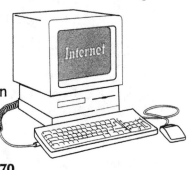

Consumer Product Safety Commission Hotline

To request information on lead in consumer products, or to report an unsafe consumer product or a product-related injury call **1-800-638-2772**. (Internet: info@cpsc.gov). For the hearing impaired, call **TDD 1-800-638-8270**.

Local Sources of Information

State Health and Environmental Agencies

Some cities and states have their own rules for lead-based paint activities. Check with your state agency (listed below) to see if state or local laws apply to you. Most state agencies can also provide information on finding a lead abatement firm in your area, and on possible sources of financial aid for reducing lead hazards.

State/Region	Phone Number		
Alabama	(205) 242-5661	Missouri	(314) 526-4911
Alaska	(907) 465-5152	Montana	(406) 444-3671
Arkansas	(501) 661-2534	Nebraska	(402) 471-2451
Arizona	(602) 542-7307	Nevada	(702) 687-6615
California	(510) 450-2424	New Hampshire	(603) 271-4507
Colorado	(303) 692-3012	New Jersey	(609) 633-2043
Connecticut	(203) 566-5808	New Mexico	(505) 841-8024
Washington, DC	(202) 727-9850	New York	(800) 458-1158
Delaware	(302) 739-4735	North Carolina	(919) 715-3293
Florida	(904) 488-3385	North Dakota	(701) 328-5188
Georgia	(404) 657-6514	Ohio	(614) 466-1450
Hawaii	(808) 832-5860	Oklahoma	(405) 271-5220
Idaho	(208) 332-5544	Oregon	(503) 248-5240
Illinois	(800) 545-2200	Pennsylvania	(717) 782-2884
Indiana	(317) 382-6662	Rhode Island	(401) 277-3424
Iowa	(800) 972-2026	South Carolina	(803) 935-7945
Kansas	(913) 296-0189	South Dakota	(605) 773-3153
Kentucky	(502) 564-2154	Tennessee	(615) 741-5683
Louisiana	(504) 765-0219	Texas	(512) 834-6600
Massachusetts	(800) 532-9571	Utah	(801) 536-4000
Maryland	(410) 631-3859	Vermont	(802) 863-7231
Maine	(207) 287-4311	Virginia	(800) 523-4019
Michigan	(517) 335-8885	Washington	(206) 753-2556
Minnesota	(612) 627-5498	West Virginia	(304) 558-2981
Mississippi	(601) 960-7463	Wisconsin	(608) 266-5885
		Wyoming	(307) 777-7391

EPA Regional Offices

Your Regional EPA Office can provide further information regarding regulations and lead protection programs.

EPA Regional Offices

Region 1 (Connecticut, Massachusetts, Maine, New Hampshire, Rhode Island, Vermont)
John F. Kennedy Federal Building
One Congress Street
Boston, MA 02203
(617) 565-3420

Region 2 (New Jersey, New York, Puerto Rico, Virgin Islands)
Building 5
2890 Woodbridge Avenue
Edison, NJ 08837-3679
(908) 321-6671

Region 3 (Delaware, Washington DC, Maryland, Pennsylvania, Virginia, West Virginia)
841 Chestnut Building
Philadelphia, PA 19107
(215) 597-9800

Region 4 (Alabama, Florida, Georgia, Kentucky, Mississippi, North Carolina, South Carolina, Tennessee)
345 Courtland Street, NE
Atlanta, GA 30365
(404) 347-4727

Region 5 (Illinois, Indiana, Michigan, Minnesota, Ohio, Wisconsin)
77 West Jackson Boulevard
Chicago, IL 60604-3590
(312) 886-6003

Region 6 (Arkansas, Louisiana, New Mexico, Oklahoma, Texas)
First Interstate Bank Tower
1445 Ross Avenue, 12th Floor, Suite 1200
Dallas, TX 75202-2733
(214) 665-7244

Region 7 (Iowa, Kansas, Missouri, Nebraska)
726 Minnesota Avenue
Kansas City, KS 66101
(913) 551-7020

Region 8 (Colorado, Montana, North Dakota, South Dakota, Utah, Wyoming)
999 18th Street, Suite 500
Denver, CO 80202-2405
(303) 293-1603

Region 9 (Arizona, California, Hawaii, Nevada)
75 Hawthorne Street
San Francisco, CA 94105
(415) 744-1124

Region 10 (Idaho, Oregon, Washington, Alaska)
1200 Sixth Avenue
Seattle, WA 98101
(206) 553-1200

CPSC Regional Offices

Eastern Regional Center
6 World Trade Center
Vesey Street, Room 350
New York, NY 10048
(212) 466-1612

Central Regional Center
230 South Dearborn Street
Room 2944
Chicago, IL 60604-1601
(312) 353-8260

Western Regional Center
600 Harrison Street, Room 245
San Francisco, CA 94107
(415) 744-2966

13

Simple Steps To Protect Your Family From Lead Hazards

If you think your home has high levels of lead:

◆ Get your young children tested for lead, even if they seem healthy.

◆ Wash children's hands, bottles, pacifiers, and toys often.

◆ Make sure children eat healthy, low-fat foods.

◆ Get your home checked for lead hazards.

◆ Regularly clean floors, window sills, and other surfaces.

◆ Wipe soil off shoes before entering house.

◆ Talk to your landlord about fixing surfaces with peeling or chipping paint.

◆ Take precautions to avoid exposure to lead dust when remodeling or renovating (call 1-800-424-LEAD for guidelines).

◆ Don't use a belt-sander, propane torch, dry scraper, or dry sandpaper on painted surfaces that may contain lead.

◆ Don't try to remove lead-based paint yourself.

Helpful Web Sites for Homebuyers

The ever-changing and competitive cyber-world gives us no guarantee that Web sites listed here will stand the test of time. These sites, however, have been among the most reliable sites over the past few years.

House Hunting *(Resale and some new)*

- Realtor.com
- HomeAdvisor.com
- HomeSeekers.com
- Yahoo!RealEstate.com
- Cyberhomes.com

New Home Sites

- HomeBuilder.com
- NewHomeNetwork.com
- NewHomes.com
- BuilderOnline.com
- mHousing.com
- manufacturedhousing.org

Home Improvement Sites

- Improve.net
- Remodel.com
- Builderonline.com

For Sale By Owner and Discount Broker Sites

- Help-u-sell.com
- Owners.com
- Americas-real-estate.com
- iOwn.com
- eBay.com

Real Estate News and Advice Sites

- RealtyTimes.com
- Inman.com
- RealtorMag.com
- Rismedia.com
- HomeStore.com

Glossary

abstract of title (abstract) History of a parcel of real estate, compiled from public records, listing transfers of ownership and claims against the property

acceleration clause Provision in a mortgage document stating that if a payment is missed or any other provision violated, the whole debt becomes immediately due and payable

acknowledgment Formal declaration before a public official that one has signed a document

acre Land measure equal to 43,560 square feet

adjustable-rate mortgage (ARM) Loan with an interest rate that changes periodically to keep pace with current levels

adjusted basis Original cost of property plus any later improvements and minus a figure for depreciation claimed

adjusted sales price Sales price minus commissions, legal fees, and other costs of selling

agent Person authorized to act on behalf of another in dealings with third parties

agreement of sale (purchase agreement, sales agreement, contract to purchase) Written contract detailing terms under which buyer agrees to buy and seller agrees to sell

alienation clause (due-on-sale, non-assumption) Provision in a mortgage document stating that the loan must be paid in full if ownership is transferred; sometimes contingent upon other occurrences

amortization Gradual payment of a debt through regular installments that cover both principal and interest

appraisal Estimate of value of real estate, presumably by an expert

appreciation Increase in value or worth of property

"as is" Present condition of property being transferred, with no guaranty or warranty provided by the seller

assessed valuation Value placed on property as a basis for levying property taxes; not identical with appraised or market value

assignment   Transfer of a contract from one party to another

assumable mortgage   Loan that may be passed to the next owner of the property

assumption   Takeover of a loan by any qualified buyer (available for FHA and VA loans)

automatic renewal clause   Provision that allows a listing contract to be renewed indefinitely unless canceled by the property owner

balloon loan   Mortgage in which the remaining balance becomes fully due and payable at a predetermined time

balloon payment   Final payment on a balloon loan

bill of sale   Written document transferring personal property

binder   Preliminary agreement of sale, usually accompanied by earnest money (term also used with property insurance)

bond   Roughly the same as *promissory note;* a written promise to repay a loan, often with an accompanying mortgage that pledges real estate as security

broker   Person licensed by the state to represent another for a fee in real estate transactions

builder sales consultant   Licensed (usually) agent who sells homes on behalf of new home builders

building code   Regulations of local government stipulating requirements and standards for building and construction

buydown   The payment of additional points to a mortgage lender in return for a lower interest rate on the loan

buyer's broker   Agent who takes the buyer as client, is obligated to put the buyer's interests above all others, and owes specific fiduciary duties to the buyer

buyers' market   Situation in which supply of homes for sale exceeds demand

cap   Limit (typically about 2 percent) by which an adjustable-rate mortgage might be raised at any one time

capital gain   Taxable profit on the sale of an appreciated asset

caveat emptor   Let the buyer beware

ceiling   Also known as *lifetime cap;* limit beyond which an adjustable-rate mortgage may never be raised

certificate of occupancy   Document issued by local governmental agency stating that property meets standards for occupancy

chattel   Personal property

client   The broker's principal, to whom fiduciary duties are owed

closing (settlement, escrow, passing papers)   Conclusion of a real estate sale, at which time title is transferred and necessary funds change hands

closing costs   One-time charges paid by buyer and seller on the day property changes hands

closing statement   Statement prepared for buyer and seller listing debits and credits, completed by the person in charge of the closing

cloud (on title)   Outstanding claim or encumbrance that challenges the owner's clear title

commission   Fee paid (usually by a seller) for a broker's services in securing a buyer for property; commonly a percentage of sales price

commitment (letter) Written promise to grant a mortgage loan under the conditions stated by the lender

common elements Parts of a condominium development in which each owner holds an interest (swimming pool, etc.)

comparable Recently sold similar property, used to estimate market value

comparative market analysis Method of valuing homes using study of comparables, property that failed to sell, and other property currently on the market

conditional commitment Lender's promise to make a loan subject to the fulfillment of specified conditions

conditional offer Purchase offer in which the buyer proposes to purchase only after certain occurrences (sale of another home, securing of financing, etc.)

condominium Type of ownership involving individual ownership of dwelling units and common ownership of shared areas

consideration Something of value given to induce another to enter into a contract

contingency Condition (inserted into the contract) that must be satisfied before the buyer purchases a house

contract Legally enforceable agreement to do (or not to do) a particular thing

contract for deed (land contract) Method of selling whereby the buyer receives possession but the seller retains title

conventional mortgage A loan arranged between lender and borrower with no governmental guarantee or insurance

cost basis Accounting figure that includes original cost of property plus certain expenses to purchase, money spent on permanent improvements, and other costs, minus any depreciation claimed on tax returns over the years

covenants, conditions, and restrictions (CC&Rs) Specific rules drawn up by a neighborhood association governing the appearance and activities of that neighborhood.

credit scoring Numeric rating system used by lenders, based on certain credit criteria, in order to review a borrower's credit status

curtesy In some states, rights a widower obtains to a portion of his deceased wife's real property

customer Typically, the buyer, as opposed to the principal (seller)

days on market (DOM) Number of days between the time a house is put on the market and the date of a firm sales contract

deed Formal written document transferring title to real estate; a new deed is used for each transfer

deed of trust Document by which title to property is held by a neutral third party until a debt is paid; used instead of a mortgage in some states

deed restriction (restrictive covenant) Provision placed in a deed to control use and occupancy of the property by future owners

default Failure to make mortgage payment

deferred maintenance Needed repairs that have been put off

deficiency judgment Personal claim against the debtor when foreclosed property does not yield enough at sale to pay off loans against it

delivery Legal transfer of a deed to the new property owner; the moment at which transfer of title occurs

depreciation Decrease in value of property because of deterioration or obsolescence; sometimes, an artificial bookkeeping concept valuable as a tax shelter

desktop underwriting Lender's electronic evaluation of buyer-verified qualification data to gain loan approval, subject to review by an underwriter

direct endorsement Complete processing of an FHA mortgage application by an authorized local lender

discretionary income Amount of money left over in a given period not earmarked for mortgage or bill payments, use of which is wholly in the hands of the earner

documentary tax stamp Charge levied by state or local governments when real estate is transferred or mortgaged

dower In some states, the rights of a widow to a portion of her deceased husband's property

down payment Cash to be paid by the buyer at closing

dual agent Agent who represents and negotiates on behalf of both buyer and seller in the same transaction

earnest money Buyer's good faith deposit accompanying purchase offer

easement A permanent right to use another's property (telephone lines, common driveway, footpath, etc.)

elevations Builder's varied selection of exterior styles of the same floor plan

encroachment Unauthorized intrusion of a building or improvement onto another's land

encumbrance Claim against another's real estate (unpaid tax, mortgage, easement, etc.)

equity The money realized when property is sold and all the claims against it are paid; commonly, sales price minus present mortgage

escrow Funds given to a third party to be held pending some occurrence; may refer to earnest money; funds collected by a lender for the payment of taxes and insurance charges; funds withheld at closing to ensure uncompleted repairs; or, in some states the entire process of closing

escrow company Neutral third party location and depository for both buyer and seller that interprets and presents contractual agreements for final endorsements and closing (not common in all states)

exclusive agency Listing agreement under which only the listing office can sell the property and keep the commission, except if the owner sells the house, in which case no commission is paid

exclusive right-to-sell Listing agreement under which the owner promises to pay a commission if the property is sold during the listing period by anyone, even the owner

facilitator One who offers real estate services without owing special fiduciary duties to either seller or buyer (see **transaction broker**)

fair market value see **market value**

Federal Fair Housing Act The Fair Housing Act, enforced by the U.S. Department of Housing and Urban Development, bars discriminatory practices in housing related to race, color, national origin, religion, sex, handicap, or familial status

fee simple (absolute) Highest possible degree of ownership of land

FHA Federal Housing Administration (HUD), which insures mortgages to protect the lending institution in case of default

FHA mortgage Loan made by a local lending institution and insured by the FHA, with the borrower paying the premium

fiduciary A person in a position of trust or responsibility with specific duties to act in the best interest of the client

first mortgage Mortgage holding priority over the claims of subsequent lenders against the same property

fixture Personal property that has become part of the real estate

foreclosure Legal procedure for enforcing payment of a debt by seizing and selling the mortgaged property

front foot Measurement of land along a street or waterfront—each front foot is one foot wide and extends to the depth of the lot

grantee The buyer, who receives a deed

grantor The seller, who gives a deed

guaranteed sale Promise by the listing broker that if the property cannot be sold by a specific date, the broker will buy it, usually at a sharply discounted price

hazard insurance Insurance on a property against fire and similar risks

homeowners policy Policy that puts many kinds of insurance together into one package

impound account Trust account from which a specified amount of monthly principal, interest, taxes, and insurance (PITI) are paid on behalf of the buyer

improvements Permanent additions that increase the value of a home

incentives Monetary bonus or credit offered by home builders to encourage buyers to make a particular decision when buying a home

index Benchmark measure of current interest levels, used to calculate periodic changes in rates charged on adjustable-rate mortgages

in-house lender Lender owned by the same corporation or entity that owns the builder, to provide new home financing for the builder's buyers

inventory home New home that is considered complete but unsold

joint tenancy Ownership by two or more persons, each with an undivided ownership—if one dies, the property goes automatically to the survivor

junior mortgage   A mortgage subordinate to another

land contract   Type of layaway installment plan for buying a house; sought by a buyer who does not have enough down payment to qualify for a bank loan or to persuade the seller to turn over title

lien   A claim against property for the payment of a debt: mechanic's lien, mortgage, unpaid taxes, judgments

lis pendens   Notice that litigation is pending on property

listing agreement (listing)   Written employment agreement between a property owner and a real estate broker, authorizing the broker to find a buyer

listing presentation   Proposal submitted orally or in writing by an agent who seeks to put a prospective seller's property on the market

loan servicing   Handling paperwork of collecting loan payments, checking property tax and insurance coverage, handling delinquencies

lock-in   Guarantee that the borrower will receive the rate in effect at the time of loan application

maintenance fees   Payments made by the unit owner of a condominium to the homeowners association for expenses incurred in upkeep of the common areas

margin   Percentage (typically about 2.5 percent) added to index to calculate mortgage rate adjustment

marketable title   Title free of liens, clouds, and defects; a title that will be freely accepted by a buyer

market value   The most likely price a given property will bring if widely exposed on the market, assuming fully informed buyer and seller

mechanic's lien   Claim placed against a property by unpaid workers or suppliers

meeting of the minds   Agreement by buyer and seller on the provisions of a contract

mortgage   A lien or claim against real property given as security for a loan; the homeowner gives the mortgage; the lender takes it

mortgagee   The lender

mortgagor   The borrower

Multiple Listing Service (MLS)   An arrangement by which brokers work together on the sale of each others' listed homes, with shared commissions

negative amortization   Arrangement under which the shortfall in a mortgage payment is added to the amount borrowed; gradual raising of a debt

net listing   An arrangement under which the seller receives a specific sum from the sales price and the agent keeps the rest as sales commission (open to abuses, illegal in most states)

non–owner-occupied   Property not occupied by its principal owners

note   see **bond**

PITI   Abbreviation for principal, interest, taxes, and insurance, often lumped together in a monthly mortgage payment

plat Map or chart of a lot, subdivision, or community, showing boundary lines, buildings, and easements

PMI Private mortgage insurance

point (discount point) 1 percent of a new mortgage being placed, paid in a one-time lump sum to the lender

portfolio loans Loans made by a bank that keeps its mortgages as assets in its own portfolio (also called *nonconforming loans*)

preapproval Formal, preliminarily (conditionally) underwritten loan approval, using a borrower's entire financial picture and credit check at the time of application; usually states the highest loan amount for which the borrower will qualify

prepayment Payment of a mortgage loan before its due date

prepayment penalty Charge levied by the lender for paying off a mortgage before its maturity date

prequalification Cursory examination of a buyer's income, assets, and creditworthiness without benefit of a formal loan application review

principal Party (typically the seller) who hires and pays an agent

procuring cause Actions by a broker that bring about the desired results

prorations Expenses that are fairly divided between buyer and seller at closing

purchase-money mortgage Mortgage for the purchase of real property, commonly a mortgage taken back by the seller

quitclaim deed Deed that completely transfers whatever ownership the grantor may have had, but makes no claim of ownership in the first place

real property Land and the improvements on it

Realtist Member of the National Association of Real Estate Brokers

REALTOR® Registered name for a member of the National Association of REALTORS®

REALTOR-ASSOCIATE® Salesperson associated with a broker who is a member of a Board of REALTORS®

redlining Practice of refusing to provide loans or insurance in certain neighborhoods

RESPA Real Estate Settlement Procedures Act, requiring advance disclosure to the borrower of information pertinent to the loan

restrictive covenant See **deed restriction**

reverse mortgage Arrangement under which an elderly homeowner, who does not need to meet income or credit requirements, can draw against the equity in the home with no immediate repayment

salesperson Holder of an entry-level license who is allowed to assist a broker who is legally responsible for the salesperson's activities (synonymous in some areas with *agent*)

seller's broker Agent who takes the seller as a client, is legally obligated to a set of fiduciary duties, and is required to put the seller's interests above all others'

sellers' market Situation in which demand for homes exceeds the supply offered for sale

settlement See **closing**

specific performance   Lawsuit requesting that a contract be exactly carried out, usually asking that the seller be ordered to convey the property as previously agreed

subagency   Legal process by which the seller who lists property for sale with a broker takes on the broker's associates and cooperating firms in a Multiple Listing System as agents

supplemental property tax bill   Tax bill sent out by the tax assessor's office after closing, adding the value of the dwelling to the land value to make a total sum of assessed value

survey   Map made by a licensed surveyor who measures the land and charts its boundaries, improvements, and relationship to the property surrounding it

time is of the essence   Legal phrase in a contract, requiring punctual performance of all obligations

title   Rights of ownership, control, and possession of property

title insurance   Policy protecting the insured against loss or damage due to defects in title: the owner's policy protects the buyer, the mortgagee's policy protects the lender; paid with a one-time premium

title search   A check of the public records, usually at the local courthouse, to make sure that no adverse claims affect the value of the title

transaction broker   A broker who offers services without owing fiduciary duties to either party, as defined by law in various states

VA   Department of Veterans Affairs (formerly Veterans Administration), which guarantees a veteran's mortgage so that a lender is willing to make the loan with little or no down payment

vendee   The buyer

vendor   The seller

warranty deed   Most valuable type of deed, in which the grantor makes formal assurance of title

zoning   Laws of local government establishing building codes and regulations on usage of property

Index